CIPS Study Matters

Level 5

Advanced Diploma in Purchasing and Supply

Management in the Purchasing Function

James Milligan and Jennifer Blockley
The Derbyshire Business School, University of Derby

THE
CHARTERED INSTITUTE OF
PURCHASING & SUPPLY

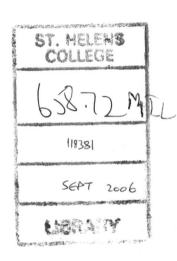

Published by

The Chartered Institute of Purchasing and Supply
Easton House, Easton on the Hill, Stamford, Lincolnshire PE9 3NZ
Tel: +44 (0) 1780 756 777
Fax: +44 (0) 1780 751 610
Email: info@cips.org
Website: www.cips.org

© The Chartered Institute of Purchasing and Supply 2006

First published July 2006

While every effort has been made to ensure that references to websites
are correct at time of going to press, the world wide web is a constantly
changing environment and CIPS cannot accept any responsibility for any
changes to addresses.

CIPS acknowledges product, service and company names referred to in this
publication, many of which are trade names, service marks, trademarks or
registered trademarks.

CIPS, The Chartered Institute of Purchasing & Supply and its logo are all
trademarks of the Chartered Institute of Purchasing & Supply.

The right of James Milligan and Jennifer Blockley to be identified as authors
of this work has been asserted by them in accordance with the Copyright,
Designs and Patents Act, 1988 in force or as amended from time to time.

Technical reviewer: Dave Wood

Instructional design and publishing project management by Wordhouse
Ltd, Reading, UK

Content management system, instructional editing and pre-press by
Echelon Learning Ltd, London, UK

Index prepared by Indexing Specialists (UK) Ltd, Hove, UK

ISBN 1-86124-158-5
ISBN 978-186124-158-0

Contents

Introduction

This course book has been designed to assist you in studying for the CIPS Management in the Purchasing Function unit in the Level 5 Advanced Diploma in Purchasing and Supply. The book covers all topics in the official CIPS unit content document, as illustrated in the table beginning on page ix.

The ability to take an overview of wider management issues and fully understand the process of management is now considered to be crucial for those pursuing a career in purchasing management.

This course book has been designed to provide a general overview of management and the business-related issues confronting managers today. It deals with the roles and tasks of managers, not only generally, but also specific to the purchasing function. It covers areas relating to organisational structure and culture, as well as managing conflict, change and performance. Within and across this framework, particular emphasis is placed upon managerial decision making, ethics and social responsibility and the impact of these on operations and (in particular) the purchasing and supply function. Further, this course book also explores how the purchasing function has evolved in recent years, and how it has been influenced and impacted by the dynamics of the 'new economy', ethics and e-business.

It provides a holistic view and understanding of the process of management, but more specifically how that process impacts on the changing role of the purchasing function. With the role of purchasing being increasingly more strategic in nature, and with its emphasis on value creation and the development of supply chain relationships and partnerships, purchasing managers must develop a wider range of technical and conceptual skills to perform their role effectively.

The course book has been structured to provide a broad representation of differing, and often conflicting, management perspectives and theories that reflects the richness of current debate among academics and practitioners in the field of management. Finally, it has also been designed to further develop the student's analytical, problem-solving and decision-making skills.

How to use this book

The course book will take you step by step through the unit content in a series of carefully planned 'study sessions' and provides you with learning activities, self-assessment questions and revision questions to help you master the subject matter. The guide should help you organise and carry out your studies in a methodical, logical and effective way, but if you have your own study preferences you will find it a flexible resource too.

v

Before you begin using course this book, make sure you are familiar with any advice provided by CIPS on such things as study skills, revision techniques or support and how to handle formal assessments.

If you are on a taught course, it will be up to your tutor to explain how to use the book – when to read the study sessions, when to tackle the activities and questions, and so on.

If you are on a self-study course, or studying independently, you can use the course book in the following way:

- Scan the whole book to get a feel for the nature and content of the subject matter.
- Plan your overall study schedule so that you allow enough time to complete all 20 study sessions well before your examinations – in other words, leaving plenty of time for revision.
- For each session, set aside enough time for reading the text, tackling all the learning activities and self-assessment questions, and the revision question at the end of the session, and for the suggested further reading. Guidance on roughly how long you should set aside for studying each session is given at the beginning of the session.

Now let's take a look at the structure and content of the individual study sessions.

Overview of the study sessions

The course book breaks the content down into 20 sessions, which vary from three to six or seven hours' duration each. However, we are not advising you to study for this sort of time without a break! The sessions are simply a convenient way of breaking the syllabus into manageable chunks. Most people would try to study one or two sessions a week, taking one or two breaks within each session. You will quickly find out what suits you best.

Each session begins with a brief **introduction** which sets out the areas of the syllabus being covered and explains, if necessary, how the session fits in with the topics that come before and after.

After the introduction there is a statement of the **session learning objectives**. The objectives are designed to help you understand exactly what you should be able to do after you've studied the session. You might find it helpful to tick them off as you progress through the session. You will also find them useful during revision. There is one session learning objective for each numbered subsection of the session.

After this, there is a brief section reproducing the learning objectives and indicative content from the official **unit content document**. This will help you to understand exactly which part of the syllabus you are studying in the current session.

Following this, there are **prior knowledge** and **resources** sections if necessary. These will let you know if there are any topics you need to be familiar with before tackling each particular session, or any special resources you might need, such as a calculator or graph paper.

Then the main part of the study session begins, with the first of the numbered main subsections. At regular intervals in each study session, we have provided you with **learning activities**, which are designed to get you actively involved in the learning process. You should always try to complete the activities – usually on a separate sheet of your own paper – before reading on. You will learn much more effectively if you are actively involved in doing something as you study, rather than just passively reading the text in front of you. The feedback or answers to the activities are provided at the end of the session. Do not be tempted to skip the activity.

We also provide a number of **self-assessment questions** in each study session. These are to help you to decide for yourself whether or not you have achieved the learning objectives set out at the beginning of the session. As with the activities, you should always tackle them – usually on a separate sheet of paper. Don't be tempted to skip them. The feedback or answers are again at the end of the session. If you still do not understand a topic having attempted the self-assessment question, always try to re-read the relevant passages in the textbook readings or session, or follow the advice on further reading at the end of the session. If this still doesn't work, you should contact the CIPS Membership and Qualification Advice team.

For most of the learning activities and self assessment questions you will need to use separate sheets of paper for your answers or responses. Some of the activities or questions require you to complete a table or form, in which case you could write your response in the study guide itself, or photocopy the page.

At the end of the session are three final sections.

The first is the **summary**. Use it to remind yourself or check off what you have just studied, or later on during revision.

Then follows the **suggested further reading** section. This section, if it appears, contains recommendations for further reading which you can follow up if you would like to read alternative treatments of the topics. If for any reason you are having difficulty understanding the course book on a particular topic, try one of the alternative treatments recommended. If you are keen to read around and beyond the syllabus, to help you pick up extra points in the examination for example, you may like to try some of the additional readings recommended. If this section does not appear at the end of a session, it usually means that further reading for the session topics is not necessary.

At the end of the session we direct you to a **revision question**, which you will find in a separate section at the end of the course book. Feedback on the questions is also given.

Reading lists

CIPS produces an official reading list, which recommends essential and desirable texts for augmenting your studies. This reading list is available on the CIPS website or from the CIPS Bookshop. This course book is one of the essential texts for this unit. In this section we describe the main characteristics of the other essential text for this unit, which you are strongly urged to buy and use throughout your course.

The other essential text is:

Management and Organisational Behaviour, 7th edition, by JL Mullins, published by FT Prentice Hall in 2005.

This text provides a multi-disciplinary approach to organisational behaviour with an engaging writing style, and presents a broad appreciation of most of the topics covered in the course book. As such it covers a significant amount of the unit content.

It provides concepts, theories, models and frameworks to help understand behaviour in organisations and is simple to follow and structured in a way that allows the reader to find subject content and supporting examples easily.

It succeeds in covering in one volume a wide field of study of management and organisational behaviour and is particularly strong in relation to management processes and organisational dynamics. Further, it contains additional activities and case studies to help students improve their understanding of the frameworks relating to these areas.

However, it is not purchasing specific and as such it therefore does not provide the student with a wider appreciation of how these areas relate to the course book. Students are therefore advised to refer to the suggested further reading section at the end of each session to help increase their knowledge and understanding.

Unit content coverage

In this section we reproduce the whole of the official CIPS unit content document for this unit. The overall unit characteristics and learning outcomes for the unit are given first. Then, in the table that follows, the learning objectives and indicative content are given in the left hand column. In the right hand column are the study sessions, or subsections, in which you will find coverage of the various topics.

Unit Characteristics

This unit is designed to enable students to manage their own area of responsibility within an organisation's internal supply chain, in line with the overall strategic business plan and the operational plan for the purchasing function.

Students should be able to implement operational plans for their own area of responsibility to achieve objectives set out in their plan. In doing so they should be able to employ a range of resources, including human, physical and financial resources, and manage and delegate tasks effectively.

This unit is about managing the expectations of the stakeholders that are directly involved in the student's own area of responsibility and will provide them with management techniques to help them to involve others, be innovative, consultative, influential and persuasive in order to achieve targets effectively.

Learning Outcomes

On completion of this unit, students will be able to:

- Evaluate the challenges facing managers in dynamic and changing organisations.
- Analyse the characteristics of different organisational structures and cultures.
- Use a range of techniques to support and implement justifiable management decisions.
- Formulate plans to effectively manage work groups and teams.
- Propose processes and systems to enable the successful implementation of change programmes to maximise purchasing efficiency and effectiveness.

Learning objectives and indicative content

1 The challenges of management. (Weighting 20%)

1.1 Define the term management and differentiate management from leadership.
- Definitions of management (Drucker & Brech)
- Management: planning, coordinating, controlling and motivating staff
- Management styles
- Leadership perspectives and styles

Study session 1

1.2 Establish the importance of stakeholder groups who directly impact upon the purchasing function and manage their expectations effectively.
- Stakeholders: employees, customers, shareholders, suppliers, government, lenders
- Identifying and fulfilling stakeholder/customer needs
- Working within ethical codes of conduct and practice

Study session 2

1.3 Contrast the key roles and functions of managers in the purchasing and supply function.
- Ensuring best value/quality at the lowest price (purchaser)
- Advising and recommending suitable purchasing and supply systems
- Building good relationships within the purchasing and supply chain
- Management of resources (human, financial, materials, equipment) to be effective in role
- Policy development

Study session 2
Study session 10

1.4 Compare the diverse purchasing management practices of the private and public sectors.
- Tendering
- Recommended suppliers
- E-commerce: Internet, E-auctions, E-catalogues, EDI
- Outsourcing
- Authority levels (i.e. purchase orders)
- Relationship Building
- Payment terms and other contracting arrangements

Study session 2

1.5 Create a set of rules for ethical behaviour.
- What is ethics?
- CIPS ethical codes

Study session 3

1.6 Propose ways of reporting effectively to senior management and securing top level support and sponsorship for initiatives and implementation of plans.
- Keeping your stakeholders informed
- Building a business case
- Report writing: structure, content and making it interesting
- Effective meetings
- Presenting your plans

Study session 4

2 Organisation structures and culture. (Weighting 20%)

2.1 Evaluate the importance of organisational structure.
Study session 5
- Rationale/background: industrial revolution to modern day — Study session 6
- Choice of different structures to aid management
- Organisational structures: conflicts between control and empowerment; autonomy and entrepreneurship
- Power

2.2 Evaluate the nature and scope of federal and network structures and the implications of such structures for the purchasing function.
Study session 6
- Local
- Regional
- National
- International
- Global

2.3 Assess and evaluate methods of job design for purchasing roles.
Study session 7
- Identifying responsibilities, associated tasks and priorities
- Updating existing roles, via job description and person specification
- Training needs analysis
- Competency frameworks
- Role mapping

2.4 Define the term culture and assess different models of culture which may exist within organisations.
Study session 8
- Definitions/terms
- Behaviour, values and assumptions
- Organisational influences of company politics, power, bureaucracy, rules and standards of behaviour
- Models of cultural strength, masculine/feminine societies, cultural values and individualism/collectivism

2.5 Evaluate methods and formulate plans for managing effectively in international or cross-cultural organisations.
Study session 8
- Stages of planning
- Methods: managerial and leadership styles, approaches, communication and media channels
- Evaluation process of research (primary and secondary), conducting pilot schemes, gathering feedback from staff and choosing most successful option
- Considerations: cultural diversity, existing structures, codes of conduct, differing goals and expectations
- Stages of planning

3.0 Management decision making. (Weighting 15%)

3.1 Evaluate and apply a range of tools to make effective management choices and decisions.
Study session 9
- Problem and decision making process
- Pareto Analysis, Ishikawa (fishbone) diagram, SWOT, decision making trees, cost/benefit analysis, risk evaluation, paired comparison analysis
- Balanced scorecard

3.2 Formulate, implement and monitor operational plans for   Study session 10
the purchasing and supply function to achieve organisational
objectives.
  * Aligning plans with strategic objectives/direction of
    organisation
  * Agreeing objectives and targets: reducing defects, improving
    lead times, reducing costs
  * SMART principles
  * Importance of and ways to involve the team in the planning
    process
  * Monitoring systems and processes including annual and
    periodic reviews
  * Reporting structures
3.3 Assess and deploy the resource requirements for the   Study session 10
implementation of operational plans for the purchasing
function.
  * People as a resource
  * Financial resources
  * Physical resources
  * Time

4.0 Managing work groups and teams. (Weighting 25%)
4.1 Evaluate the concept of authority, delegation and accountability   Study session 11
when managing the purchasing function.
  * Understanding of key concepts: taking ownership, decision
    making, empowerment and responsibility
  * Reasons: workload, prioritising, developing individuals and
    the team, minimising blame and achieving results
  * Good time management
  * The delegation process
4.2 Apply techniques for building, motivating and managing   Study session 15
successful teams within the purchasing and supply function.
  * What is a team/group?
  * Stages of team development (Tuckman & Jensen model)
  * Team Roles (and Meredith Belbin's research)
  * Building a balanced team
  * Motivational determinants: innate drive, desire, fulfilling
    need
  * Satisfying individual and team needs: praise, rewards,
    recognition, responsibility, promotion, pay
  * Building relationships through leadership, with trust,
    fairness, equal opportunities, ethics and respect
4.3 Manage the sources of conflict which may arise within the   Study session 12
purchasing function.   Study session 13
  * Disagreement about needs, goals, values, priorities and
    interests
  * Poor communication
  * Lack of trust in leadership
  * Lack of direction
  * Lack of clarity in role
  * Scarcity of resources
  * Interpersonal and hygiene issues

Study session 1
Introduction to management

Introduction

'Managers do things right, while leaders do the right thing.'
Bennis and Nanus (1985)

It is through the process of management that the efforts of members of the organisation are coordinated, directed and guided towards the achievement of organisational goals. Management is therefore an integral part, and fundamental to the successful operation, of the organisation.

This session provides students with an overview of organisation and management, and an insight into how the understanding of organisational behaviour can help managers to develop their people in the pursuit of these organisational goals and objectives. It also explores the similarities and differences between the roles of managers and leaders.

Session learning objectives

After completing this session you should be able to:

1.1 Define the terms 'organisation' and 'management' and explain why each is important.
1.2 Distinguish between management and organisational behaviour.
1.3 Demonstrate understanding of the nature of organisational behaviour and the importance of the people–organisation relationship.
1.4 Explain how and why management is regarded as an integrating activity.
1.5 Explain key differences between management and leadership.

Unit content coverage

This study session covers the following topic from the official CIPS unit content document:

Learning outcome

Evaluate the challenges facing managers in dynamic and changing organisations.

Learning objective

1.1 Define the term 'management' and differentiate management from leadership.

Prior knowledge

Level 3, Understanding the Purchasing Environment.

1

Timing

You should set aside about 7 hours to read and complete this session, including learning activities, self-assessment questions, the suggested further reading (if any) and the revision question.

1.1 Organisations and management

Learning activity 1.1

Drawing on your own experience, explain what an organisation is and why it exists. Your answer can be in the form of a short report or key points or a bullet list (250–300 words maximum).

Feedback on page 12

What is an organisation?

At the simplest level, an organisation is a collection of people working together to achieve a common purpose, that is, usually organisational objectives. In doing so, this collection (or group) of people are able to accomplish tasks that are far beyond the reach of anyone acting individually. Furthermore, the purpose of any organisation is to produce goods and/or provide services that satisfy the needs of customers or clients, that is, to provide something useful for society.

Today, a clear sense of mission – or purpose – tied directly to product quality and customer service is now increasingly viewed as an essential organisational strength and source of (hopefully *sustainable*) competitive advantage.

Cole (2000) states that 'there are some commonly accepted features of organisations such as purpose, people and structure.' Other leading writers on organisations provide further definitions and explanations:

- 'Organisations are intricate human strategies designed to achieve certain objectives.' (Argyris, 1960 cited in Cole, 2000)
- 'Since organisations are systems of behaviour designed to enable humans and their machines to accomplish goals, organisational form must be a joint function of human characteristics and the nature of the task environment.' (Simon, 1976 cited in Cole, 2000)
- 'Organisations are systems of inter-dependent human beings.' (Pugh, 1990 cited in Cole, 2000)
- 'Organisations are set up to achieve purposes that individuals cannot achieve on their own. Organisations then provide a means of working with others to achieve goals…likely to be determined by whoever is in the best position to influence them…a key characteristic of organisations is their complexity.' (Stewart, 1994 cited in Cole, 2000)

We have all been part of one type of organisation or another, whether it is a school, college or university; a sports team; a theatrical group, or a company. Each of these types of organisation have specific goals, objectives or purposes, for example to win a league championship, to entertain an audience, or of course, to sell a product. Without specific goals or objectives, organisations would have little or no reason to exist. Thus, all organisations develop some strategy or method of achieving their goals or objectives. Without clear direction in terms of the route to achieving their goals, or some plan for what it must do, no organisation is therefore likely to be effective.

Furthermore, organisations must also acquire and allocate the necessary resources (human, financial, physical and so on) to help them achieve their goals in the most cost-effective way, for example an appropriate playing field or rehearsal hall for a sports or theatrical organisation; the requisite plant, equipment and transport facilities for a manufacturing organisation; and the finances necessary to pay for overheads such as heating, lighting and other power, and of course payment for employees.

In essence, it is how an organisation uses its people that counts in terms of its level of success. In addition, most (if not all) organisations are also heavily dependent on other supply and distribution organisations for the resources they need, and for transportation of their goods/services to their customers and/or end users.

Note: For the purchasing or procurement officer, this buyer–supplier–distribution chain is very important. Without it – and the inter-organisational relationships that exist – organisations themselves would find it extremely difficult to compete effectively in their relevant industry or market.

Why are organisations important?

There are a number of reasons why organisations are important. However, these can be summarised in generic terms:

- Organisations serve society. Organisations are important because they are social institutions that reflect certain culturally accepted values and needs, allowing us to live together in a civilised way and to accomplish goals as a society.
- Organisations help us to reach objectives. Consider for a moment how many organisations were involved in bringing us the paper on which this book is printed. Loggers, a sawmill, equipment and supplies manufacturers, transport firms, the postal service, banks and other financial institutions and so on have all contributed to the process. Individuals alone could not achieve this quickly or effectively enough to serve the needs of the customers and remain competitive.
- Organisations provide careers. Organisations are important because they provide employees with a sense of purpose, livelihood and (depending on the style and effectiveness of their managers) perhaps even personal satisfaction and self-fulfilment.
- Organisations preserve knowledge. Organisations add to our knowledge by developing new and more efficient ways of doing things.

What is management?

A number of definitions of **management** exist. The following three writers offer definitions which have similar elements:

1

'Management is a social process…the process consists of…planning, control, coordination and motivation.' (Brech, 1957 cited in Mullins, 2005)

'Management is concerned with the systematic organisation of economic resources and its task is to make these resources productive.' (Drucker, 1955)

'Management is the process of planning, organising, leading, and controlling the efforts of organisation members and of using all other organisational resources to achieve stated organisational goals.' (Mescon, cited in Stoner and Freeman, 1992)

Why is management important?

Essentially, management's responsibility is to help an organisation achieve high performance through the utilisation of all its resources, both human and material. This is achieved through the process of management – most often defined as planning, organising, leading and controlling the use of resources to accomplish the organisation's objectives. Without effective management – or managers – organisational objectives are unlikely to be realised.

What is a manager?

A manager is someone who is responsible for the work performance of one or more other persons in an organisation. Serving in positions with a wide variety of titles, for example supervisor, team leader, division head or vice-president (depending on the type of organisation), managers are persons to whom others (staff or subordinates) usually report.

Self-assessment question 1.1

Research as many different authors' definitions of 'management' and 'organisation' as you can and draw up a list of the common terms used in those definitions. Then write your own definitions/short description of what you now understand those terms to mean.

Feedback on page 12

1.2 Management and organisational behaviour

Organisational behaviour

According to Pugh (1971), **organisational behaviour** is:

> 'the study of structure, functioning and performance of organisations, and the behaviour of groups and individuals within them.'

Organisational behaviour (OB) is a multidisciplinary field that seeks knowledge of behaviour in organisational settings by systematically studying individual, group and organisational processes. This knowledge is then used by scientists interested in understanding human behaviour and by practitioners in order to enhance organisational effectiveness and individual well-being. For example, researchers have shed light on such practical questions as:

- How can goals be set to enhance people's job performance?
- How are jobs designed so as to enhance employees' feelings of satisfaction?
- Under what conditions do individuals make better decisions than groups?
- What can be done to improve the quality of organisational communication?
- What steps can be taken to alleviate work-related stress?
- How can leaders enhance the effectiveness of their teams?

To fully understand behaviour in organisations, organisational specialists do not focus exclusively on individuals acting alone since in organisational settings people frequently work together in groups or teams. Also, people – alone and in groups – influence and are influenced by their work environments. With this in mind, it is therefore not surprising to learn that the field of organisational behaviour focuses on three distinct levels of analysis:

1 individuals
2 groups
3 organisations.

Encompassing all of this is the study of organisations as a whole, in terms of:

- the way they are structured;
- how they operate in their environments;
- the effects of their operations on the individuals and groups within them.

Learning activity 1.2

Discuss critically what you believe are the main factors to bear in mind with, and particular difficulties presented by, the study of management and organisational behaviour. Where possible, give practical examples based on your own organisation or experience.

Feedback on page 12

Self-assessment question 1.2

Explain the significance of an understanding of organisational behaviour.

Feedback on page 13

1

1.3 Organisational behaviour and the people–organisation relationship

Learning activity 1.3

'A company's most valuable resource are its employees.'

Evaluate this statement using appropriate examples from your own organisation or experience. Outline your answer in the form of a key-points list.

Feedback on page 13

Human behaviour is unpredictable, and therefore scientific methods or principles of behaviour cannot be applied reliably. Bassett's research on job satisfaction (Mullins, 2005) revealed that there was a lack of universal generalisations regarding worker dissatisfaction that permit easy management policy solutions to absenteeism and turnover problems. There are almost never any exact conditions of cause and effect in the realm of human behaviour.

It has been widely observed that you cannot study the behaviour of people without changing it. Patterns of behaviour are influenced by a complex combination of individual, social and cultural factors. Tensions, conflicts and politics are inevitable, as are informal structures of organisation and unofficial working methods.

Therefore, we need to remind ourselves of the human aspects of organisations and the idiosyncratic behaviour of individuals, referred to by Egan (Mullins, 2005) as:

> 'the importance of the shadow side of the organisation: that is, those things not found on organisation charts or in company manuals – the covert, and often undiscussed, activities of people which affect both the productivity and quality of working life of an organisation.'

In general, the majority of people originally come to work with the attitude of being eager to do a good job and perform well and to the best of their abilities. Further, people generally respond in the manner in which they are treated. Where actual performance fails to match the ideal this is usually a result of how staff perceive they are treated by management and the management function.

Thus, many problems in the people–organisation relationship arise not so much from what management does, but from the manner in which it is done, and it is not necessarily the intent but the manner of implementation that is the root cause of staff unrest and dissatisfaction. For example, staff may agree on the need to introduce new technology to retain the competitive edge of the organisation, but feel resentment about the lack of pre-planning, consultation, retraining programmes, participation in agreeing new working practices and pay rates, and similar considerations arising from the manner of its introduction.

A heavy responsibility is therefore placed on managers and the activity of management in terms of its processes, systems and style. Careful attention to the work environment and appropriate systems of motivation, job satisfaction and rewards is important to ensure that organisational performance improves through its people.

Management should try to create the right organisational climate in which people work willingly and effectively. This means they must try to achieve a balance between the interrelated elements which make up the whole organisation, and to mould these into coherent patterns of activity which allow the organisation to best respond to and operate within its external (competitive) environment.

Organisations are made up of groups of people. The two (organisations and people) are not mutually exclusive. Therefore, attention needs to be focused on improving the people–organisation relationship. Management is a key part of this relationship and should serve to balance the needs of people at work with the requirements of the organisation.

Nowadays, management processes tend to be much more behavioural in nature, focusing on the key human resource-related issues: learning, team-based visions, driving human resource processes, incentives to enhance growth, holistic budgeting and proactive controls. One significant aspect of this and the relationship between individuals and the organisation is the concept of the psychological contract, described as follows:

- It is not a written document, but implies a series of mutual expectations and satisfaction of needs arising from the people–organisation relationship.
- It involves a process of giving and receiving by the individual and by the organisation.
- It covers a range of expectations of rights and privileges, duties and obligations, which do not form part of a formal agreement but still have an important influence on people's behaviour.

And this is explained by the following key points:

- The nature and extent of individuals' expectations vary widely as do the ability and willingness of the organisation to meet them.
- It is difficult to list the range of implicit expectations that individuals have and they change over time.
- These expectations are notwithstanding any statutory requirements placed upon the organisation; instead they relate more to the idea of a social responsibility of management.
- The organisation will also have implicit expectations of its members.
- The organisational side of the psychological contract places emphasis on expectations, requirements and constraints that may differ from, and may conflict with, an individual's expectations.

In summary, it is unlikely that all expectations of the individual or of the organisation will be met fully because there will be a continual process of balancing and explicit and implicit bargaining. Further, the nature of these expectations is not easy to define formally, and although the individual

1

member and the organisation may not be aware consciously of them, they still affect relationships between them and have an influence on behaviour.

Self-assessment question 1.3

A prominent management guru once stated that organisations are made up of people – and people are emotive.

Explain why you think this might be relevant when discussing the relationship between organisations and their employees. Use appropriate examples to support your answer.

Feedback on page 13

1.4 Management as an integrating activity

Learning activity 1.4

Using your own or another organisation as an example, describe in no more than 300 words how people in the organisation are managed towards the pursuit of functional and organisational objectives. For example, are management approaches to directing and controlling people directive or participative in nature? Please justify your answers.

Feedback on page 13

In recent years, the general movement towards flatter organisation structures, flexible working and greater employee involvement has placed increasing emphasis on an integrating rather than a hierarchical/controlling style of management.

At the heart of successful management is the challenge of integrating the individual and the organisation, and this requires an understanding of both human personality and formal organisations. Regardless of the individual's orientations to work, it is through the process of management that the efforts of members of the organisation are coordinated, directed and guided towards the achievement of organisational goals. Management is an integral part of, and fundamental to, the successful operation of the organisation.

Organisations can only achieve their aims and objectives through the coordinated efforts of their members. This involves the effective management of human resources. However, it is important always to remember that it is people who are being managed and people should be considered in human terms. Unlike physical resources, people are not owned by the organisation. People bring their own perceptions, feelings and attitudes towards the organisation, systems and styles of management, their duties and responsibilities, and the conditions under which they are working.

There are many aspects to management in work organisations, but the one essential ingredient of any successful manager is the ability to handle people effectively. The manager needs to be conversant with social and human skills, and have the ability to work with and through other people. As His Royal Highness, the Duke of Edinburgh (and patron of the Institute of Management) suggests:

'The fact is that management ultimately depends on an understanding of human nature. I suggest it goes much further than that. In the first place, good management depends on the acceptance of certain basic values. It cannot be achieved without honesty and integrity, or without consideration for the interests of others. Secondly, it is the understanding of human foibles that we all share, such as jealousy, envy, status, prejudice, perception, temperament, motivation and talent, which provides the greatest challenge to managers.' (March 1998, 'In Celebration of the Feel-good Factor', *Professional Manager*, p6.)

Self-assessment question 1.4

Explain how the basic elements in the management process are interrelated and outline the impact on the organisation if they were unrelated.

Feedback on page 14

1.5   Management and leadership

Learning activity 1.5

You have been asked to prepare a short talk for first-year students at your local college on 'The management/leadership debate'. Draw up a short briefing paper (in bullet or list form) that outlines and explains the differences between the two terms from an organisational (behavioural) theory perspective.

Feedback on page 14

There are almost as many different definitions of leadership as there are people who have attempted to define it. In simple terms, leadership is the process of directing and influencing the task-related activities of group members. There are three important implications of this definition:

- Leadership involves other people – subordinates or followers. By their willingness to accept directions from the leader, group members help define the leader's status and make the leadership process possible; without subordinates, all the leadership qualities of a manager would be irrelevant.
- Leadership involves an unequal distribution of power between leaders and group members. Group members are not powerless; they can

and do shape group activities in a number of ways. Still, the leader will usually have more power. Where does a manager's power come from? The greater the number of these power sources available to the manager, the greater his or her potential for effective leadership. Yet it is a commonly observed fact of organisation life that managers at the same level – with the same amount of legitimate power – differ widely in their ability to use reward, coercive, referent or expert power.

- Leadership is the ability to use the different forms of power to influence followers' behaviours in a number of ways. Indeed, leaders have influenced soldiers to kill and influenced employees to make personal sacrifices for the good of the company. For this reason, many believe that leaders have a special obligation to consider the ethics of their decisions.

Although it is highly related to and important to management, leadership and management are by no means the same concepts. Managers perform functions in organisations and hold a particular formal title. A typical example is a divisional marketing manager, responsible for the marketing of a product range in a geographical territory; or a personnel manager responsible, for example, for the recruitment and selection staff for a single site organisation.

Leaders, on the other hand, aim to influence and guide others into pursuing particular objectives or visions of the future and to stimulate them into wanting to follow. Leadership demonstrates the power of one individual over others and is not necessarily related to hierarchical position. Informal leaders exist at all levels of an organisation. Zaleznik (1977) is of the opinion that managers adopt a less emotional and more passive attitude than leaders and are more concerned with seeking compromise in conflicting positions and with conserving order than in initiating transformation.

Kotter (1990) also believes that leadership is more concerned with the human, visionary, inspirational, motivational and dynamic aspects of the total management/leadership role whereas management tends to focus on the tasks identified by Fayol (1949), that is, planning, organising and controlling, together with problem solving and maintaining a degree of predictability and stability.

It is not always the case that individuals are either managers or leaders. It is likely, for example, that a manager may show leadership qualities on particular occasions. Indeed, Mintzberg (1973) refers to leadership roles as one of his ten roles of management. Other academics suggest that leadership is merely part of the broader role of management and principally concerned with interpersonal aspects of the role. Similarly, a leader, focused on attitudinal and organisational change, employing all the political, emotional and symbolic tools of leadership, might also conduct normal managerial responsibilities.

Nevertheless, individuals may have a tendency towards either a managerial or a leadership disposition. Given the challenges presented by today's ever-changing and dynamically competitive environments, many organisations now put a premium on managers who also possess effective leadership skills.

1 Introduction to management

Self-assessment question 1.5

The Chinese philosopher Lao Tzu said: 'When the best leader's work is done, the people say, "We did it ourselves".'

Explain in no more than 400 words what this means in the context of working in your own organisation.

Feedback on page 14

Revision question

Now try the revision question for this session on page 247.

Summary

This study session has covered the following points:

- At the simplest level, an organisation is a collection of people working together to achieve a common purpose – usually organisational objectives. In doing so, this collection (or group) of people are able to accomplish tasks that are far beyond the reach of anyone acting individually. Furthermore, the purpose of any organisation is to produce goods and/or provide services that satisfy the needs of customers or clients. Most organisations therefore exist to provide something useful for society.
- Organisations are important because they serve society, help us to reach objectives, provide careers, and preserve knowledge by developing new and more efficient ways of doing things.
- Management is the process of planning, organising, leading and controlling the efforts of the organisations' members to help achieve organisational objectives.
- Organisational behaviour is 'the study of structure, functioning and performance of organisations, and the behaviour of groups and individuals within them.' (Pugh, 1971)
- Organisational behaviour focuses on three distinct levels of analysis: individuals, groups and organisations in terms of the way they are structured, how they operate in their environments, and the effects of their operations on the individuals and groups within them.
- It is the responsibility of managers and the activity of management to ensure that organisational performance improves through its people. Management therefore needs to create the right organisational climate in which people work willingly and effectively.
- Nowadays, management processes tend to be much more behavioural and focus on human resource related issues: learning, team-based visions, driving human resource processes, incentives to enhance growth, holistic budgeting and proactive controls.
- Leadership is the process of directing and influencing the task-related activities of group members. Leadership involves other people and an

unequal distribution of power between leaders and group members, and it is the ability to use different forms of power to influence followers' behaviour in a number of ways.

- Although it is closely related and highly important to management, leadership and management are by no means the same concepts. Managers perform functions in organisations and hold a particular, formal title, whereas leaders aim to influence and guide others into pursuing particular objectives or visions of the future and to stimulate them into wanting to follow.

Suggested further reading

Buchanan and Huczynski (2004), chapter 21.

Mullins (2005), chapter 6.

You could also read the relevant sections of Drucker (1989), Gosling and Mintzberg (2003), Handy (1976) and McGregor (1960).

Feedback on learning activities and self-assessment questions

Feedback on learning activity 1.1

You should explain what organisations are and why they exist, including some narrative on the key functional areas within them. This should then serve as a basis for you explaining the management task(s) within and across organisations and the key roles that management per se, and managers in particular, play within organisations. Definitions of management in terms of how it is perceived and manifest should be an integral part of your answer.

Note: Your ideas and examples may be culturally specific and parochial (local) in nature. This is acceptable as long as you can show evidence of understanding the theory, concept and application of these.

Feedback on self-assessment question 1.1

You are expected to draw on a wide range of authors' work on the subject and compare and contrast – with explanation where necessary – the definitions and/or explanations they provide. You should pay particular attention to similarities and differences between the various theorists' work. You can then give a summary definition and explanation on the basis of your findings.

Feedback on learning activity 1.2

You should define what is meant by organisational behaviour and its importance within organisations. This then provides a platform on which you can develop your discussion regarding the similarities, but more importantly perhaps, the specific differences between individuals and groups, and their behaviour. This should lead to further discussion on the disparity that exists within and across organisations and the levels of complexity surrounding the study of management and OB. It is expected that you will provide some detail based on your own organisation, including aspects of *how* people are managed and the ways in which they are motivated/controlled and so on.

Having completed this learning activity you should now attempt self-assessment question 1.2.

Feedback on self-assessment question 1.2

Your answer should relate to differences in management style and people's behaviour in different organisations. These differences serve as the basis for assessing the organisation's health, in human terms, and how this is managed effectively towards the achievement of the organisation's objectives.

Feedback on learning activity 1.3

You should explain that employees, as perhaps *the* key resource in organisations, should be managed appropriately for both the effectiveness and efficiency of the organisation. You should also clearly identify the relationships that exist between people and functions in terms of the required skills (levels) and knowledge, and the responsibilities of employees in contributing to organisational success and development.

Feedback on self-assessment question 1.3

You should be able to evaluate this statement in terms of what you consider Tom Peters meant, and explain that the effective management of different individuals and groups – however different and idiosyncratic – is essential for organisational success. Some reference to the consistency of management – in dealing with different individuals in a similar and equitable manner – should also be made.

Feedback on learning activity 1.4

You should structure your answer around the functional areas of the organisation (on the basis that different functional 'specialist' managers, for example, will probably have different management styles or approaches). This should provide the basis for specific discussion on each approach and its relative advantages and disadvantages. Part of your discussion should relate to the different types of organisational activity and the employees involved. For example, employees with specialist knowledge and/or skill may require a particular management style which is more participative and consultative because of the nature of their tasks, roles and responsibilities. Conversely, people in the organisation who perform more standardised tasks, for example machine operators where the operation is simply performed, may be managed through straightforward direction from management.

Feedback on self-assessment question 1.4

You should include planning, directing, controlling, monitoring and so on as the basis for your answer and explain how each of these applies across – and at each level – in an organisation (or your own organisation). In addition, you should explain the direct relationships of these areas and the link to functional areas. Unrelatedness would mean problems for any organisation. Suitable explanation and examples of the impacts of this should be given as part of your overall answer.

Feedback on learning activity 1.5

You should provide a comparative list or table that highlights the specific differences according to the principal writers on the subject. Many textbooks on management outline and explain the similarities and differences between leadership and management. You should be able to show evidence of research and, through their justification, an understanding of each.

Feedback on self-assessment question 1.5

The quotation refers to the fact that effective managers and leaders empower their employees through effective delegation of authority and responsibility, which in turn leads to employees being self-motivated to the point where they (hopefully) achieve both personal objectives and those set for them. Further, they do this without interference or coercion from their manager. It explains the role of an effective manager/leader in terms of how they manage their staff for good performance.

Managers – key roles and functions

Introduction

How successfully an organisation achieves its objectives, satisfies social responsibilities, or both, depends to a large extent on its managers. If managers do their jobs effectively, the organisation will probably achieve its goals. In addition, if a nation's major organisations achieve their goals, the nation as a whole will prosper.

You cannot manage what you cannot see! The Charge of the Light Brigade was ordered by a general who was not there surveying the field of battle at the time.

Session learning objectives

After completing this session you should be able to:

2.1 Describe the process, roles and tasks of management.
2.2 Compare the diverse purchasing management practices of the private and public sectors.
2.3 Explain the importance of stakeholder groups who directly impact upon the purchasing function.
2.4 Explain how stakeholder expectations can be managed effectively.

Unit content coverage

This study session covers the following topics from the official CIPS unit content document:

Learning outcome

Evaluate the challenges facing managers in dynamic and changing organisations.

Learning objective

1.2 Establish the importance of stakeholder groups who directly impact on the purchasing function and manage their expectations effectively.
1.3 Contrast the key roles and functions of managers in the purchasing and supply function.
1.4 Compare the diverse purchasing management practices of the private and public sectors.

Prior knowledge

Study session 1.

2

Timing

You should set aside about 7 hours to read and complete this session, including learning activities, self-assessment questions, the suggested further reading (if any) and the revision question.

2.1 Management – process, roles and tasks

Learning activity 2.1

List the basic activities in the management process and explain how they are interrelated. In your opinion, what would be the impact on an organisation if they were unrelated?

Feedback on page 26

The management process

Management has been called 'the art of getting things done through people'. This definition calls attention to the fact that managers achieve organisational goals by arranging for others to perform whatever tasks may be necessary – not by performing the tasks themselves.

In fact, management is so much more that no one simple definition has been universally accepted. Moreover, definitions change as the environments of organisations change. Our discussion will start with a fairly complex definition so that we may call your attention to important aspects of managing:

Management is the process of planning, organising, leading and controlling the efforts of organisation members and of using all other organisational resources to achieve stated organisational goals. We define management as a process because all managers, regardless of their particular aptitudes or skills, engage in certain interrelated activities in order to achieve their desired goals. In the rest of this section we describe and explain these four main management activities.

Planning

Planning implies that managers think through their goals and actions in advance, that their actions are based on some method, plan or logic rather than on a hunch. The first step in planning is the selection of goals for the organisation. Then objectives are established for the organisation's sub-units – its divisions, departments and so on. Once objectives are determined, programmes are established for achieving them in a systematic manner. Of course, in selecting objectives and developing programmes, the manager considers their feasibility and whether they will be acceptable to the organisation's other managers and employees.

Organising

Organising is the process of arranging and allocating work, authority and resources among an organisation's members so they can achieve the planned organisational goals efficiently.

Leading

Leading involves directing, influencing and motivating employees to perform essential tasks.

Controlling

Finally, the manager must be sure that the actions of the organisation's members do in fact move the organisation toward its stated goals. This is the controlling function of management and it involves four main elements:

- establishing standards of performance;
- measuring current performance;
- comparing this performance to the established standards; and
- taking corrective action if deviations are detected.

Thus, through the controlling function, the manager keeps the organisation on its chosen track.

In practice, the management process does not involve four separate or loosely related sets of activities but a group of interactive functions. In reality, various combinations of these activities usually take place simultaneously. Furthermore, managers are limited by internal factors, for example their place in the organisation hierarchy, limited resources and the need to coordinate their actions with others. Managers must also adapt to the environment in which their organisation operates.

Types of managers

Managers are usually classified by:

- the range of organisational activities for which they are responsible (so-called functional and general managers); and
- their level in the organisation (so-called first-line, middle and top managers).

The functional manager

The **functional manager** is responsible for only one organisational activity such as production, marketing or finance. The people headed by a functional manager are engaged in a common set of activities. The general manager oversees a complex unit such as a company, a subsidiary or an independent operating division. He or she is responsible for all the activities of that unit such as its production, marketing and finance.

The first-line manager

First-line managers can also be referred to as supervisors, team leaders, section heads or leading hands, the latter being traditionally used in the manufacturing industry. At the simplest level, Bennett (1997) defines a first-line manager as 'a manager who controls non-managerial employees but is controlled by other managers'. In other words, the first-line manager represents the lowest level in the management hierarchy and acts as an intermediary between senior management and the workforce, balancing the demands of the two.

Middle management

Middle managers direct the activities of lower-level managers and sometimes those of operating employees as well. Middle managers' principal responsibilities are to direct the activities that implement their organisations' policies and to balance the demands of their superiors with the capacities of their subordinates.

Top managers

Composed of a comparatively small group of executives, **top management** is responsible for the overall strategic direction of the organisation. It establishes operating policies and guides the organisation's interactions with its environment. Typical titles of top managers are chairman, managing director and chief executive officer. (Actual titles tend to vary from country to country and from one organisation to another and are not always a reliable guide to membership of the highest management classification.)

Management level and skills

First-line managers and other levels of management are similar in the respect that they are responsible for the work of others, whereas subordinates are responsible for their own actions. Miller et al (in Cheng: 2000) made the observation that whilst managers perform similar functions, their time devoted to each task varies, which distinguishes senior management from first-line managers. Senior management tend to be involved in strategic decision making regarding the direction of the business. In contrasting, first-line managers are concerned with operational decisions relating to the daily running of the business to meet the objectives set by higher management.

According to Katz (in Stoner and Freeman, 1992), managers can be distinguished by the different sets of skills required for each level, which include technical, human and conceptual. He suggests that managers need all three skills.

- **Technical skill** is the ability to use the procedures, techniques and knowledge of a specialised field. Surgeons, engineers, musicians and accountants all have technical skills in their respective fields.
- **Human skill** is the ability to work with, understand and motivate other people as individuals or in groups.
- **Conceptual skill** concentrates on corporate and organisational planning, policy and systems.

Katz suggests that although all three of these skills are essential to a manager, their relative importance depends mainly on the manager's rank in the organisation. Technical skill is most important in the lower levels. Human skill, by contrast, is important for managers at every level. Because managers must work primarily through others, their ability to tap the technical skills of their subordinates is more important than their own technical proficiency. Finally, the importance of conceptual skill increases as one rises through the ranks of a management system based on hierarchical principles of authority and responsibility. (See figure 2.1.)

Figure 2.1: Skill distribution at various management levels

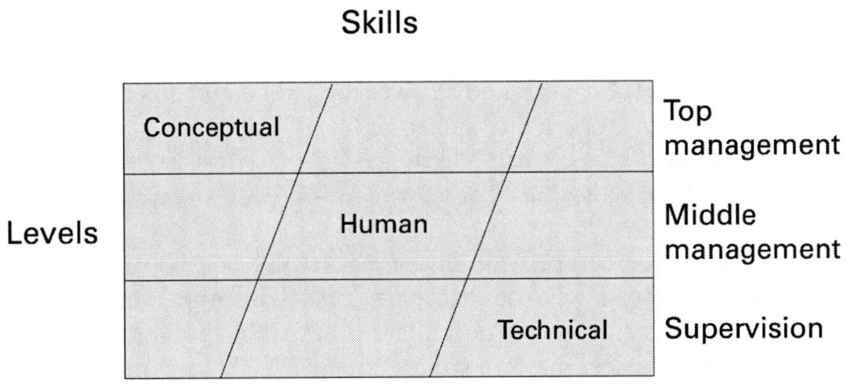

Skills

Source: Adapted from Katz, cited in Stoner and Freeman (1992)

Self-assessment question 2.1

Use Katz' typology of management skills to critically evaluate the attributes and skills of a managerial role in your own organisation and explain the extent to which these add value to your organisation.

Feedback on page 27

2.2 Purchasing management – public and private sector approaches

Learning activity 2.2

Draw up a table that compares the roles and responsibilities of purchasing managers in both private and public sector organisations.

Feedback on page 27

The private sector model

Public and private sector management both entail producing value for 'actors' in their environments, utilising resources and capabilities. However, they differ in the nature of that value and of those resources, capabilities and environments in ways which have implications for making and implementing strategy.

Ideally, private sector management requires the manager to:

- use organisational capabilities (for example staff, buildings, equipment) to produce particular goods and services;

- sell these goods and services to those in the organisation's environment who desire them, namely customers; and
- obtain resources (that is, money) from these customers (and from other providers of funds, that is, investors) in order to maintain or acquire organisational capabilities.

In this private sector model, the manager's task is to perform these functions as effectively as possible, by:

- producing the kinds of goods and services desired by customers (that is, the most useful, the best quality and so on);
- producing as much of them as desired; and/or
- doing so at minimal cost and hence at the lowest price to customers.

This model assumes that competition in the marketplace acts as a constant incentive for managers to maximise their performance in these respects. Resources only flow to the organisation if it is producing what the customers want at the prices they are willing to pay (that is, the measure of value of the goods and services produced is exchange value in markets).

At the strategic level, therefore, the private sector executive seeks to position or define the business (that is, decide to produce particular products for particular markets) in a way which aligns with the environment in that it maximises the flow of resources from customers and from investors, who perceive that this positioning is one that will earn them a good return on their investment. Thus, the money that the manager obtains from customers and investors is not only a resource with which to purchase productive capabilities, but also a signal that he or she is producing the right kind and amount of value. If customers do not get what they regard as value for money, they take their money elsewhere. Alternatively, the manager may seek to enhance the organisation's capabilities to produce more or better value.

The public sector management approach

The circumstances of ideal (or typical) public sector management are similar in form but more diverse in content. The public sector manager is also engaged in a process of converting resources into tangible or intangible things of value. However, they are more diverse in that each part of the process embraces a wider array of possible elements than in the private sector, such as in:

- the range of values produced;
- the productive capabilities deployed;
- the resources called upon;
- the composition of the environment in which they occur; and
- the nature of their interactions with that environment.

Each public manager faces a different mix of these elements, but they include inescapably public features to a greater or lesser extent.

Firstly, the public sector manager is responsible for ensuring the production of not only private but also *public* value – that is, value which is consumed by the public collectively (Moore, 1995; Stewart and Ranson, 1988). Of course, there is much debate about what public value is and should be. But the mainstream political consensus is that it includes:

- The provision of the legal framework which underpins law and order as well as providing the preconditions for the operation of the market, such as reinforcing property rights and contracts; this is the core of the free-market libertarians' minimal state (Nozick, 1974).
- Remedying various kinds of market failure, through the provision of public goods, and intervening to counter negative externalities, to minimise transactions costs or to curb excessive market power (Stokey and Zeckhauser, 1978).
- The promotion of equity. There is much disagreement about what equity means and how it can best be advanced, but there is broad consensus that it is important and needs to be facilitated (Stone, 1988).

Public value often tends to be perceived in different terms to private value which usually takes the form *of outputs* (that is, products and services). Public value usually registers in the public mind in the form *of outcomes*, that is, in terms of impacts on social groups or conditions.

The second difference is that public managers produce this value for a more complex cast of actors in their environments. Public value is 'consumed' by the *citizenry* rather than by paying customers, who consume private value. The citizenry expresses its needs and wants through the political process, which is subject to the influences of a diverse group of stakeholders, who convey their preferences by the mechanism of voice rather than exit (Hirschman, 1970). Thus, the public manager faces an *authorising* environment rather than a market one, which is often turbulent (Lax and Sebenius, 1986; Moore, 1995).

Also, some of the consumers of *private* value are not paying customers, but rather either *beneficiaries* (who receive private value but do not pay for it, for example welfare recipients), or *obligatees* (who have consumer-like interactions with the agency but in the process are being subjected to legal obligations, backed by the coercive power of the state, for example prisoners).

Thirdly, public sector managers use more diverse resources. In the private sector model, resources are unambiguously *economic*, that is, money provided as revenue or investments which provides the means of acquiring or renewing labour, equipment and raw materials. In the public production process, however, not only is public money a resource, but so too is *public power*.

Public managers use the legitimate authority of the state, as well as money, in order to carry out their tasks. Just as significantly, public power underpins the use of public money, in that public power is used to compel the collection of taxes. Therefore, the task of the public manager is to maximise benefits for the public while minimising resource costs.

Finally, public sector managers tend to utilise a wider range of productive capabilities, whereas private sector managers utilise organisational capabilities such as labour, equipment, buildings, raw materials and so on. These are controlled by owners or managers, or can be purchased by them with money, and are at the manager's disposal to be used in a variety of ways to optimise production. Public management, however, often entails tapping a wider range of productive capabilities which are available both within and outside the organisation.

Self-assessment question 2.2

Compare and contrast the roles and responsibilities of the purchasing manager in your own organisation with that of say, the production manager (if applicable) or finance manager. Make a note of the similarities and differences. Apart from functional expertise, what else do you think might differentiate each of these managers' roles?

Feedback on page 28

2.3 Purchasing function – impact of stakeholder groups

Learning activity 2.3

Identify the key stakeholders for your own or another organisation and the level of influence they might have.

Feedback on page 28

The concept of organisational stakeholders is now long established and the implications to management across all functional areas are well understood. In particular, it reminds managers of the following:

- Different stakeholders may have commonality of purpose at a very general level (for example 'providing quality services' or 'improving the quality of life for the community') but at more detailed levels they would wish to impose different purposes and priorities on an organisation. Therefore, purposes and priorities emerge from the political interplay between different stakeholder groups.
- Both politicians and strategic managers must understand the political context in detail and be able to develop and implement organisational strategies which are politically viable as well as rational.

What are stakeholders?

Organisational stakeholders are any individuals or groups (a collection of individuals) that have an interest in an organisation. These stakeholders can be both internal and external to the organisation and they can influence – and will be influenced by – the organisation in various ways. Figure 2.2 shows a number of key stakeholders for organisations.

Figure 2.2: Organisations – key stakeholders

For the purchasing function, the key *external* stakeholders that have a direct impact or influence are customers, suppliers, shareholders and perhaps in some circumstances competitors. However, the purchasing function also has to consider its *internal* stakeholders in addition to managers and employees, such as other functional areas in the organisation. In this respect, the purchasing manager has to consider manufacturing or service operations, sales and marketing, the cost and/or finance department among others. Each of these, to a greater or lesser extent, will have some influence on the decisions that the purchasing manager makes in the exercise of his role to provide the requisite materials for the organisation's operations.

Identifying stakeholders – stakeholder mapping

According to Johnson and Scholes (1999):

'Stakeholder mapping can be a powerful and useful tool of analysis but managers using it for the first time often find it a little more difficult than they expected. Like most practical tools of analysis, stakeholder mapping is most useful if it strikes a sensible balance between being too simplistic/generic and so detailed that it is difficult to interpret.'

They suggest that the following guidelines should be helpful:

* Avoid plotting long lists of stakeholders who 'in principle' or 'potentially' could have an influence on the (organisation's) strategy. This is a particularly important guideline in relation to powerful groups such as the ministry, the unions and so on.
* Remember that the mapping is done in relation to specific strategies, so a judgement must be made as to whether these groups are likely to exercise their power in relation to this particular strategy.
* This is clearly a matter of judgement of their level of interest. Groups that certainly will remain indifferent to the strategy probably could be excluded from the analysis.

Stakeholders: sources and indicators of power

Johnson and Scholes (1999) assert that it is important to identify where stakeholder power derives, and what the indicators of that power might be. They suggest that the source of power derives from the following:

* Within organisations:
  - the hierarchy (formal power), for example autocratic decision making

- influence (informal power), for example charismatic leadership
- control of strategic resources, for example strategic products
- possession of knowledge and skills, for example computer specialists
- control of the environment, for example negotiating skills
- involvement in strategy implementation, for example by exercising discretion.
- For external stakeholders:
  - control of strategic resources, for example materials, labour, money
  - involvement in strategy implementation, for example distribution outlets, agents
  - possession of knowledge (skills), for example subcontractors
  - through internal links, for example informal influence

They further suggest that the indicators of power derive from the following:

- Within organisations:
  - status
  - claim on resources
  - representation
  - symbols.
- For external stakeholders:
  - status
  - resource dependence
  - negotiating arrangements
  - symbols.

Self-assessment question 2.3

Having listed, in the learning activity, the key stakeholders relative to your own/another organisation, now rank each in the order of the level of influence they might have on the decision process(es) within your organisation, with 'most influence' ranking highest. Over time, how might this ranking change?

Feedback on page 28

2.4 Managing stakeholders

Learning activity 2.4

Explain how and why these different types of stakeholders (employees, customers, shareholders, suppliers, government, lenders and others) might affect decisions made within the purchasing function in your organisation.

Feedback on page 29

In order to manage stakeholders and their expectations, it is first necessary to identify who they are and then consider their level of power and interest. This can be done by using a power-interest matrix (shown in figure 2.3) to identify whether their level of power and interest is low or high.

Figure 2.3: The power-interest matrix

Level of interest

	Low	High
Low	Category A Minimal effort	Category B Keep informed
High	Category C Keep satisfied	Category D Key player

Power (vertical axis label)

Source: Johnson, Scholes and Whittington (2005)

Analysing stakeholders

- Stakeholders with high level of power and high level of interest (D): these tend to be the key players in the organisation who are often involved in managing the organisation and its future. Usually senior managers (or external bodies), they have power to block proposed plans and implement their own alternative agendas. These 'players' should be given serious consideration in the development of long-term plans and the future direction of the organisation.
- Stakeholders with high level of power and low level of interest (C): these tend to be mostly institutional shareholders and companies have to work hard to keep them satisfied. Often they remain compliant as long as they receive acceptable returns on their investment. Should returns be poor they may withdraw their support in terms of their financial investment in the organisation.
- Stakeholders with low level of power and high level of interest (B): these stakeholders exert relatively little power in influencing the organisation and its actions, but they do maintain a high level of interest in the organisation's health and well-being. They are quick to voice their concerns if that interest is not being considered and they usually do this via lobbying or the use of petitions with and from other interested parties.
- Stakeholders with low level of power and low level of interest (A): stakeholders in whom the organisation only invests minimal effort, for example small customers, small suppliers or non-direct organisations in the local community etc.

Self-assessment question 2.4

Imagine your purchasing and supply department is to go through a major change as part of refocusing the business to be more competitive. Explain how conducting a stakeholder analysis can help in planning this change.

Feedback on page 29

Revision question

Now try the revision question for this session on page 247.

Summary

In this study session we have looked at the following points:

- The key tasks of management in an organisation are to plan, organise, lead and control.
- Managers are usually classified by the range of organisational activities for which they are responsible (so-called functional and general managers) and their level in the organisation (so-called first-line, middle and top managers).
- Managers should possess three types of skills in order to carry out their role(s) effectively. Katz classifies these as technical, human and conceptual skills.
- Public and private sector management both entail producing value for 'actors' in their environments, but they differ in the nature of that value and in the way they deploy resources, capabilities and so on in their different environments in ways which have implications for the making and implementation of strategy.
- Organisational stakeholders are those individuals or groups – internal and/or external – that have an interest in an organisation. They can influence – and be influenced by – the organisation in various ways. We use stakeholder mapping to identify key stakeholders, and a power-interest grid to assess each stakeholder's level of power and influence on the organisation. This helps organisational decision making in that key stakeholders can be included in either the process itself or considered in relation to the impacts and/or outcomes of decisions made by the organisation.

Further reading

Van Weele (2005), chapter 19.

Feedback on learning activities and self-assessment questions

Feedback on learning activity 2.1

You should include planning, directing, controlling, monitoring and so on as the basis for your answer and explain the direct relationships of these areas to one another and to functional areas. You should be able to explain that unrelatedness would mean problems for any organisation and you should provide suitable explanation and examples of the impacts of this. Specific examples you might include are:

- Planning – this might involve developing a mission and setting objectives and actions to achieve those objectives. This requires decision making, that is, choosing from among alternative future courses of action and so on.

- Directing (organising) – relates to establishing intentional roles for people to fill in the organisation; designing appropriate structure and defining tasks and roles in relation to abilities and motivations of staff and so on.
- Leading and coordinating – influencing people to work in harmony so that they contribute to organisational and group goals.
- Controlling and monitoring – measuring and correcting the activities of staff to ensure that outcomes conform to plans and so on.

Feedback on self-assessment question 2.1

You should identify a specific management role in your organisation or purchasing function and evaluate the conceptual, technical and human skills necessary to carry out the role effectively. Also, you should attempt to evaluate whether or not these skills add value to the role identified. Some of the key skills you might include are:

- Conceptual – management skills in relation to decision making; problem identification; formulating alternative courses of action; evaluating alternative courses of action; selection of 'best choice' alternative. Thus the ability to rationally process and interpret information is important.
- Technical – skills in relation to applying specialist knowledge and expertise to the specific task in hand. All jobs require some specialist expertise, and technical skills can be learned on the job whether relating to design, use of technology, operations processes, testing, manufacturing and so on.
- Human – skills relating to the ability to work with, understand and motivate other people, both individually and in groups. Interpersonal skills such as listening and understanding the needs of others, managing conflict, communicating effectively, motivating and delegating are all examples of human skills.

Feedback on learning activity 2.2

Table 2.1 provides some examples of appropriate comparisons.

Table 2.1 Roles and responsibilities of purchasing managers in private and public sector organisations

Private sector	Public sector
Providing value through specialised utilisation of resources and capabilities	Providing value via a more diversified approach to utilising resources and capabilities
Purchasing managers are likely to have a narrower group of stakeholders	Purchasing managers have to provide value for a more complex cast of 'actors' in their environment, that is, a wider range of different stakeholder groups
Use organisational capabilities to provide goods and services demanded by customer groups	Outsource or purchase direct from suppliers of products and/or services. Do not purchase for manufacture
Maintain lowest cost/best (competitive) price for value to customers. If customers do not get value for money they find another supplier	Provide efficient and effective services and/or utilities to the public.

(continued on next page)

Table 2.1 *(continued)*

Private sector	Public sector
Private sector procurement policies tend to be organisation specific and are not subject to specific directives	Public sector procurement tends to follow legislatory directives

Feedback on self-assessment question 2.2

Where possible you should draw on real job roles and job descriptions in your own organisation to make the comparisons required and clearly identify the similarities and differences that exist within and across the roles chosen. You should clearly identify and explain any other relevant differentiating factors (perhaps specific to your organisation). The following examples provide some generic roles of purchasing and finance managers:

- Purchasing manager: Determine specification of goods and services to be bought; selecting suitable suppliers and devising procedures ad routines for their selection; negotiating with suppliers to establish agreements and prepare contracts; placing orders with suppliers; developing efficient purchase order and handling systems; monitoring and controlling orders to secure supply; follow-up and evaluating (settling claims, maintaining supplier records, supplier rating and ranking and so on).
- Finance manager: Procurement, allocation and utilisation of funds; careful selection of the source of capital; determining the debt to equity ratio; designing a proper capital structure for the organisation; financial planning including assessing the funds requirement, identifying and sourcing funds, allocation of funds and income and controlling the use or utilisation of funds towards achieving the primary goal of profit/wealth maximisation; preparation of financial plans etc.

Feedback on learning activity 2.3

You should identify key stakeholders such as shareholders/investors, employees, customers, management, suppliers, local authorities, community groups and any others that are directly relevant. For each one you should be able to explain the level of influence that they have on the organisation in terms of their involvement in planning and decision making relating to your organisation's strategic direction/goals and so on, or whether they are stakeholders with minimal influence but high interest in your organisation's activities. For example, these might be community or special interest (for example environmental) groups, certain customers or suppliers. It is important that you identify which groups directly or indirectly influence your organisation's direction and development.

Feedback on self-assessment question 2.3

You should identify that ranking, in terms of their level of influence, will be in accordance with the organisation and the stakeholders identified. Over time, the levels of influence by stakeholders may alter due to changes in organisational goals and objectives, strategy and direction, and the product or service-to-market relationships (that is, customer bases and supply bases may change over time).

Feedback on learning activity 2.4

You should identify the key stakeholder relationships that affect or influence your purchasing function or department, for example managers, customers, suppliers, other functional areas and so on. Each of these stakeholder groups will have a varying degree of influence – either directly or indirectly – on decisions made within the purchasing function.

You should explain which stakeholders have the most influence, the nature of this influence and why the stakeholders are important to the organisation. For example, important customers will have considerable influence over decisions made in the function, particularly if there is the threat (real or perceived) of them sourcing another supplier if they are not satisfied. Thus, relationships with these customers must be maintained well.

Certain suppliers might also have a high degree of influence – particularly if they are specialist suppliers who can command a high price for their products. This will undoubtedly influence your organisation in terms of its relationship with such suppliers.

You might also wish to consider the issue of the *internal customer*, that is, your production or service facility. They are obviously key stakeholders in your organisation and as such also have to be given priority or due consideration when circumstances dictate.

Feedback on self-assessment question 2.4

You should explain that stakeholder analysis will help your organisation identify where its priorities might lie in terms of who their key stakeholders are and to what extent they can influence the organisation's direction. In pursuing a new strategy to be more competitive, emphasis might be placed on relationships with those stakeholders who have a direct contribution to make to this, for example suppliers, distributors, financiers, internal production and operations, sales and marketing and so on. The mix will obviously depend on the type and nature of the organisation and the strategies it is pursuing.

2

Ethics and social responsibility

'If business is not based on ethical grounds, it is of no benefit to society, and will, like all other unethical combinations, pass into oblivion.'
Max Killan (cited in David, 1999)

Introduction

An organisation must have a purpose for it to exist. Put quite simply: if you have not got a goal, how do you know you have reached where you want to be? Establishing goals and strategies to achieve goals is essential if an organisation is to function effectively and efficiently.

Business ethics is a form of applied ethics that examines ethical rules and principles within a commercial context; the various moral or ethical problems that can arise in a business setting; and any special duties or obligations that apply to persons who are engaged in commerce. This session explores both organisational purpose (that is, achievement of goals) and the various ethical doctrines and approaches that exist.

Session learning objectives

After completing this session you should be able to:

3.1 Assess the importance of organisational goals and strategy for the operations and management of organisations.
3.2 Explain the concept of 'social responsibility and business ethics' and how this links directly (or otherwise) to an organisation's strategies and goals.
3.3 Create a set of rules for ethical behaviour.

Unit content coverage

This study session covers the following topics from the official CIPS unit content document:

Learning outcome

Evaluate the challenges facing managers in dynamic and changing organisations.

Learning objectives

1.5 Create a set of rules for ethical behaviour.

Prior knowledge

Study sessions 1 and 2.

Timing

You should set aside about 6 hours to read and complete this session, including learning activities, self-assessment questions, the suggested further reading (if any) and the revision question.

3.1 Organisational goals and strategy

The importance of goals has been the subject of many authors' work in recent times.

- Goals give the company direction and promote good organisation. Goals encourage purposeful behaviour. De Wit and Meyer (2004) stipulate, 'Plans give organisations a sense of direction. Without objectives and plans organisations would be adrift.' Without a clear sense of direction, any activity would be acceptable. Job roles/demarcations would be ambiguous and consequently the company would be ineffectual.
- Goals help to coordinate the company's activities. Having a specific goal allows the organisation to work together. If activities are agreed at the beginning, there will be less confusion and tension within the organisation at a later date. It also helps to avoid duplication of work.
- Goals make the best use of available resources. Deciding on a goal and then a strategy gives managers the opportunity to take stock of their resources and allocate them to the most appropriate activity.
- Goals help break down big tasks into small chunks. Having a goal allows managers to break up an activity into smaller tasks. It also means that it is possible to make detailed plans to ensure that the goal is achieved.
- Goals can act as motivators. By reaching a goal, employees can be fuelled with confidence and strive to attain other goals. Although, Etzioni (1964, cited in Mullins, 2005) is very cynical and points out that organisations 'rarely achieve their goals with any degree of finality and can, therefore, almost always be reported as a failure'.
- Goals help measure success/progress and monitor change. Simon (1964, cited in Mullins, 2005) views goals as a hindrance rather than a help. He views goals as constraints which the organisation must deal with, for example attaining a certain level of profit or providing job satisfaction for employees. He believes that goals actually prevent decision making at the lower levels of an organisation.

Having goals is a necessity, but depending on the environment, the goals of the organisation may have to change in order to sustain competitiveness. This is underpinned by Mullins (2005) who comments, 'It is important, however, that the organisation does not restrict innovation but is ready to respond positively to changing circumstances and, increasingly, to anticipate future change.'

Learning activity 3.1

Brooks (2003) argues 'that in dynamic environments annual objectives or individual goals often fail to embrace the need for change and flexibility'.

(continued on next page)

3

3

Learning activity 3.1 *(continued)*

Using your own or another organisation to illustrate your answer, draw up a list of reasons why this argument might be true.

Feedback on page 39

The goal-setting theory proposed by Locke (1968) believes that:

- Challenging goals lead to a higher level of performance than basic ones.
- Specific goals should be assigned as they lead to higher levels of performance than those that are ambiguous. Buchanan and Huczinski (2004) makes the valid point that 'it is easier for us to change our behaviour when we know precisely what is required of us'.
- Involvement and participation in setting goals also improves the level of performance. It makes employees feel included and important and therefore they are likely to commit themselves to a particular goal.
- Feedback is essential. As Buchanan and Huczinski (2004) highlighted, we can alter our behaviour if we know what is expected of us.

Above all, goals should be **SMART**: specific, measurable, attainable, realistic and time related. If goals are not SMART they can actually have a negative impact upon employees and hence the organisation. For example, if an employee is set an unrealistic goal which is too demanding, the employee is unlikely to reach the intended goal and therefore may feel awkward and demotivated.

Most importantly, in order to have the desired effect the goals must be communicated clearly and accepted by those responsible for implementation. Participative goal setting as opposed to management merely dictating the terms is particularly useful as it helps to set realistic goals and it involves employees at lower levels which is likely to empower them. This in turn helps to nurture a healthy culture. Brooks (2003) comments, 'organisational bureaucracies often make goal setting difficult, and, hence, dissipate the potential motivational benefits from processes such as management by objectives (MBO)'. Finally, feedback should be provided.

Self-assessment question 3.1

Critically evaluate the following statement:

'The most fundamentally important part of the management process is the setting of realistic goals and objectives'.

Use your own organisation to support your discussion.

Feedback on page 40

3.2 Social responsibility and ethics

Learning activity 3.2

Prepare a list of examples giving instances where your organisation acts ethically. Explain where improvements can be made.

Feedback on page 40

Generally speaking, business ethics is a **normative discipline**, whereby particular ethical standards are assumed and then applied. Business ethics makes specific judgements about what is right or wrong, which is to say, it makes claims about what ought to be done or what ought not to be done. While there are some exceptions, business ethicists are usually less concerned with the foundations of ethics (**meta-ethics**) or with justifying the most basic ethical principles, and are more concerned with practical problems and applications, and any specific duties that might apply to business relationships.

Ethics is the study of moral values and moral behaviour. Ethical behaviour is acting in ways consistent with one's personal values and the commonly held values of the organisation and society. A number of definitions exist:

- 'The study of ethics is not what is legal but of the application of moral standards to business decisions.' Jennings (1996)
- 'Ethics is concerned with the study of morality: practices and activities that are considered to be importantly right or wrong, together with the rules that govern those activities and the values to which those activities relate.' Mullins (2005)
- 'Corporate social responsibility is the obligation of an organisation to behave in ethical ways in the social environment in which it operates … Current concerns include protecting the environment, promoting worker safety, supporting social issues and investing in the community.' (Nelson and Quick, 1996)
- 'Being socially responsible implies playing more than just an economic role in society. Increasingly, firms are expected by society to play a direct role in meeting community needs in the Arts and education, in health and environmental matters, and in social welfare, and in addition to their roles as employers and producers.' (Cole, 1996)

Unethical behaviour includes:

- stealing
- lying/not telling the truth
- engaging in conflict of interest
- divulging information
- taking advantage of others.

To date, no *universal* code of ethics is in existence. Some companies develop their own code of ethics as did Rotary International (in Nelson and Quick, 1996). They believe it is ethical behaviour if:

- it is the truth
- it is fair to all concerned
- it will foster goodwill and better friendships
- it will be beneficial to all concerned.

Some firms 'volunteer' to be socially responsible, but in some cases social responsibility is enforced by the law. As Cole (1996) states:

> 'In Britain, as in most other states, the law plays an important, though not dominant, role in regulating the relationships between firms and their various stakeholders. So for example, there are laws designed

to protect the community from less-welcome effects of commercial activities, such as industrial pollution, unsightly building developments and hazardous products'

By voluntarily being socially responsible, firms can benefit as well as society. For example, a major pharmaceutical company might contribute funds to their local hospital. By doing this, a company can foster good public relations and promote an altruistic reputation whereby the company is an asset to the community. The vice-chairman of a well-known advertising agency stresses 'the only sustainable competitive advantage any business has is its reputation' (Jennings, 1996).

Many companies devote a great deal of time to their ethical behaviour and behaving ethically can have a positive impact upon an organisation's performance. However, interpretation of *what is ethical* varies quite considerably. For example, some organisations believe that the social responsibility of business is principally to generate as much profit as possible for their shareholders and within certain guidelines. Others take a wider perspective, believing that a business exists for all of its stakeholders.

On the other hand, some companies choose to behave unethically, for example exploiting labour in order to retain a large profit margin. However, the longevity of these companies might be considered debatable. Although savings may be made, in the long-run these decisions will be detrimental to the company both in terms of image and its long-term competitiveness.

Moody Jennings (1996) supports this. She argues that 'a business lacking an ethical commitment will eventually bring about its own demise', and continues to say that:

> 'examining the fates of companies such as Union Carbide, Beech-Nut, E.F. Hutton, Soloman Brothers, Johns-Manville, Exxon, Phar-Mor, and others whose ethical mishaps resulted in public exposure supports the notion that a lack of commitment to ethical behaviour is a lack of commitment to a firm's success.'

Self-assessment question 3.2

Draft an outline report in explaining *why* organisations should conduct their business in an ethical and socially responsible way.

Feedback on page 41

3.3 Ethical codes and rules

According to the Institute of Management (in Cole, 1996), a code of ethics is:

> 'a set of moral principles or values, used by organisations to steer the conduct both of the organisation itself and its employees, in all their business activities, both internal and in relation to the outside world'.

Such codes exist in most professions and some organisations to guide interactions between specialists with advanced knowledge (for example doctors, lawyers, engineers, stonemasons) and the general public. These codes are often not part of any more general theory of ethics but accepted as pragmatic necessities. Ethical codes are distinct from moral codes that apply to the education and religion of a whole society.

A code of ethics is a formal statement of the company's values on ethics and social issues. Some set out general principles about the company's beliefs on matters such as quality, employees or the environment. Others set out the procedures to be used in specific ethical situations, such as conflicts of interest or the acceptance of gifts. The effectiveness or otherwise of such codes of ethics depends on the extent to which management supports them with sanctions and rewards.

Ethical codes establish trade-offs and rationale for making decisions for the greater good. Some of these resemble a moral code, most are less strict and make no special claim to actually distinguish right from wrong in any absolute sense. The ethical code is concerned with weighing all of the negative and positive results of an action, and making a decision based upon the greater good for a greater number.

Ethical issues and approaches

Philosophers and others disagree about the purpose of a business in society. For example, some suggest that the principal purpose of a business is to maximise returns to its owners or, in the case of a publicly traded concern, its shareholders. Thus, under this view, only those activities that increase profitability and shareholder value should be encouraged. Some believe that the only companies that are likely to survive in a competitive marketplace are those that place profit maximisation above everything else. However, some point out that self interest would still require a business to obey the law and adhere to basic moral rules, because the consequences of failing to do so could be very costly in fines, loss of licence or company reputation. The economist Milton Friedman is a leading proponent of this view.

Other theorists contend that a business has moral duties that extend well beyond serving the interests of its owners or stockholders, and that these duties consist of more than simply obeying the law. They believe a business has moral responsibilities to so-called stakeholders, people who have an interest in the conduct of the business, which might include employees, customers, vendors, the local community or even society as a whole. They would say that stakeholders have certain rights with regard to how the business operates, and some would even suggest that this includes rights of governance.

Learning activity 3.3

Prepare a list of detailed reasons why an organisation's code of ethics should consider all of its stakeholders rather than just its shareholders.

Feedback on page 41

Ethical issues can arise when companies must comply with multiple and sometimes conflicting legal or cultural standards, as in the case of multinational companies that operate in countries with varying practices. For example, should a company obey the laws of its home country, or should it follow the less stringent laws of the developing country in which it does business? To illustrate this, for example, US law forbids companies from paying bribes either domestically or overseas. However, in some other parts of the world, bribery is a normal, accepted way of doing business. Similar problems can occur with regard to child labour, employee safety, work hours, wages, discrimination and environmental protection laws.

Corporate ethics policies

Many companies have formulated internal policies pertaining to the ethical conduct of employees. These policies can be simple exhortations in broad, highly generalised language (typically called a corporate ethics statement), or they can be more detailed policies, containing specific behavioral requirements (typically called corporate ethics codes). They are generally meant to identify the company's expectations of workers and to offer guidance on handling some of the more common ethical problems that might arise in the course of doing business. It is hoped that having such a policy will lead to greater ethical awareness, consistency in application and the avoidance of ethical disasters.

In creating a set of rules for ethical behaviour, most organisations would (indirectly) follow a set of historical philosophical doctrines, such as:

- Deontological ethics, or deontology (from the Greek word *deo*, meaning obligation), is an ethical theory considered solely on duty and rights, where there is an unchanging moral obligation to abide by a set of defined principles. Thus, the ends of any action never justify the means in this ethical system. If someone were to do their moral duty, then it would not matter if it had negative consequences.
- Utilitarianism (from the Latin word *utilis*, meaning useful) is a theory of ethics based on quantitative maximisation of some good for society or humanity. It is a form of consequentialism. This good is often happiness or pleasure, though some utilitarian theories might seek to maximise other consequences. Utilitarianism is sometimes summarised as 'The greatest happiness for the greatest number'.
- Teleology is the supposition that there is design, purpose, directive principle or finality in the works and processes of nature, and the philosophical study of that purpose.
- Ethical egoism is the ethical doctrine that holds that individuals ought to do what is in their self-interest. Ethical egoism does not necessitate that individuals disregard the well-being of others, nor does it require that an individual refrain from taking the well-being of others into consideration. It allows for the possibility of either as long it is efficacious in satisfying self-interest.

Not everyone supports corporate policies that govern ethical conduct. Some claim that ethical problems are better dealt with by depending upon employees to use their own judgement. Others believe that corporate ethics policies are primarily rooted in utilitarian concerns, and that they are mainly

3

to limit the company's legal liability, or to win favour from the public by giving the appearance of being a good corporate citizen.

Sometimes there is a disconnection between the company's code of ethics and the company's actual practices. Thus, whether or not such conduct is explicitly sanctioned by management, at worst this makes the policy duplicitous, and at best it is merely a marketing tool. To be successful, most ethicists would suggest that an ethics policy should be:

- Given the unequivocal support of top management, by both word and by example.
- Explained in writing and orally, with periodic reinforcement.
- Do-able, that is, something employees can both understand and perform.
- Monitored by top management with routine inspections for compliance and improvement.
- Backed up by clearly stated consequences in the case of disobedience.

Self-assessment question 3.3

Explain your organisation's approach to 'ethical purchasing', and also the extent to which you consider this to be based upon the dominant culture of your organisation/country. Explain how this approach might differ in other organisations.

Feedback on page 41

Revision question

Now try the revision question for this session on page 247.

Summary

- Clear goals give a company direction and promote good organisation; help coordinate the company's activities; help make best use of available resources; help break down big tasks; can act as motivators and help measure progress and monitor change within the organisation. For organisations to stay ahead of their competition, they must be adaptable. This may mean that they have to rethink and devise new goals.
- Goals must be SMART: specific, measurable, attainable, realistic and time related. If goals are not SMART, they can have a negative impact upon employees and hence the organisation. If employees are set an unrealistic goal, it is likely that the employee will feel demotivated.
- Goals must be clearly communicated and accepted by those responsible for implementing them. Participative goal setting, rather than management dictating the objectives, is particularly useful as it makes employees feel involved and gives them a sense of responsibility. This is

likely to empower them. Feedback is essential as it allows employees to get back on track should they deviate from their goal.

- Ethics is the study of moral values and moral behaviour. Ethical behaviour means acting in ways consistent with an individual's own personal values and the commonly held values of the organisation and society.
- 'Corporate social responsibility is the obligation of an organisation to behave in ethical ways in the social environment in which it operates … Current concerns include protecting the environment, promoting worker safety, supporting social issues and investing in the community'. (Nelson and Quick, 1996)
- Interpretations of 'what is ethical' varies quite considerably. For example, some organisations are of the belief that the social responsibility of business is principally to generate as much profit as possible for their shareholders, and within certain guidelines. Others take a wider perspective, believing that a business exists for all of its stakeholders.
- Jennings (1996) argues that 'a business lacking an ethical commitment will, eventually bring about its own demise'.
- According to Cole (1996), a code of ethics is 'a set of moral principles or values, used by organisations to steer the conduct both of the organisation itself and its employees, in all their business activities, both internal and in relation to the outside world'.
- Deontology is the logic of moral obligation.
- Utilitarianism is the ethical doctrine that the greatest happiness of the greatest number should be the criterion of the virtue of action.
- Teleology is an approach to ethics that studies actions in relation to their ends or utility.
- Egoism (or ethical egoism) is the belief that the correct basis for a moral code is every person's concern for their own best interests, or the doctrine supporting this belief.

Suggested further reading

Deresky (2006), pp63–70 and pp71–73.

Feedback on learning activities and self-assessment questions

Feedback on learning activity 3.1

There are likely to be a variety of reasons why this may be true depending on the context of your organisation. However, it is important to consider the following points:

- If an organisation sets annual objectives, they are usually developed based on previous years' performance and figures. This annual planning cycle usually means that the organisation is unlikely to deviate from its plans until the next review.
- Functional, departmental and individual objectives usually coincide with organisational objectives. Therefore, it is likely that these objectives will also be pursued within the same planning period.

- Changes in competitive dynamics have no fixed time frames. Organisations therefore need to be flexible and prepared to revise their goals and objectives in line with their environment. However, with the aforementioned fixed or annual planning approaches, organisations may be 'locked in' to achieving the objectives they have set and may not be prepared for change. For example, a firm may have invested a large amount of money and time into a certain product, activity system or specific technology. If there is a change in the environment, the firm is likely to be hesitant and reluctant to immediately change with the environment as, according to De Wit and Meyer (2004), any deviation from the past investment 'will increase the risk of not earning back [recouping] the sunk cost'. Also a company may have allocated set budgets for each function over a financial year and may not have the resources available to accommodate responses to change within that period. The impact of this may be an inability to compete or to take advantage of opportunities that may arise.

Feedback on self-assessment question 3.1

This is an open discussion vehicle but you should think carefully about the detail associated with this task. You should be able to explain why it is important to set realistic goals and targets as the basis for organisational development through business-level plans and strategic plans etc. The issue of interdependence of functions in the achievement of goals should also be discussed. In reality, businesses with no clear sense of direction lose their way and competitiveness is affected.

A good answer is likely to include the following points:

- Goals that are too ambitious will inevitably lead to failure, low morale and demotivation of staff.
- If goals are realistic they are likely to be met, which makes future planning easier (it smoothes out the planning process).
- Realistic goals, if met, can motivate staff further to reach other desired goals and objectives.

Feedback on learning activity 3.2

The meaning of the word 'ethical' is open to interpretation. Examples of ethical behaviour will vary and may be company specific. For example, your organisation might:

- Provide outplacement services and compensation/severance pay when redundancies have to be made to help employees cope with the situation and find alternative employment.
- Help/invest in the local community by either making donations or allocating a day where they help with countryside tasks or something similar.
- Promote worker safety.
- Generate as much profit as possible for its stakeholders!
- Treat employees fairly and with respect.

Feedback on self-assessment question 3.2

Important points to consider include:

- It fosters good public relations as well as helping with the local community's needs.
- It helps create a certain reputation.
- Consumers are more likely to purchase goods and services from ethical companies, therefore sales will be increased.
- Research shows that unethical companies have no long-term future.

Feedback on learning activity 3.3

If attention is paid only to investors of the business, with the intention of maximising its profits, then the company is in fact stifling its profits. If the company focuses all its attention on its investors, the business could be neglecting its most valuable resource – its employees. Theaker (2002) states that 'one of the most important groups of stakeholders is a company's employees'. If employees are content at work, the fact that the company is good to work for and that it values and cares for its employees will spread by word of mouth. Also it has been observed by a well-known firm of accountants that investors' decisions to buy or sell their shares is based upon factors other than financial performance, such as the ability to attract and retain talented employees, as well as corporate strategy and innovation. Therefore, employees can have a significant impact on the share price.

It is important to consider all stakeholders; however, in practice it is impossible. Companies must therefore prioritise their stakeholders.

Feedback on self-assessment question 3.3

Your answers to this will be primarily subjective. However, your answers should include some detailed reference to the principles governing purchasing practice in your organisation or culture. For example:

- To what extent does your organisation's ethical approach approximate to the doctrines explained in this session, that is, deontology, teleology, ethical egoism or utilitarianism?
- Does your organisation have clearly defined policies that govern ethical conduct throughout the organisation, for example through your purchasing policy documents or statements, or your code of conduct for doing business with not only suppliers but also customers.
- Does your organisation always purchase from approved vendors who can guarantee the quality, safety and reliability of goods supplied? To what extent might your organisation be inclined to purchase from unapproved sources, and for what reason?
- Does the dominant national culture dictate the principles and practices that exist in your organisation? For example, are there recognised trading standards and associations which govern and monitor organisational practices from an ethical standpoint?

3

Management reporting

Introduction

Effective reporting, through the most efficient communication channels and by the best communication methods, is essential if an organisation is to achieve its goals and objectives. Reporting or communicating to management is basically the exchange of information (messages) from a *sender* to a *receiver*, by a variety of means and through a number of different kinds of networks, in order to achieve common meaning between the two parties.

This session examines the nature of managerial communication, the basic components of the communication process, and the use of negotiation as a means of gaining senior management support for new initiatives and ideas.

At the start of the first round of the 1972 British Open Golf Championship, Tony Jacklin said to his partner Lee Trevino: 'I don't want to talk.' Trevino replied: 'You don't have to talk, just listen.'

Session learning objectives

After completing this session you should be able to:

4.1 Determine ways of reporting effectively to senior management.
4.2 Explain the ways in which the purchasing manager might secure top-level support and sponsorship for initiatives and implementation of plans in the purchasing and supply function.

Unit content coverage

This study session covers the following topic from the official CIPS unit content document:

Learning outcome

Use a range of techniques to support and implement justifiable management decisions.

Learning objective

1.6 Propose ways of reporting effectively to senior management and securing top-level support and sponsorship for initiatives and implementation of plans.

Prior knowledge

Study sessions 1 – 3.

Timing

You should set aside about 4 hours to read and complete this session, including learning activities, self-assessment questions, the suggested further reading (if any) and the revision question.

4.1 Communicating and reporting to management

Learning activity 4.1

Identify and describe the various forms of communication that exist within your own organisation or one with which you are familiar.

Feedback on page 56

Managerial communication

Managerial decision making is based on the acquisition of appropriate, relevant and timely information that provides the manager (decision maker) with the means to make *informed* decisions. Managers often lack vital information or have too much indiscriminate information which must be sifted through for its salient points.

The effectiveness of reporting in organisations is dependent on the communication flows that exist in the organisation:

- Downward – from people at higher levels to those at lower levels throughout the organisation.
- Upward – from subordinates or staff to superiors or senior officers in the organisation.

Crosswise – either horizontally, via people on the same level; or diagonally, between people at different levels who have no direct reporting relationships.

Figure 4.1: Communication flows in an organisation

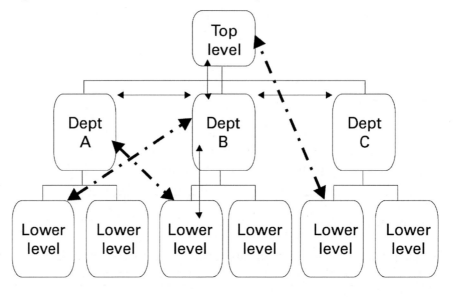

Figure 4.1 shows vertical, horizontal (or lateral) and crosswise (or informal) lines of communication in an organisation.

Essentially, communication is the exchange of messages between people for the purpose of achieving common meanings, and generally managers use two types of communication in their work, as follows.

Verbal communication

Using words to communicate:

- In written form – including letters, memos, reports, newsletters, policy and instructional manuals etc. Advantages are that there is a record of the communication, delivery can be assured, and the writer has time to think the message through. It is also permanent, less liable to misinterpretation and encourages the sender to think before despatch (Cole, 1996). Disadvantages are that written messages are longer, sometimes costly, liable to misinterpretation and can be of poor quality.
- Orally – through face-to-face conversations, meetings or by telephone. This may lack the thought that is given to written communication but the advantages here are that oral communication is usually faster and provides for immediate feedback. In the case of face-to-face meetings, it has the added advantage of being reinforced by various forms of non-verbal behaviour such as facial expressions, gestures and body posture. The disadvantages are that conversations are time consuming and difficult to terminate, and that additional time may be needed to document what has been said. Also, according to Cole (1996):

'one of the major difficulties associated with oral communication is its transience – the spoken word is a sound, and lasts only so long as it takes to pronounce it. Thus people are often able to deny, or to qualify what they have, in fact, said.'

(Cole makes the point that this is one of the main reasons for the importance of minutes at committee meetings – to provide true and accurate records of what has been discussed, by whom, and so on.)

Non-verbal communication

Non-verbal communication is usually conveyed from sender to receiver by means of various elements and behaviours that are not coded into words, such as:

- Kinesic behaviour – this includes body movements such as gestures, facial expressions and so on.
- Proxemics – the influence of proximity and space on communication, for example the influence of a large desk between a manager and employee.
- Paralanguage – this includes vocal aspects of communication that relate to how something is said rather than to what is said.
- An object language – communication through the use of material things, including clothing, cosmetics, furniture and architecture.

4

Factors that impede or enhance individual communication

Perception

The perception of people is affected by factors such as experiences, needs, personality and education. Distorted perceptions can cause communication problems for managers because of:

- Stereotyping – the tendency to attribute characteristics to an individual on the basis of an assessment of the group to which the individual belongs.
- The halo effect – the tendency to use a general impression based on one or a few characteristics of an individual in order to judge other characteristics of that same individual.
- Projection – the tendency of an individual to assume that others share their thoughts, feelings and characteristics.
- Perceptual defence – the tendency to block out or distort information that appears to be threatening or that challenges an individual's beliefs.
- Self-serving – the tendency to perceive oneself as responsible for successes and others as responsible for failures.

Semantic blocks

These are blockages or difficulties in communication that arise from word choices. These occur because both senders and receivers of messages have different **semantic nets** (that is, the network of words and word meanings that individuals have available for recall), and **semantic blocks** (which arise because senders and receivers of messages have different *semantic nets*). Examples of these include where professional jargon (language related to a particular profession) is used that is unfamiliar to others outside the profession. Organisation-specific language can build cohesiveness within the organisation but can be confusing to newcomers.

Paying attention to non-verbal parts of messages

Non-verbal elements reinforce verbal messages in four ways:

- Repeating the verbal message, for example pointing out a direction.
- Complementing, or adding to, the verbal message, for example looking embarrassed.
- Accenting, or emphasising, a verbal message, for example pounding the table.
- Regulating the verbal message, for example nodding to signal another to start or stop speaking.

Non-verbal communication elements can also substitute for the verbal message (such as using gestures) and contradict the verbal message (looking angry while stating that you are not).

Listening and feedback

These are skills that can be developed by managers as they tend to spend a great deal of their time engaged in oral communication.

Active listening

Managers can develop this by:

- Listening patiently and signalling simple acceptance of what is being said.
- Trying to understand feelings as well as cognitive content.
- Encouraging other people to keep talking.
- Allowing time for discussion and avoiding confrontative questions or assertions.
- Encouraging exposition of topics that are of interest.
- Listening for omissions.
- Offering honest opinion only if it is elicited.
- Listening: not planning what they will say next.
- Not making judgements until all information is conveyed.

Giving feedback

This is a continuous part of managing and an essential part of the communications process. Most feedback that managers give is to their staff or subordinates, and a few simple guidelines can help develop this more effectively:

- Focus on relevant behaviours or outcomes, not on the individual as a person.
- Deal with specific, observable behaviour, not generalities.
- Label perceptions, reactions and opinions as such.
- Spell out what can be done to improve performance.

Managers must also be able to receive feedback themselves, and should:

- Paraphrase what is said to check perceptions.
- Ask for clarification or examples regarding points that are unclear or with which they disagree.
- Avoid reacting defensively.

Barriers to communication

Barriers to communication can exist in the sender, the transmission of the message, the receiver or in feedback. The most common barriers are:

- Lack of planning – communicating without thinking first or stating purpose.
- Underlying assumptions in messages, that is, unstated parts of a message that the sender believes the receiver will understand.
- Semantic distortion, either deliberate or accidental.
- Poorly expressed messages – lack of care and precision in articulating meaning and content.
- Communication in the international environment – different meanings in different cultures.
- Loss by transmission and poor retention – information is less accurate if repeated by person to person, details may not be remembered.
- Poor listening and premature evaluation – internal focus by the receiver instead of on the sender or the message, judging instead of understanding.

- Impersonal communication instead of willingness by superiors to be open in communicating.
- Distrust, threat and fear, which undermine communication.
- Insufficient period for adjustment to change – forcing before people can adjust.
- Information overload – causing the receiver to disregard information, make errors, delay, filter only bits of information, or escape from the task of communication.

Other barriers include:

- Selective perception – receiving what they expect to receive.
- Attitude – influencing what is received.
- Status and power differences – if information goes through several levels.

Types of reporting

In business situations there are two widely used communication methods: written reports and presentations.

Written reports

Written reports are basically outcomes of a study of facts and implications of particular situations and are intended to summarise the facts relating to those situations, relate them to what the organisation is doing, draw appropriate conclusions and make useful recommendations.

Betts (2000) defines a report as 'a written account of an event or situation, together with relevant facts, figures and recommendations, where required'.

Reports can range from short, one-page summaries to detailed works of many thousands of words. Either way, reports usually follow a generic format that allows the writer to assemble their data and ideas into a logical order:

1 Title, name of author(s) and date.
2 Terms of reference.
3 Introduction.
4 Findings.
5 Implications for the organisation.
6 Conclusions.
7 Recommendations.
8 Appendices.
9 Bibliography and references (usually in academic reports).

(Adapted from Cole, 1996)

Basic/key requirements of a report are:

- The report should be timely (that is, it should be presented at the required time).
- The report should contain information that is relevant and accurate.
- The report should not be discriminatory.

- The report should have a clear objective and be concise throughout. Cole (1996) argues that 'a clear well-argued report will stand a far higher possibility of acceptance than one which is rambling and verbose, however relevant its content'.
- The report should be readable, that is, any terminology/abbreviations used should be explained.
- The report should be in a logical order, with a clear layout, and it should be complete.
- The report must be interesting.
- The report should be of appropriate length and detail.

Koontz and Weihrich (1990) state:

'common problems in written communication are that writers omit the conclusion or bury it in the report, are too wordy, and use poor grammar, ineffective sentence structure, and incorrect spelling.'

Presentations

Widely used in selling situations and management planning exercises, presentations can also be used for major reports or to disseminate information relating to new ideas or proposals to colleagues, suppliers or customers. The three main elements of any presentation are:

- Preparation – this is vital for any presentation.
- Content – what to include and what to leave out in relation to the type of audience receiving the presentation.
- Delivery – *how* the presentation will be made. Some audiences expect presentations to be short, sharp and to the point (for example, top management). Others require further detail and explanation (for example, shop-floor workers receiving technical information). Also, most presentations benefit from illustrations and the use of visual aids such as flipcharts, videos, films, overhead transparencies etc.

According to Cole (1996), when making presentations the manager (or presenter) should:

- Consider their audience and their needs.
- Assemble their facts and ideas, having considered the audience and their needs, and take into account the complexity of the material.
- Develop sufficient and suitable visual aids.
- Consider what other information should be made available (drawings, specifications and so on).
- Explain to their audience what they are about to tell them, tell them, and then tell them what they told them!
- Be enthusiastic about the subject.
- Be natural wherever possible.
- Maintain eye contact with their audience.
- Be prepared for questions both during and after the presentation.

Improving communication

- Senders must clarify in their minds what they want to communicate.

- Words and symbols should be familiar to the receiver and the sender.
- Planning should not be done in a vacuum, others should be consulted.
- The needs of the receivers of the information must be considered.
- Tone of voice, choice of words and congruency all influence communication.
- Feedback is required to ensure the message has been understood.
- Responsibility for the communication lies with the receiver as well as the sender.
- The sender and receiver engage in **active listening**: this is the key to understanding.

Improving written communication

Use:

- Simple words and phrases and short, familiar words.
- Personal pronouns when appropriate.
- Illustrations and examples (charts, tables and so on).
- Short sentences and paragraphs.
- Active verbs.

Avoid unnecessary words.

Effective communications in committees

Committees, whether formal or informal, require certain components for effective communication to be realised. In general, committees should:

- Have the authority to define known responsibilities.
- Be of an appropriate size, that is, large enough to promote deliberation, but not so large as to waste time or foster indecision.
- Have an appropriate membership: members should be representative of the interests they are intended to serve, they should possess the required authority and be able to contribute to committee discussion.
- Limit subject matter to what can be handled in group discussion.
- Have a chairperson who can plan and conduct the meeting effectively.
- Keep accurate records of discussions via minutes: these should be prepared in order to avoid misunderstanding and should be followed up for approval.
- Be cost effective: any committee meeting must be worth its cost.

Using electronic media

Telecommunications occur via telephone, cable, radio, TV and microwave.

Teleconferencing is where groups of people interact with one another from different parts of the country – or globe – using audiovisual media with still or moving pictures. This has advantages in that it:

- Reduces costs of travel time and other associated expenses, for example hotel bills, taxis fares and so on.
- Can be used when the need arises. No long-term advance planning is needed.
- Can be used frequently, thus improving communications.

The disadvantages are:

- It should not be over-used, that is, teleconferencing should only be used for essential and important meetings or dissemination of information. Overuse may have a detrimental effect on cost.
- The equipment may not be reliable.
- It is not a substitute for face-to-face communication.

Using computers for information handling

Computers allow the communication of appropriate and timely information via intra-, inter- and extranets. (See study session 20.) This facilitates speedy communications and decision making in organisations.

Effective meetings

Cole (1996) maintains that:

'to use the time spent on meetings more effectively, a number of simple questions can be asked:
- Is a meeting necessary to deal with this issue? That is, could a telephone call, fax or memo suffice?
- What is the purpose of the meeting?
- How can we prepare for this meeting?
- How can we ensure that the meeting is going to be worthwhile to those attending?
- How long should the meeting last?
- Who should be invited to attend?
- How will action points be captured and dealt with?'

Self-assessment question 4.1

Evaluate the effectiveness of the various forms of communication in your organisation and suggest how instances of poor communication can or should be remedied.

Feedback on page 56

4.2 Securing top-management support

Learning activity 4.2

Describe, in around 250–300 words, how you would engage the support of your immediate line manager for an idea or initiative that you would like adopted or implemented in your department or functional area.

Feedback on page 56

The basics of negotiating

In order to secure top-management support for new ideas or initiatives within the purchasing function or across the organisation as a whole, it is important that managers/employees not only have the requisite communication skills, but also good negotiating skills.

According to Cawthray (1984), negotiation is 'a transaction involving the voluntary consent of two parties to reach a most favourable outcome, free of potential veto'.

Normally, negotiation takes place in our everyday working lives when buying goods, when selling goods and services, when making contracts and when settling disagreements. The common dilemmas associated with negotiating in these situations relate to:

- How much to ask for.
- Knowing what the other party will accept.
- How far to move in the negotiation.
- How long to 'hang on' for a favourable outcome.
- How to avoid deadlock.
- The other party's expectations.

Movement and concessions in negotiating

Movement involves the parties moving towards a compromise situation.

Concessions – or give-aways – may produce movement (opening 'goodwill' concessions usually display weakness and tough negotiators will harden).

Starting proceedings

In opening negotiations it is important to avoid weakening the opening by agreeing to concessions (see above) and showing eagerness to settle quickly. This produces an imbalance in the buyer:seller relationship associated with the negotiation. It is also important to avoid time constraints because this concentrates the negotiation towards a quick outcome, sometimes unfavourably. It is much better to ask questions relating to different scenarios and outcomes (for example, 'what ifs') and outline the terms of the negotiation or contract and deal in packages initially rather than specific detail.

Dealing in packages means prefacing the negotiation with phrases such as 'If …', 'If you …' and 'I will …'. The purpose is to maintain ground in terms of the arguments and ideas that are being presented – to develop new packages to facilitate movement. There should be no 'give and take' or 'equal moves' in negotiations. The objective is to develop fair and equitable transactions.

Avoiding deadlock

During the negotiation process, it is important to refrain from saying or doing things that strengthen the resolve of the other party:

- Do not verbally attack the other party in any way as this only strengthens their defence.

- Do not take a rigid stance on a particular aspect of the negotiation as this can be seen as a form of attack.
- Avoid emotive language or rhetoric as this is distracting, wastes energy and can escalate any dissatisfaction in the other party to the negotiation.

It is better to keep talking and maintain dialogue, open up new areas for discussion, use open questions, suggest remedies or alternatives or trade-offs and, finally, search for new 'packages'.

People problems

When entering into a negotiation, it is important to remember that people all have their own hopes, prejudices and grievances and that, from time to time, everybody may exhibit offensive and/or provocative behaviour, all of which may lead to deadlock and hinder any settlements.

Aspects of negotiating – power

It is important to understand the part that power plays in negotiating situations. Power is manifest in many ways, such as:

- It is partly psychological.
- It is perceived by the other party – that is, you have power if the other party *thinks* you have. Conversely, thinking that your opponent has power weakens you!
- Power is subjective – subjective perceptions are usually stronger than objective circumstances.
- Beware self-induced intimidation. Power is often given away by self-induced intimidation. (The opposition is seldom as formidable as they seem. Influencing and intimidation often work against an opponent.)
- Suspect illusions of grandeur – an opponent's outward 'trimmings' are usually intended to impress and intimidate in a negotiation situation.

Objectives of negotiating

The objective of negotiating is simple – to try to reach a favourable outcome. In order to do this, it is important to try to alter the other party's perception of *your* power, credibility and strength. In addition, it is also important to try to alter the opponents' perception of *their* power, credibility and strength by seeking anomalies in their case to reduce their credibility and test their authority to negotiate. The object is to try to facilitate movement in your favour and to reach a favourable outcome following established rules and rituals.

Types of negotiator

Negotiators are either tough or soft. Tough negotiators usually:

- Open with high demands.
- Have high expectations.
- Stick to (or near) their demands.

- Move infrequently.
- Make few concessions. When they do, concessions are usually small, never large.
- Are not scared of deadlock and time constraints.
- Take more time than they give.
- Do not succumb to threats and sanctions (because they do not believe they will be implemented).

On the other hand, soft negotiators usually:

- Open modestly.
- Move considerably.
- Make frequent concessions.
- Are scared of deadlock and time constraints.
- End up giving more than they wanted to.
- Succumb to threats or suggestions or sanctions. (See below for 'Use of threats in negotiating'.)

Skills and tactics in negotiating

Wherever possible, when negotiating, it is important to try to uncover the opponent's boundaries (the extent of their authority in the negotiation) whilst concealing your own or erecting boundaries that are difficult for opponents to circumvent. Another tactic in negotiating is to act as an agent for absent principals, for example as representative for a larger body of people pursuing a particular goal through the negotiation process. Here, you speak for others rather than yourself and make use of different negotiating language such as 'my members have instructed me to …' and so on. Alternatively, making use of skilled negotiators or agents helps protect parties who are inexperienced in negotiating.

Use of threats in negotiating

Use of threats and counter-threats usually accelerates potential deadlock in negotiations. For example, *compliance threats* ('do it or else') compel action, and *deterrence threats* ('if you do … I'll') deter action. Sometimes, the use of threats implies you are more powerful than you actually are, and in this situation, opponents may test your credibility and challenge you to implement any threats you make. The question is: can you, and at what cost? Where threats are made by an opponent it is important to try and search for an outcome that satisfies both parties and avoids a situation where one party loses to the other. Threats tend to produce a negative or hostile response and will sour negotiations.

Self-assessment question 4.2

Describe some of the common barriers to effective negotiation, and for each of these explain how the barriers may be overcome.

Feedback on page 56

Revision question

Now try the revision question for this session on page 247.

Summary

- Reporting to or communicating with management is basically the exchange of information (messages) from a *sender* to a *receiver*, by a variety of means and through a number of different kinds of networks, in order to achieve common meaning between the two parties.
- Managerial decision making is based on the acquisition of appropriate, relevant and timely information that provides the manager (the decision maker) with the means to make *informed* decisions. Managers often lack vital information or have too much indiscriminate information which must be sifted for its salient points.
- Communication flows in organisations are generally *downward* – from people at higher levels to those at lower levels throughout the organisation; *upward* – from subordinates or staff to superiors or senior officers in the organisation; and *crosswise* – horizontally, via people on the same level or diagonally, between people at different levels who have no direct reporting relationships.
- Verbal communication is where we use words to communicate in either *written form* (letters, memos, reports, newsletters, policy and instructional manuals and so on) or *orally* through face-to-face conversations and meetings or by telephone.
- Non-verbal communication is conveyed from sender to receiver by means of various elements and behaviours that are not coded into words, for example *kinesic behaviour* (body movements, gestures, facial expressions), *proxemics* (the influence of proximity and space on communication), *paralanguage* (relates to *how something is said* rather than what is said), *object language* (communication through the use of material things, including clothing, cosmetics, furniture and architecture).
- Key factors that impede or enhance individual communication are perception, semantic blocks, attention to non-verbal parts of messages, listening and feedback.
- The most common barriers to communication are: lack of planning; unclarified assumptions; semantic distortion; poorly expressed messages; cultural differences; loss by transmission and poor retention; poor listening and premature evaluation; impersonal communication; distrust, threat and fear; insufficient period for adjustment to change; information overload.
- In business situations there are two widely used communication methods: written reports and presentations. Written reports are basically outcomes of a study of facts and implications of particular situations, and presentations are usually widely used in selling situations and management planning exercises.

Suggested further reading

You could read the relevant sections of Betts (2000) and Elsayed-Elkhouly, Lazarus and Forsythe (1997).

Feedback on learning activities and self-assessment questions

Feedback on learning activity 4.1

You should first describe the communication flows (up, down and across) your organisational hierarchy. This will provide a basis for you describing specific forms of oral/verbal, written and non-verbal communications. Each of these should be described in some detail (for example, oral/verbal reporting, meetings, interviews and so on) and in relation to their level of use and effectiveness. Where a specific form is perhaps culturally specific, you should explain why.

Once you have done this, you should compare your answer with the text in this session.

Feedback on self-assessment question 4.1

You should outline which forms can be improved and explain why they may need improvement. You should highlight each form of communication, its relative merits and problems, and explain why the problems exist. You should then make appropriate suggestions for improving those aspects of poor communication in terms of both *what* needs to be done and *how* you would do it.

Feedback on learning activity 4.2

You should outline what is currently done to get top-management support for new ideas, explain the extent to which current approaches work, and make some suggestions for improving the process of negotiation. Having done this, you should then compare your organisation's approach with those suggested in this session.

Feedback on self-assessment question 4.2

You might start by listing some of the common barriers to communication, such as: lack of planning, unclarified assumptions, semantic distortion, poorly expressed messages, communication in the international environment, loss by transmission and poor retention, poor listening and premature evaluation, impersonal communication, distrust, bias, threat and fear, and information overload.

Here are some of the factors that help improve and overcome these barriers:

- Senders must clarify what they want to communicate.
- Words and symbols should be familiar to the receiver and the sender.
- Planning should not be done in a vacuum, others should be consulted.
- You should consider the needs of receivers of the information.
- Tone of voice, choice of words and congruency all influence communication.
- Encourage feedback to ensure messages are understood.

Organisational structures

5

Introduction

According to Mintzberg (1979), an organisation is:

> 'the sum total of the ways in which it divides its labour into distinct tasks and then achieves coordination between them.'

In essence, Mintzberg believes that most organisations are in a state of tension as a result of the need to be both differentiated and integrated. Essentially, once an organisation grows beyond the point where its owners can exercise direct influence and control, then some degree of specialisation or integration is inevitable. As a result, most organisations have to answer a number of questions about the type of structure that will best support the organisation in the pursuit of its objectives.

In this context, according to Cole (1996), the most frequent questions that require answers are:

- To what extent should we encourage the specialisation of roles?
- What degrees of standardisation should be imposed on behaviour and methods, or what degree of discretion (empowerment) should be allowed to individual job holders?
- How much formality should be encouraged?
- How many levels of authority should we establish?
- To what extent should decision making be centralised or decentralised?

As Cole summarises:

> 'there is no perfect answer to any of these questions, but there are a number of viable options which, taken together, can produce an optimum design for an organisation.'

This session explores the various forms of organisational structure and outlines the importance of appropriate structure for effective organisational management and performance.

Session learning objectives

After completing this session you should be able to:

5.1 Evaluate the importance of organisational structure.
5.2 Evaluate common forms of organisational structures.
5.3 Explain the nature and importance of structure for effective management and organisational performance.
5.4 Describe the relationship between organisational structure and people.

5

Unit content coverage

This study session covers the following topics from the official CIPS unit content document:

Learning outcome

Analyse the characteristics of different organisational structures and cultures.

Learning objective

2.1 Evaluate the importance of organisational structure.

Prior knowledge

Study sessions 1 and 2.

Timing

You should set aside about 6 hours to read and complete this session, including learning activities, self-assessment questions, the suggested further reading (if any) and the revision question.

5.1 Organisational structure

The role of structure

- It shows established patterns of relationships between parts and members of an organisation.
- It separates decisions into different levels of management.
- It identifies the form the decision process will take.

Learning activity 5.1

Give three further reasons why structure is important in organisations.

Feedback on page 69

Organisational 'shape'

Nowadays, in most organisations, this is usually depicted by lines of *authority, responsibility, communications* and *function*. We can contrast this modern approach to organisational structure with Henri Fayol's scalar organisation or chain (1916, in Fayol 1949) as shown in figure 5.1.

Figure 5.1: Fayol's scalar chain

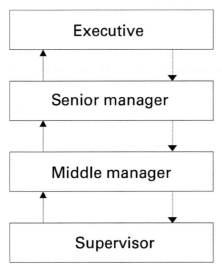

Source: Fayol, 1916 (in Fayol 1949)

5

Fayol's approach followed a 'one man one boss' rule (after Urwick, 1956), where lateral or functional relationships do not exist. As figure 5.1 shows, this is strictly hierarchical and 'line-management' in design.

The study of organisational design was further defined by Burns and Stalker (1961) who identified two contrasting types of structure:

- A mechanistic structure, which:
  - is designed for relatively stable conditions;
  - clearly identifies management tasks and specialisms (regarded as restrictive);
  - depicts a clear hierarchy of control;
  - shows that responsibility for coordination resides at the top of the organisation;
  - emphasises only vertical communication and interaction.
- An organic structure, which:
  - is able to adapt to unstable conditions when new and unfamiliar situations arise;
  - allows for structural changes to meet new conditions;
  - depicts management as being contributive rather than restrictive;
  - breaks down interaction and communication within and across levels and functional areas.

Contingency theory (an extension of the systems approach to management that implies that the structure of the organisation and its success are dependent upon the nature of the tasks which are undertaken and the nature of environmental influences) argues that there is no one best way to structure or manage organisations; rather it must be dependent upon the contingencies of the situation. This holistic view, in contrast to Burns and Stalker (1961), suggests that in designing organisations, management:

- should reject earlier theories of universal models for designing formal structures;
- should assess each situation separately, that is, that designing for the 'whole' is restrictive;

- should understand that, implied within organisations, bureaucratic, matrix and divisionalised units may operate; and
- should realise that 'effective' design relates to task performance and individual and group satisfaction.

Formal and informal organisations

Formal organisation is defined by Etzioni (cited in Mullins, 2005) as being 'A social unit deliberately constructed to seek specific goals', and this is characterised by:

- planned divisions of responsibility;
- power centres which control its efforts;
- substitution of personnel;
- an ability to combine personnel in different ways.

Further, formal organisations have:

- an explicit hierarchy in a well-defined structure;
- job specifications – clearly defined;
- communications channels – clearly defined.

In contrast to this, informal organisations:

- are loosely structured, flexible and spontaneous;
- tend to be membership based (this may be gained consciously or unconsciously and it is difficult to determine when a person becomes a member);
- also exist within formal organisations with varying degrees of complexity.

As John Child argued (in Mullins, 2005):

> 'One of the facts of life for organisations is that as they grow, they become more formalised...Just as growth sets up pressures for delegation, so it is also accompanied by formalisation.'

This is supported by Larry E. Greiner (1972) who, in his paper 'Evolution and revolution as organisations grow', explains the reasons for formalisation are that 'with growth, structure develops from being simple [for example sole trader and so on] to highly complex [for example multinational-type organisations]'. He maintains that organisations move through distinct phases of development as they increase in size and complexity, and as a result they become more formalised.

Self-assessment question 5.1

Which structure – mechanistic or organic – does your organisation most closely resemble and why? Also, how conducive is it in helping the organisation achieve its objectives? Give reasons to support your answer.

Feedback on page 69

5.2 Structural design or 'form'

So, which structural design or form is best? It can be argued that there is no one optimal design of structure for a given strategy or type of organisation, although firms in a given industry tend to organise along similar lines, for example:

- small firms tend to organise by function (a centralised approach);
- medium-sized firms tend to be organised divisionally (a decentralised approach);
- consumer goods firms tend also to be divisional, that is, 'structure by product'.
- large firms tend to be organised into strategic business units (SBUs) or based on a matrix structure.

These various forms are explained in more detail below

Functional structure

Figure 5.2: A functional structure

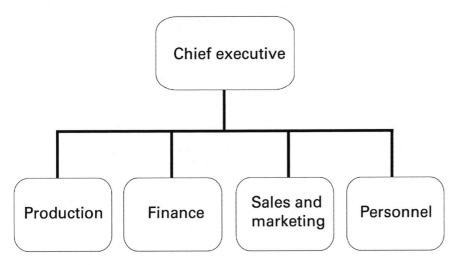

The *advantages* of this type of structure are that it is simple and it promotes specialisation and encourages efficiency. Also, communication lines are short which allows for rapid decision making.

The *disadvantages* are that there is a tendency for functions to operate independently; focus tends to be in an upward direction and its inflexibility makes it difficult to cope with diversity. There is also a risk of low employee morale, interdepartmental conflicts and senior managers focusing more on functional rather than strategic issues.

Divisional structure

Figure 5.3: A divisional structure

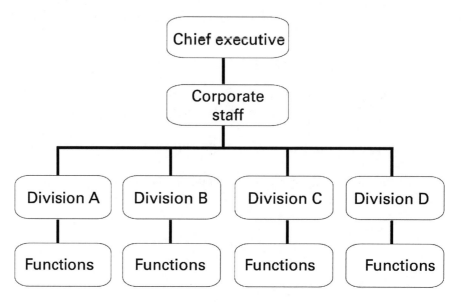

The *advantages* here are that the divisional structure allows for concentration on specific business (or product-market) areas where there is clear accountability, and (perhaps) improved morale. It also encourages general management development and helps facilitate organisational change (either through growth or divestment). Thus senior managers focus more on strategy.

The *disadvantages* are that there might be duplication of effort (in terms of some business activities and processes) and also conflict between and across divisions (because it provides the basis for inter-trading within the organisation). It is also costly and requires complex coordination by centralised control or headquarters.

Geographic (matrix) structure

Figure 5.4: A geographic or matrix structure

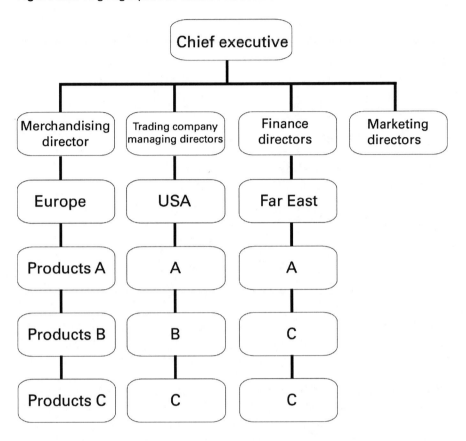

The *advantages* of a geographical or matrix structure relate to the quality of decision making; the direct contact (between product/manufacturing divisions and their markets) instead of bureaucracy; and the opportunities it provides for manager development.

However, there are considerable *disadvantages* to a matrix system of organisation. For example, the length of time for decisions is increased; there tends to be a confusion of responsibilities (in terms of who reports to whom), conflicts of interest, dilution of priorities and a tendency for increasing bureaucracy.

Devolved structure (strategic business unit (SBU))

Figure 5.5: A devolved (or strategic business unit) structure

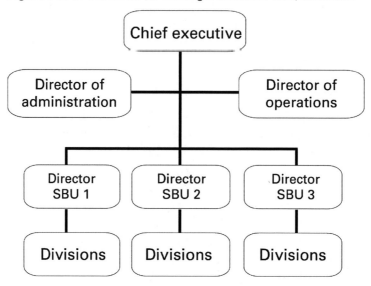

The devolved structure has a number of *advantages*. For example, individual business units (SBUs) have a high degree of autonomy, there is an increased potential for improved coordination and control and thus possible improved accountability. Also, this structure allows SBUs to be highly responsive to local circumstances because they are free from *direct* headquarters control.

The *disadvantage*s of this form of structure tend to relate to the increased costs associated with managing a group of individual (and possibly specialised) business units, and the confusion of roles that might arise between business unit directors and their superiors (for example administrations and operations directors).

Learning activity 5.2

Having read the material on organisational structure and design, identify which type or form your organisation's structure takes.

How does it compare with those you have studied? Identify the strengths and weaknesses of your structure compared to those outlined here and suggest suitable recommendations for improvement.

Feedback on page 69

Having completed this learning activity, you should now attempt self-assessment question 5.2 below.

Self-assessment question 5.2

Explain the main factors to be considered in the design of organisational structure.

Feedback on page 69

5.3   Structure and organisational performance

The management task of organisation relates to the level of (managerial) authority over the activities in an organisation, for example structuring work and getting jobs done. This in turn determines the degrees of efficiency and inefficiency in the organisation. It is therefore vitally important that the organisational structure or form provides for the achievement of organisational or corporate objectives.

In 1962, in his classic work *Structure and Strategy*, Alfred Chandler argued that 'Structures should be designed to facilitate the strategic pursuit of a firm and, therefore, follows strategy'. (See figure 5.6.)

Figure 5.6: Chandler's strategy–structure relationship

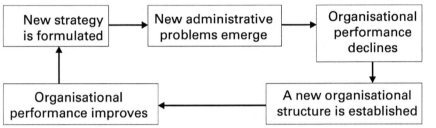

Source: Adapted from Chandler (1962)

Chandler argued that changes in strategy often require changes in structure. His reasons for this are that:

- Structure largely dictates how objectives and policies are established, for example where structure is based, say, on product groups, then objectives and policies will be stated in product terms.
- Structure also dictates how resources will be allocated, for example functional structures are therefore resourced by functional area.
- If new strategies require major structural change, then problems will arise.

In addition, Luffman et al (1996) argued that:

'in making a choice of consistent strategies, structure must be based on two dimensions:

1   the rate of change of the organisation's (market and industry) environment, and;
2   the complexity of processes within an organisation'.

Essentially, what this means for organisations that operate in dynamic and volatile competitive environments is that they must design structure to be equally dynamic, in that it can be reconfigured relatively easily to cope with changing situations. Also, it means that if their internal processes and practices are deeply embedded and difficult to change, the organisation will not be able to adjust quickly enough to remain competitive.

Some of the symptoms of a poor or inefficient structure, which inevitably would adversely affect an organisation, are as follows:

- growth of many levels of management, hence work creation;
- frictional or unprofitable overheads, for example coordinators, assistants-to and so on;

- need for special coordinating measures – appointment of liaison officers or coordinating committees;
- tendency to go through channels rather than to person(s) directly;
- a lopsided management age structure.

Each of these symptoms has a tendency to add cost rather than add value to an organisation. Therefore, in designing or redesigning structure to create any competitive advantage, management should attempt to avoid their occurrence.

Learning activity 5.3

With reference to your own organisation, assess the extent to which its structure serves to maximise both departmental and organisational performance.

Feedback on page 70

You should now attempt self-assessment question 5.3 below.

Self-assessment question 5.3

Alfred Chandler (1962) argues that 'strategic goals should be determined first and structure designed to ensure goals are reached'.

Critically evaluate this statement, drawing on relevant examples to support your answer.

Feedback on page 70

5.4 People: employees and structure

Learning activity 5.4

Evaluate the impacts (positive and negative) that formal and informal structures might have on an organisation's employees. Provide your answer in the form of a list with the headings 'formal' and 'informal' organisations.

Feedback on page 70

Structure is important – not only for productivity and economic efficiency but also for the morale and job satisfaction of employees. It is therefore also very important to get the structure right. It should be designed to encourage the willing participation of employees and as a basis for effective organisational performance.

The activities and relationships within organisations exist independently of the members (or employees) who carry out the work. It must be borne in mind, however, that personalities are an essential part of the working of the organisation as a whole. Thus, an organisation's operations and success in meeting its goals or objectives depends upon the behaviour of employees.

Many writers on human relations criticise the formal organisation and tend to favour a structure where there is:

- an emphasis on participation from people at all levels and across all functions of the organisation; and
- greater freedom for the individual and more meaningful work organisation and relationships.

Argyris (1960) in particular, argues that:

> 'the formal, bureaucratic organisation restricts individual growth and self-fulfilment and, in the psychologically healthy person, causes a feeling of failure, frustration and conflict...and...that the organisation should provide a more "authentic" relationship for its members.'

This view stresses the importance of the human element in the design of structure. Consequently, managers need to consider how appropriate structural design and methods of work organisation will affect the behaviour and subsequent performance of employees. Ultimately, organisational performance will be affected both by robust structural design and by the individuals occupying the various positions within the structure.

It is important that management recognises that within any structure an informal organisation will exist which arises from the relationships between employees. The operation of the organisation and actual working arrangements will therefore be influenced by the style of management and the informal organisation.

In summary, it seems obvious that building an organisation involves more than solely a concern for structure, methods of work and operational efficiency. Successful organisations focus attention on the human element; that is, to the development of an organisational culture which helps foster a sense of belonging, commitment and job satisfaction.

Self-assessment question 5.4

To what extent would you agree with the contention that a logical structure for organisation is better for efficiency and morale than a structure allowed to develop around personalities?

Feedback on page 71

Revision question

Now try the revision question for this session on page 247.

5

Summary

In this session we have shown that:

- Structure shows established patterns of relationships between parts and members of an organisation; it separates decisions into different levels of management and identifies the form that the decision process(es) will take in the organisation.
- Organisational 'shape' is usually depicted by lines of *authority, responsibility, communication* and *function*.
- Burns and Stalker (1961) identified two contrasting types of structure: mechanistic (designed for relatively stable conditions; clearly identifies management tasks and specialisms; shows a clear hierarchy of control; shows that responsibility for coordination resides at the top of the organisation; and emphasises vertical communication and interaction), and organic (able to adapt to unstable conditions; allows for structural changes to meet new conditions; shows management as contributive not restrictive; breaks down interaction and communication within and across levels and functional areas).
- Informal organisations exist within formal organisations.
- Firms tend to organise along similar lines (for example, small firms tend to organise by function, medium-sized firms tend to be organised divisionally, consumer goods firms tend to structure by product and large firms tend to be organised into strategic business units (SBUs) or based on a matrix structure), each of which have significant advantages and disadvantages.
- The management task of organisation relates to the level of authority over an organisation's activities, which determines the degrees of *efficiency* and *inefficiency*. Structure or form thus provides for the achievement of organisational objectives.
- The Chandler strategy–structure model highlights that structure should always be designed to facilitate the strategic pursuits of the firm, and so should follow strategy. Also Luffman et al argued that 'in making a choice of consistent strategies, structure must be based on two dimensions: (1) the rate of change of the organisation's environment and (2) the complexity of processes within an organisation'.
- Managers should consider how appropriate structural design and methods of work organisation will affect the behaviour and performance of employees, and recognise that within any structure an *informal* organisation exists, arising from the relationships between employees. Thus the operation of the organisation and actual working arrangements will be influenced by the style of management and the informal organisation. (Successful organisations focus attention on the human element and development of a culture which helps foster a sense of belonging, commitment and job satisfaction.)

Suggested further reading

Brooks (2003), chapter 7.

You could also read the relevant sections of Buchanan and Huczynski (2004), Chandler (1962), Greiner (1972) and Mullins (2005).

Feedback on learning activities and self-assessment questions

Feedback on learning activity 5.1

You should consider the role of structure in an organisation-wide context. Some of the reasons you should consider are:

- Appropriate structure helps the organisation work more effectively towards its objectives.
- Structure also shows role demarcation – it defines roles of employees in the organisation.
- Structure shows levels of authority and responsibility.
- It shows division of functions and specialisation.
- It shows formal lines of communication – it can be used to assess effectiveness of same throughout the organisation.

Feedback on self-assessment question 5.1

Here, you should use Burns and Stalker's structural types to assess you own organisation. Think carefully about whether or not your structure follows *either* a mechanistic *or* an organic type only, or whether there are elements of both. Also, you should, in assessing your organisational structure, explain the extent to which it is a formal or an informal organisation. For example, your organisation might resemble a mechanistic structure – designed for relatively stable conditions – but its competitive environment may be dynamic, not stable. This means the organisation might not be flexible and adaptable enough to sustain any real level of competitiveness. Also if it were organic – hence flexible and adaptable – but in a relatively stable competitive environment, its opportunities for competition would be limited.

Feedback on learning activity 5.2

You should identify the structural form of your organisation and weigh its advantages and disadvantages in relation to those given in this section. You should also consider the costs and benefits associated with your particular form or structure, and how it might add value to the organisation overall. Where you identify any weaknesses or shortcomings, you should make suitable recommendations for a change of structure or parts thereof. For example, you may work in a globalised firm that does not have a suitable geo-matrix or devolved structure. It is important to consider the relationship the organisation has within and across its product-market groups in some cases.

Feedback on self-assessment question 5.2

You should make reference to structure being supportive of strategic objectives, with appropriate levels of authority and responsibility across divisions of function or specialisation. Structural form should relate to the environmental dynamics facing the firm. If operating in volatile, highly

5

competitive markets, structure should reflect the organisation's capability to respond and adapt to changes. If operating in stable environments, the structure should be such that the organisation can respond within that context *and* be flexible enough to adapt to any changes in those dynamics.

Feedback on learning activity 5.3

Where possible, you should use your company's organisation chart or structure diagram – if it has one – as a basis for this assessment. In organisations it is important that structure allows for good functional and overall performance. Thus, the structure should provide for interdependency between functions where functional relationships create value for, and reduce costs to, the organisation as a whole. The structure should also facilitate the maximisation of the labour and capital utilisation ratios (that is, where all people and capital equipment, assets and so on are fully employed to add value to the organisation). Poor or ineffective structures would, in some ways, prevent this from happening.

Feedback on self-assessment question 5.3

Use Chandler's strategy–structure model as a starting point to explain what he means by the statement; that is, that structure should always be designed to facilitate the strategic pursuits of the firm and so should follow strategy. Discuss why this is important and also the consequences of firms trying to pursue new strategic objectives with a structure that will not see their objectives realised. Some level of criticality of evaluation is essential here. You should be able to discuss the pros and cons of Chandler's model as well as the impact on organisations who do not follow his reasoning.

Feedback on learning activity 5.4

You should note that informal organisations can exist within formal organisations. You should consider some of the following key points:

- Formal organisations:
    - Positive: employees may be glad to know their place within the organisation, be appreciative of direction and clear lines of authority. Therefore, this structure could actually be considered to motivate its employees in certain cases.
    - Negative: formal organisations are largely based on control and involve rigid job specifications which can demotivate staff and in turn stifle creativity. Employees may feel frustrated that decisions tend to be top down and generally imposed from above.
- Informal organisations:
    - Positive: informal organisations encourage participation and communication at all levels, and give employees greater autonomy based on appropriate delegation of authority and responsibility etc. Communication is usually more efficient. It can mean that work is more interesting and challenging, which can lead to increased job satisfaction.
    - Negative: informal organisations can also create communication problems as a result of the grapevine effect where employees might

bypass formal communication channels. There is also the problem of to whom employees should report. For example, they may for some reason report or respond to a manager from another department, thus ignoring the formal line structure.

Feedback on self-assessment question 5.4

You should consider the following.

An organisation should not be structured on the basis of personalities. It should be structured according to the organisation's objectives and the knowledge, skills and experience of those managers and employees required to fulfil functional roles at all levels. Should an organisation not possess the right people with the right skills and expertise, its performance will most likely be sub-optimal. Further, with the right people, skills and so on, the organisation is likely to be more efficient and possibly more successful. The morale of the workforce is likely to be high as a result. Conversely, morale will suffer if managerial and leadership knowledge and expertise is lacking.

Structure: implications for purchasing and supply

Introduction

Academic literature stresses the value of developing positive relations with suppliers. It is argued that through better understanding of buyer/seller needs and capabilities, and through developing cooperative strategies, quality of output to the end customer may be enhanced at lower overall cost. The process of developing products and services is seen as a continuous one with suppliers as an overall extension of the local firm's business environment. But just how close should this cooperation or 'partnering' be, and how does organisational structure either facilitate or hinder the purchasing function in the pursuit of its objectives in this area? This session explores the impact of organisational structure – both internal and external (in terms of its wider business networks or relationships) – on the purchasing function.

'Structure should be designed to facilitate the strategic pursuits of a firm, and as such, follows strategy.'
Chandler (1962)

6

Session learning objectives

After completing this session you should be able to:

6.1 Evaluate the nature and scope of federal and network structures and the implications of such structures for the purchasing function.

Unit content coverage

This study session covers the following topic from the official CIPS unit content document:

Learning outcome

Analyse the characteristics of different organisational structures and cultures.

Learning objective

2.1 Evaluate the importance of organisational structure.
2.2 Evaluate the nature and scope of federal and network structures and the implications of such structures for the purchasing function.

Prior knowledge

Study session 5.

Timing

You should set aside about 4 hours to read and complete this session, including learning activities, self-assessment questions, the suggested further reading (if any) and the revision question.

6.1 Suppliers – partnerships or independence?

Organisational structure – internal approaches

For organisations that have several geographically dispersed manufacturing or operational sites, the purchasing function or activity could be either centralised or decentralised. Alternatively, a hybrid of these two approaches might be followed.

Centralised purchasing

Where purchasing is centralised, all purchased items for every operational division are procured through one department or operating site. According to Waller (2003) the advantages of this are:

- Buying in larger quantities usually means it is possible to obtain more attractive prices from suppliers.
- Purchasing in large quantities often means the supplier is more attentive to the order.
- It permits a standardisation of purchased products and thus guarantees a constant quality throughout the organisation.
- Larger purchasing departments, as a result of ordering for many manufacturing sites, means that the company can afford more staff specialisation, leading to greater purchasing competence and lower material cost.
- Combining small orders reduces administrative costs, time taken to negotiate orders, billing time, customs procedures where appropriate, and thus overall cost.
- Relation with suppliers is simplified.
- Reduction in transport costs since orders are shipped in larger quantities.

Decentralised purchasing

Where purchasing is decentralised, each operational division makes its own purchasing decisions. Waller (2003) suggests the advantages of this approach are:

- Less bureaucracy means a quicker response.
- Lower transportation costs if the supplier is located close to the division making the purchase.
- Possibly better responsiveness to operational needs by local purchasing.
- Reduction in inventory costs – divisions only purchase the quantity required.
- Risk is reduced by buying in smaller quantities.

A mix (or hybrid) of purchasing functions

A mixed purchasing organisation (hybrid of centralised and decentralised purchasing activities) may be established depending on the items to be purchased, for example:

- Small or rush orders, or those specific to a particular sites needs, are purchased locally (decentralised).
- High-cost capital equipment, high-volume materials, standardised products which are used for several operating companies, goods with a high technical content or those purchased overseas are purchased by the head office (centralised).

Organisation chart

The type of organisation chart for a purchasing department depends very much on the size of the organisation, its range of activities and whether it is centralised or decentralised. A basic structure might contain a purchasing director and various purchasing managers who report to the purchasing director for, say, services, raw materials and sub-assemblies or critical components. There might be a varying number of buyers reporting to each of these purchasing managers depending on the nature and size of the operating function or manufacturing division.

For a large company that manufactures non-ferrous (copper and copper alloy) tubes for a wide range of domestic and industrial applications for example, the structure may resemble that shown in figure 6.1.

Figure 6.1: Example of purchasing function structure for non-ferrous tube company

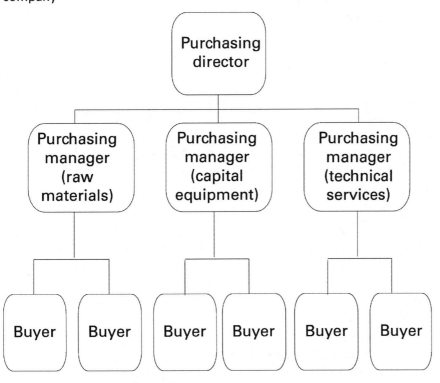

Buying

In many organisations, it is the (specialist) buyers who have direct contact with supplying organisations. Specialisation allows buyers to become experts at purchasing their particular commodity or range of materials etc. Further, according to Waller (2003):

> 'the quality of the buyers is enhanced if they are knowledgeable in:
> - Their own company, in terms of products and processes, sales and other company policy.
> - The price structure of the purchased goods or products, in terms of their (buyers) knowledge of the market and current or "going" price of the commodity available.
> - The price structure of the end product, that is, the cost structure of the finished products.
> - Laws relating to contracts, misrepresentation and fraud, infringement of patent rights, damage claims against suppliers, product safety, and more specifically, those pertaining to foods and pharmaceuticals etc.
> - Human relations, in terms of their interpersonal skills in dealing with representatives from both suppliers and customers.'

The value chain

It is important that the (internal) organisation structure is such that the organisation can continue to create and add value whilst reducing the cost of provision of goods and/or services. Thus, the organisation's 'value chain' should be managed to achieve this. The purchasing function, along with other functions, must operate cost effectively whilst adding value to both the organisation and its customers, and where possible, create value for its suppliers.

The concept of the value chain is based on the process view of organisations, the idea of seeing a manufacturing (or service) organisation as a system, made up of sub-systems each with inputs, transformation processes and outputs. Inputs, transformation processes and outputs involve the acquisition and consumption of resources – money, labour, materials, equipment, buildings, land, administration and management. How value-chain activities are carried out determines costs and affects profits.

Most organisations engage in hundreds or even thousands of activities in the process of converting inputs to outputs. These activities can be classified generally as either primary or support activities that all businesses must undertake in some form figure 6.2.

According to Porter (1985), the primary activities are:

- **Inbound logistics**, which involve relationships with suppliers and include all of the activities required to receive, store and disseminate inputs.
- **Operations** are all the activities required to transform inputs into outputs (products and services).
- **Outbound logistics**, which include all of the activities required to collect, store and distribute the output.
- **Marketing and sales activities**, which inform buyers about products and services, induce buyers to purchase them and facilitate their purchase.
- **Services**, which includes all the activities required to keep the product or service working effectively for the buyer after it is sold and delivered.

Secondary activities are:

- **Procurement**, which is the acquisition of inputs, or resources, for the firm.
- **Human resource management**, which consists of all activities involved in recruiting, hiring, training, developing, compensating and (if necessary) dismissing or laying off personnel.
- **Technological development**, which pertains to the equipment, hardware, software, procedures and technical knowledge brought to bear in the firm's transformation of inputs into outputs.
- **Infrastructure**, which serves the company's needs and ties its various parts together. It consists of functions or departments such as accounting, legal, finance, planning, public affairs, government relations, quality assurance and general management.

Figure 6.2: Porter's generic value chain

Primary Activities

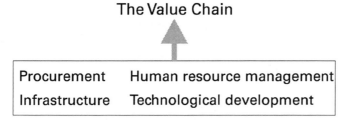

The Value Chain

Support Activities

Networks and inter-organisational relationships

In the value-chain model in figure 6.2, *procurement* is clearly a secondary or support activity to the organisation's primary operations. However, in the wider context of networks and inter-organisational relationships, the emphasis on the purchasing function changes considerably when the organisation engages in:

- **Backward (vertical) integration**: increased ownership or control of suppliers or supply chain activities.
- **Forward (vertical) integration**: increased ownership or control of distribution channels.
- **Lateral (horizontal) integration**: increased ownership or control of competitors – usually through mergers or acquisitions.

These integrative strategies or buyer–supplier relationships increase an organisation's chances to add value since, in the long term, they reduce the costs associated with operating independently. Here, the amount or level of control that the organisation has over cost, prices, production, delivery and other areas of the operation is greatly increased. Thus they can operate cost effectively, add value and maintain price competitiveness in the marketplace. This relationship of value chains is illustrated in figure 6.3.

Figure 6.3: Chain of buyer–supplier relationships

2nd Tier   1st Tier

Customers or
Suppliers   Suppliers   Organisation   Distributers

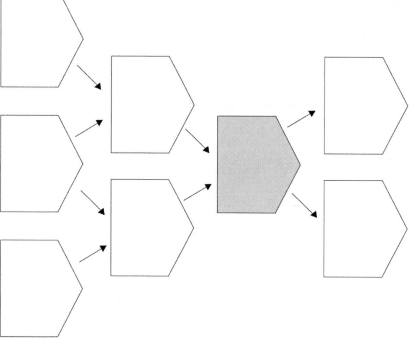

Case study: Toyota

Organisations such as the Toyota Motor Manufacturing Co. place great value on building relationships with suppliers and, where appropriate, distributors or dealerships. As Vollman and Cordon (1998) suggest, it is:

> 'demand-chain management (as opposed to supply chain management), that is one of the most promising avenues for improving company competitiveness. Many companies see the supply chain as primarily concerned with improving purchasing, usually through applying muscle power to the suppliers.'

However, they argue that 'demand-chain management starts with the customer(s), working back through the entire chain, to the suppliers of the suppliers', with the objective of creating synergy in the overall chain to achieve larger benefits than are possible by each entity in the chain acting independently.

Toyota Motor Manufacturing Co. (UK) has around 200 suppliers across the UK and Europe, of whom approximately half are dedicated suppliers, that is they are wholly or partially owned by Toyota. Their relationships with their suppliers are based on long-term trust, mutuality of goal setting and commitment. This approach allows Toyota to maintain a high level of quality and reliability in terms of its products, but at a low unit cost. Thus it enjoys the benefits of economies of scale which allow it to compete at a comparable price level with its main rivals. It would not be able to do this if both its internal structure and its external relationships were not managed in this way.

This 'partnership sourcing' approach relies on organisations having robust but flexible internal structures that allow the purchasing (and other) function(s) to become, as Mason-Jones and Towill (1997) suggest, 'smart [supply-]chain managers ensure continuous improvement to stay competitive'.

The importance of an appropriate structure to support *intra-functional* relationships cannot be understated. An organisation's structure must permit all functions to operate interdependently, and as such, the purchasing function is an essential part of this. However, external to the organisation, there is also a need to build a wider (network) structure which provides for both cost-effectiveness and the creation of value to the firm and its partner organisations. From a supply chain (or 'demand-chain') perspective, the purchasing function has an important part to play in this.

Learning activity 6.1

Draw a diagram to show the value chain of your own organisation and list those areas where you could possibly reduce cost and add value.

Feedback on page 81

Having identified the value chain of your own organisation and listed where cost can be reduced and value added, you should now attempt self-assessment question 6.1 below, which requires you to develop the learning activity in much greater detail.

Self-assessment question 6.1

'Interdependence of functions within an organisation is essential for that organisation's effectiveness and to ensure it achieves its overall aims and objectives.'

Critically evaluate this statement using your own (purchasing) function or organisation as an example to support your answer.

Feedback on page 81

Revision question

Now try the revision question for this session on page 248.

Summary

- For organisations that have several manufacturing or operational sites, the purchasing function or activity might be completely centralised or decentralised. Alternatively, a hybrid of these two approaches might be practised.
- Advantages of centralised purchasing: bulk purchasing leads to more attractive prices; the supplier is more attentive to the order; it allows for standardisation and constant quality of purchased products; more staff specialisation leads to greater purchasing competence and lower material cost; reduced administrative costs and reduction in transport costs.
- Advantages of decentralised purchasing: each division makes its own purchasing decisions; less bureaucracy; lower transportation costs if the supplier is located close to the area of purchase; better responsiveness to operational needs by local purchasing; reduction in inventory costs; reduced risk of buying smaller quantities.
- A mixed purchasing organisation (a hybrid of centralised and decentralised) can cater for both: (a) small or rush orders, or those specific to a site needs, are purchased locally (decentralised); and (b) situations where high-cost capital equipment, high-volume materials, standardised products, goods with a high technical content, or those purchased overseas are purchased by the head office (centralised).
- A basic organisational structure might contain a purchasing director, to whom various purchasing managers report. Depending on the nature and size of the organisation, varying numbers of buyers may report to the purchasing managers.
- Specialist or 'expert' buyers have direct contact with supplying organisations. These buyers should understand their own company in terms of products and processes, sales and other company policy; the price structure of the purchased goods or products; the price structure of the *end product*; laws relating to purchasing, for example contracts, misrepresentation and fraud, infringement of patent rights and so on; and human relations in terms of dealing with representatives from both suppliers and customers.
- The purchasing function, along with other functions, must operate cost effectively whilst adding value to both the organisation and its customers and, where possible, it should create value for its suppliers.
- External 'structural' relationships and networks are based on integration that is vertical (backward and forward to suppliers and distributors) and lateral (horizontal with competitors).
- These integrative strategies or buyer–supplier relationships increase an organisation's chance to add value by reducing the costs associated with operating independently. Thus they can operate cost effectively, add value and maintain price competitiveness.

Suggested further reading

You could read the relevant sections of Milligan, Longbottom, and Ellis, (February 1999), Van Weele (2005) and Waller (2003).

6

Feedback on learning activities and self-assessment questions

Feedback on learning activity 6.1

You should draw the value-chain diagram and include all the requisite areas of your organisation and then identify and explain which areas could reduce costs and make a better contribution to value.

For example, it could be that a reduction in the cost of procuring raw materials or sub-assemblies or other items will make a significant contribution to reducing the overall cost of production. Alternatively, the cost of distribution might be reduced by contracting in a specialist transport and logistics firm rather than employing your own transport fleet/department. Hence, the overall cost through the value chain will be reduced.

Your answer will of course depend on your own type and form of organisation.

Feedback on self-assessment question 6.1

You should explain why organisational functions must work in consort, that is as a team, rather than being independent of one another. It would lead to organisational dysfunctionality if functions did not communicate and coordinate with one another. Failure to do this would affect the overall competitive position of the organisation and its ability to respond to external changes or pressures from its competitive and industry/market environments. The ability to achieve organisational objectives depends on coherence and interdependence of functions and their level of flexibility and responsiveness to change.

6

6

Span of control and job design

Introduction

The principle of **span of control** is one of Urwick's Ten Principles of Management (Mullins, 2005). It is based on the concept that 'no person should supervise more than five, or at the most, six direct subordinates whose work interlocks'.

This session defines span of control, explains the key ideas behind its development and provides students with a comparison of different types of organisational structure, their advantages and disadvantages, and the role and types of job design in organisations.

'There's the real possibility that paying attention to span of control could usher your business into a new era of rapid, sustained, profitable growth. You could even find running your business easier and more fun.'
Mark Hendricks (January 2001) 'Span control', *Entrepreneur*

7

Session learning objectives

After completing this session you should be able to:

7.1 Define 'span of control' and explain the role and importance of span of control in organisations.
7.2 Determine the different spans of control within organisational structures.
7.3 Compare and analyse older methods of job design – job rotation, job enlargement, job enrichment and so on with broader approaches (for example the quality of working life, work–life balance, employee involvement and empowerment, self-managed work groups and so on) and explain the implications for the purchasing function.

Unit content coverage

This study session covers the following topic from the official CIPS unit content document:

Learning outcome

Analyse the characteristics of different organisational structures and cultures.

Learning objective

2.3 Assess and evaluate methods of job design for purchasing roles.

Prior knowledge

Study sessions 2, 5 and 6.

Timing

You should set aside about 6 hours to read and complete this session, including learning activities, self-assessment questions, the suggested further reading (if any) and the revision question.

7.1 Span of control

Span of control (also referred to as span of management) dates back to the work of Henri Fayol around 1906 (summarised and published in 1949) and is simply defined as 'the number of subordinates reporting directly to a manager'.

A number of those who have written about organisations have tried to suggest precise figures on the minimum, maximum and optimum span. One in particular, Graicunas (Mullins, 2005) even developed a mathematical formula to provide an exact number by calculating the number of social relationships involved. Urwick agreed with Graicunas and suggested that at most, six subordinates or staff are sufficient if their work interrelates or overlaps. However, more recent studies show considerable variation and suggest spans of between ten and 80 subordinates.

Learning activity 7.1

Devise a list of all the variables which can affect the span of management (the number of employees a manager can supervise), for example the nature of work. It is easier to manage a large group of people if the tasks they carry out are simple/standardised in nature.

Feedback on page 91

There are a number of variables which can affect the span of control, such as:

- the nature and context of organisation;
- the capabilities of managers and employees;
- the complexity of work tasks;
- the training available to all employees;
- the time available to managers when dealing with subordinates;
- the levels of employee morale and motivation;
- the physical and/or geographical spread of subordinates;
- the length of the chain of command, that is, the number of different levels in the structure of the organisation.

Each of these factors will have an influence on whether the span of control is tall (narrow) or flat (wide). Figure 7.1 shows a tall structure (where few employees report to each manager and the span of control of each of the managers is narrow). In contrast, figure 7.2 shows a flat structure (where many employees report to each manager and the span of control of each of the managers is wide).

7

As figure 7.1 shows, the tall structure represents a narrow span of control and is characterised by:

- decentralised authority – where authority is devolved throughout the organisation;
- many authority levels and therefore long communication lines;
- a high degree of functional specialism such as marketing, HR, finance;
- a high degree of delegation – where subordinates are given autonomy of decision making.

Tall structures promote close supervision and strong discipline, which corresponds to the bureaucratic model discussed in study session 5. This structure does not allow for quick response to change and therefore it is more suitable in stable conditions. It has been subject to much criticism as it closely resembles McGregor's (1960) 'theory X' style of management, where employees are considered to be inherently lazy and have to be continually coerced and controlled to carry out their work. This philosophy also suggests that individuals avoid responsibility and lack ambition.

Figure 7.1: A tall organisational structure

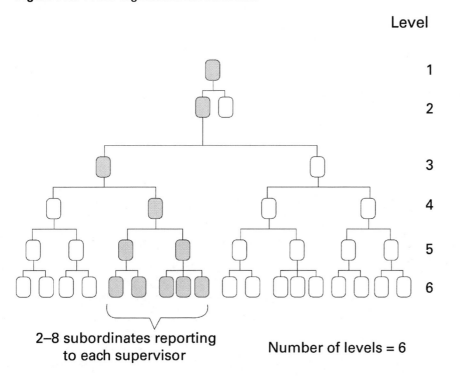

In contrast, the flat structure shown in figure 7.2 represents a wide span of control and is characterised by:

- centralised authority – where authority is retained by top management;
- few authority levels and therefore fewer communication and coordination difficulties;
- low degree of functional specialism, that is, job specifications tend to be more general;
- low delegation – where managers retain decision-making rights.

A flat structure resembles an organic structure (see study session 5), and provides for a quick response to change, making it ideally suitable for more dynamic competitive situations. This structure is flexible and informal and encourages innovation and empowerment. However, it is more reflective of McGregor's 'theory Y' style of management, whereby employees exercise self discipline, take pride in their work and relish responsibility.

Figure 7.2: A flat organisational structure

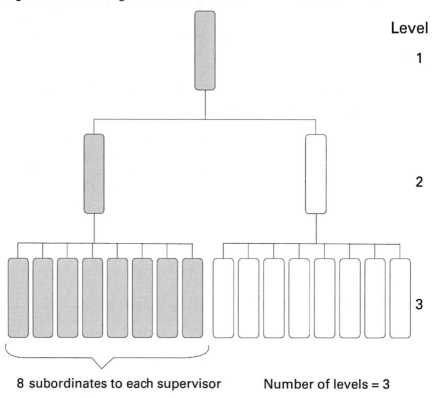

8 subordinates to each supervisor   Number of levels = 3

Self-assessment question 7.1

Critically evaluate the statement: 'As the span of control increases, so does the problem of control and coordination.'

Feedback on page 91

7.2   Spans of control – advantages and disadvantages

Learning activity 7.2

Make a list of the advantages and disadvantages relating to the span of control for your organisation.

Feedback on page 92

Whilst there are both advantages and disadvantages to wide and narrow spans of control, certain factors need to be taken into account. For example, if the span of control is too narrow (that is, there are many levels in the organisational hierarchy), it can overly complicate communication and as a result the organisation can be slow to respond to decisions. This can prove costly to the organisation, as Koontz and Weihrich (1990) assert:

> 'levels are expensive…as they increase, more and more effort and money are devoted to managing, because of the additional managers, the staffs to assist them and the necessity of coordinating departmental activities, plus the costs of facilities for the personnel.'

Another criticism of narrow spans of control relates to the issue of supervision. Closer supervision of employees can mean they feel restricted, which in turn could stifle their use of initiative and creativity.Conversely, whilst a wide span of control promotes empowerment, if it is too wide (that is, the manager has too many subordinates) it can be difficult for the manager to supervise effectively. Having a wide span of control can sometimes place too much pressure upon the manager, leaving them little time for other aspects of their job such as planning and organising work. Hence, there is a possibility that overloaded managers can become barriers or bottlenecks to decision making. For this reason, having too wide a span of control may also result in the organisation being slow to adapt to change.

Also, with a wide span there is a danger that managers could lose their control. For example, Mullins (2005) argues that 'with larger groupings, informal leaders and sub-groups or '*cliques*' are more likely to develop, and these may operate contrary to the policy of management.'

Betts (2000) points out that with the organisational pyramid flattened, power is pushed towards the supervisory level. Literature surrounding the authority of the *first-line manager* in particular is replete with claims that the span of control of the first-line manager has actually increased. This is debatable. There is much evidence to support the argument that, since the removal of middle management layers from organisations in recent years, the responsibilities of those managers have now been delegated to the first-line manager.

The implication of this has been that the first-line manager has become increasingly accountable for the middle manager's concerns, such as managing subordinates' performance, taking care of property and equipment, counselling staff, as well as perhaps managing and controlling budgets and undertaking the work themselves. However, this increase in accountability has not been commensurate with the same levels of authority. On the contrary, the former middle manager's authority has actually been entrusted to senior management.

Despite the evidence that organisations are de-layering, decentralising and devolving responsibility (which was initially designed to make organisations more responsive to consumer needs as well as empowering its employees), Knowles and Hales (2003) remain cynical. They are of the opinion that organisations are actually trying to *preserve* their structures because management want to retain control and are therefore reluctant to abdicate responsibility. They assert that:

> 'the function of managers, including first-line managers, is seen as *preventative* rather than *facilitative*, and therefore primarily concerned with monitoring and control.'

7

7.3 Job design

The structure of an organisation has a direct impact upon the ways that jobs are designed. For example, narrow structures tend to imply little authority, whereas flat structures imply more autonomy over decision making. Job design is important for two main reasons:

- to provide job satisfaction, which ultimately improves organisational performance; and
- to make efficient and effective use of the organisation's resources.

Job design dates back to classical (or scientific) management (1800s) where job specialisation was encouraged. Freeman and Stoner (1992) refer to this approach to job design as mechanistic in nature, as traditionally jobs were made as simple as possible for maximum efficiency. This often meant that the jobs were very monotonous. The renowned classical theorist Frederick Taylor (1856–1915) viewed employees as merely tools of production (machines) who were motivated solely by monetary rewards. However, Taylor's theories have been subject to much scrutiny. For example, Arnold (1998) argued that:

> 'the classical approach to jobs, with its emphasis on fragmenting jobs and reducing workers' autonomy and discretion, is counter-productive to both individual fulfilment and organisational performance. This is because boring, monotonous and meaningless jobs lead to poor mental health and feelings of dissatisfaction. In turn this can result in lack of motivation, absenteeism, labour turnover and even industrial unrest.'

Job design takes many forms, for example:

- Job rotation – where an employee is moved from one job to another with the intent of making the employee's role more interesting. Mullins

(2005) argues that job rotation is not strictly job design as 'neither the nature of the task, nor the method of working is restructured', although this is not strictly true. In certain organisations, temporary positions are advertised internally (often as a result of maternity leave), and that is called a secondment. This encourages multiskilling of the workforce and helps employees to understand the challenges faced by other employees within the organisation.

- Job enlargement – this goes against the logic of Taylor by giving employees more yet similar functions to perform. This is intended to break up the monotony of the job by adding variety. It means enlarging the scope of the job by performing similar tasks, but it does not mean increased responsibility. An example of this would be a production line worker who assembled a whole machine rather than one element of the machine. This approach to job design is often criticised as jobs designed is this manner remain fairly tedious for employees. Despite the fact that it may give the employee more to do, it gives the employee little sense of satisfaction.

- Job enrichment – this is not the same concept as job enlargement (as some academics would suggest). It gives employees autonomy over their work. They are accountable for the way they perform tasks and are permitted to work at their own pace. Employees have a sense of responsibility and involvement. Hertzberg (in Burnes, 2004), comments:

'Job enrichment, which concentrates on increasing workers' responsibilities previously borne by supervisors and support staff are given to individuals or, more often, semi autonomous work groups.'

There are two other explicit terms used to describe job enrichment:

- Empowerment – another term used to describe job enrichment. Empowerment has been defined as:

'The delegation of power and responsibility to subordinates' (Burnes, 2004).

'Where employees are made responsible for their own actions by giving them the appropriate authority to apply discretion and make decisions concerning their work. Such productive potential gives employees the opportunity to use initiative and to develop a feeling of ownership over their jobs. It also provides power to satisfy customer quality and allows employees to fully participate and achieve a high fulfilment at work' (Betts, 2000).

- Self-managed work groups are a form of job enrichment where a group/team is responsible for their own actions. A supervisor is available for guidance and support but not to control. Goals will be set for the group, however, it is up to the group to how they reach their objectives. This form of job design has the added advantage of being very cost effective for the organisation as less managers are needed to supervise the employees. In addition to this, self managed work groups often feel a 'team spirit' which can act as a motivator. Employees in self managed teams also feel motivated from the point of view that they are responsible and in control of their own work. Sceptics however, point out that teamwork often fall short of achieving improved performance.

Work–life balance – job design today takes a more holistic view, looking at the employee's life in its entirety, which is called work–life balance. There is a lot of interest surrounding the issue of the quality of working life and work–life balance. Academics such as Kellaway (in Mullins, 2005) go as far as suggesting that rather than working as many hours as possible, employees should be encouraged to finish work on time, instead of taking on extra responsibility. Evidence suggests that by using this analogy, home life does not suffer as much and productivity at work was found to actually increase! Jobs today exhibit more flexibility with more people than ever before working from home. Flexi-time, for example, is used by many companies enabling employees to work hours to suit themselves providing they work their contracted hours. This is particularly beneficial to those with children.

Summers and Nowicki (see Mullins, 2005) believe that the more secure the organisation and the more stable the environment, the more latitude the manager has to encourage employees to lead balanced lives. However, today, relatively few firms operate in stable environments.

Self-assessment question 7.3

A survey conducted by *Management Today* (2001) concluded that 'the introduction of flexible working schedules has not had the expected effect of relieving pressure and improving the sense of balance'. Drawing on your own experiences or relevant examples, explain why the use of flexible working practices might have a detrimental effect on employees.

Feedback on page 93

Revision question

Now try the revision question for this session on page 248.

Summary

- The principle of span of control is one of Urwick's Ten Principles of Management and is simply defined as 'the number of subordinates reporting directly to a manager'.
- There are a number of variables which can affect the span of control, and each of these has an influence on whether the span of control is tall (narrow) or flat (wide).
- A *narrow* span of control is characterised by decentralised authority, many authority levels and long communication lines, a high degree of functional specialism, and high degree of delegation.
- In contrast, *wide* span of control is characterised by centralised authority, few authority levels and therefore fewer communication and coordination difficulties, a low degree of functional specialism and low delegation – where managers retain decision-making rights.

7

- If spans are too narrow, the slowing of communication can result in the organisation being slow to respond to decisions. This can prove costly to the organisation. Conversely, if the span is too wide it can be difficult for the manager to supervise effectively and there is a possibility that overloaded managers could become barriers or bottlenecks to decision making.
- The removal of middle management layers from organisations in recent years has meant that the responsibilities of those managers have now been delegated to *first-line managers*, who have become increasingly accountable for the middle manager's concerns (managing and counselling subordinates; managing performance, property and equipment; controlling budgets and so on).
- In order to provide job satisfaction, improve organisational performance and make better use of an organisation's resources, the *design* of jobs is an important consideration. The classical or traditional forms of job design were based on job rotation, job enlargement and job enrichment, whereas the more modern approach is centred around job enrichment by *empowerment* and the use of *self-managed work groups*, and trying to provide employees with a better *work–life balance*.

Suggested further reading

You could read the relevant sections of Bell and McLaughlin (1977), Bohte and Meier (2001), Buchanan and Huczynski (2004), Davison (2003), Garen (1999) and Mullins (2005).

Feedback on learning activities and self-assessment questions

Feedback on learning activity 7.1

In your answer you should consider the following variables affecting the span of management:

- the nature and context of organisation;
- the capabilities of managers and employees;
- the training available to all employees;
- the time available to managers when dealing with subordinates;
- the levels of employee morale and motivation;
- the physical and/or geographical spread of subordinates;
- the length of the chain of command, that is, the number of different levels in the structure of the organisation.

Feedback on self-assessment question 7.1

You should consider the issues relating to how effective control and coordination can be maintained as span of control increases. Some discussion is required relating to management or supervisory ability to control diminishing as spans increase. The implications relating to slower decision making, poorer/slower communications and the notion that control becomes problematical should also be discussed. This should lead you to comment on issues relating to cost, quality and speed of response (or service) to customers being affected.

Feedback on learning activity 7.2

Your answer should state whether the span of control within your organisation is narrow or wide. Possible advantages and disadvantages of each structure are as follows.

Advantages of wide span of control:

- Communication can be more effective as there are less layers of management through which to pass a message, so it is less likely to be misinterpreted. The message will also reach the employee faster.
- It costs less money to run a wider span of control because a business does not need too many managers.
- It promotes empowerment.

Disadvantages of wide span of control:

- It can be difficult for a manager to supervise effectively.
- Managers may lose control and sub-groups may develop which may operate contrary to management policies.

Advantages of narrow span of control:

- Promotional opportunities.
- Managers may feel in total control.

Disadvantages of narrow span of control:

- Management layers are costly.
- Decisions can take a long time to reach the bottom of the hierarchy.
- Employees may feel restricted which can stifle creativity and use of their initiative.

Feedback on self-assessment question 7.2

You should identify that taller, increasingly layered organisations will have a longer chain of command and therefore longer communication channels. It is argued that the more layers the more process-driven an organisation might become – hence an increase in bureaucracy. The results are poorer response to internal and external changes, slower decision making, management by committees, more rules to follow, and operational and managerial dysfunctionality.

Feedback on learning activity 7.3

Your answer to this can include reference to traditional approaches to job design such as: job rotation, job enrichment and job enlargement, and/or the more holistic approach that is work–life balance to increase your job satisfaction. Detailed explanation of how the redesign will also make more efficient use of resources is required. For example, will it make better use of your time and skills, will new technology be required to support the role (use of e-commerce, e-procurement and so on).

Feedback on self-assessment question 7.3

Your answer to this is likely to be subjective. However, the following reasons are all feasible:

- Some employees may not exercise self-discipline in managing their workload, which may result in them trying to do too much in a short space of time.
- Some employees may commit themselves to other activities outside of work which may increase rather than relieve their pressures.
- Flexible working practices in one department may create conflict with other departments that do not employ flexible working.
- Working flexible hours does not necessarily benefit all employees. For example, if a particular member of staff requires assistance but the person required is not available, then bottlenecks will occur.
- Flexible working arrangements can create difficulties with planning and scheduling meetings.
- Variances in operating hours also create communication problems.

If flexible working schedules are *too flexible*, planning and control can become problematic. For example, despite the fact that employees' hours have changed, customers' requirements and deadlines do not change. In some cases this will increase pressure on both employees and their colleagues in terms of how they coordinate their workloads to meet customer needs.

7

7

Culture

Introduction

The concept of culture was first explored in the early 1950s by the likes of Jacques. However, Handy, Brown, Deal and Kennedy and, in particular, Peters and Waterman, are responsible for stimulating the current fascination with the topic. The way we perform at work is attributed to the organisation's culture. Burnes (2004) illustrates this nicely: '[the] work and the way it is done is governed, directed and tempered by an organisation's culture – the particular set of values, beliefs, customs and systems that are unique to that organisation'.

This session explores culture in further detail.

'Culture defines how those in the organisation should behave in a given set of circumstances ... [It] legitimises certain forms of action and proscribes other forms.'
Burnes (2004)

8

Session learning objectives

After completing this session you should be able to:

8.1 Define the term 'culture' and describe the different types of culture which may exist within organisations.
8.2 Explain the importance of understanding culture and climate in organisations (the cultural 'web').
8.3 Appraise methods and approaches for managing effectively in international or cross-cultural organisations.

Unit content coverage

This study session covers the following topic from the official CIPS unit content document:

Learning outcome

Analyse the characteristics of different organisational structures and cultures.

Learning objectives

2.4 Define the term 'culture' and describe the different models of culture which may exist within organisations.
2.5 Evaluate methods and formulate plans for managing effectively in international or cross-cultural organisations.

Prior knowledge

Study sessions 5 – 7.

Timing

You should set aside about 7 hours to read and complete this session, including learning activities, self-assessment questions, the suggested further reading (if any) and the revision question.

8

8.1 Culture in organisations

What is **culture**?

Imagine that you enter a restaurant. What are your first impressions of the surroundings? You may observe how expensive it is to eat there, how the employees are dressed, or how they address their customers, colleagues and managers. All of these aspects contribute to create the culture of the organisation. All organisations have something (for example, a personality, philosophy, ideology or climate) which goes beyond economic rationality, and which gives each of them a unique identity. In literature, definitions of culture vary, but all have recurring themes, for example:

> 'Culture is how things are done around here. It is what is typical of the organisation, the habits, the prevailing attitudes, the grown-up pattern of accepted and expected behaviour.' (Drennan, 1992)

> Culture is shaped by several factors. An organisation's artefacts such as its physical structure, for example the shape of the building, by its norms such as dress codes and how employees address their superiors. Ethical codes, symbols and slogans all contribute to a company's culture. (Brown, 1995)

> 'Culture is the collective programming of the human mind that distinguishes the members of one human group from those of another. Culture in this sense is a system of collectively held values.' (Hofstede, cited in Senior, 2002).

Hofstede's interpretation of culture differs slightly in that it is used to differentiate between national cultures. In this context, 'human groups' actually refer to different nationalities. The remaining definitions refer to corporate culture.

In agreement with Brown, Johnson and Scholes (1999) believe that culture comprises several elements as illustrated in his cultural web (see figure 8.1), and that these have a bearing on how culture is manifest in organisations.

Figure 8.1: The cultural web

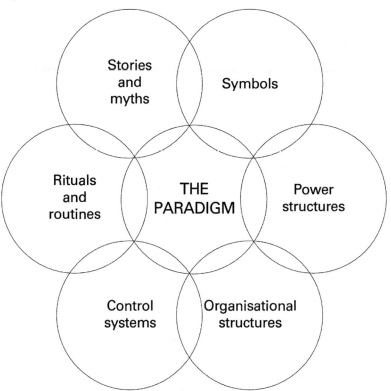

Johnson describes these elements thus:

- **The paradigm**: what the organisation is about; what it does; its mission; its values.
- **Control systems**: the processes in place to monitor what is going on. Role cultures would have vast rulebooks. There would be more reliance on individualism in a power culture.
- **Organisational structures**: reporting lines, hierarchies and the way that work flows through the business.
- **Power structures**: who makes the decisions, how widely spread the power is, and what the power is based on.
- **Symbols**: these include the logos and designs, but would extend to symbols of power, such as car-parking spaces and executive washrooms!
- **Rituals and routines**: management meetings, board reports and so on may become more habitual than necessary.
- **Stories and myths**: these develop about people and events, and convey a message about what is valued within the organisation.

It should be noted that these elements may overlap. For example, power structures may depend on control systems, which may exploit the very rituals that generate stories.

Learning activity 8.1

List seven factors that can influence the development of culture.

Feedback on page 104

Many academics are of the opinion that culture is directly related to performance (Deal and Kennedy, 1982; Kotter and Heskett (cited in Bamford and Forrester, 2003); Peters and Waterman, 1982). However, Keuning (cited in Burnes, 2004) places the emphasis more on the fact that culture is important because it provides stability by having set methods of handling and solving problems.

Culture has a major impact on organisations *even at the point of recruitment of staff*. For example, Robbins (2003) believes that:

> 'who receives a job offer to join the organisation, who is appraised as a high performer, and who gets the promotion are strongly influenced by the individual – organisational "fit" – that is whether the applicant or employee's attitudes and behaviours are compatible with the culture.'

However, hiring employees because of 'organisational fit' is a paradox in itself. If a company is to move with the times and to improve its performance, it should welcome diversity.

Strong and weak cultures

A strong culture is said to exist when the organisation's core values are shared throughout the organisation. Conversely, a weak culture exists where there is little alignment with organisational values, and control must be exercised through extensive procedures and bureaucracy.

It should be noted that a strong culture is not always advantageous. Cultures which are too cohesive can be a liability in that they create a major barrier to change. For example, in a stable environment, consistency of behaviour is likely to be an asset to an organisation. However, Robbins (2003) points out that consistent behaviour can also actually 'burden an organisation that operates in a dynamic environment'.

Classifying organisational culture

Several authors have attempted to classify organisational culture, for example:

1   Geert Hofstede demonstrated that there are national and regional cultural groupings that affect the behaviour of organisations. He identified five characteristics of culture in his study of national influences:
    (a)   power distance – the degree to which a society expects there to be differences in the levels of power. A high score suggests that there is an expectation that some individuals wield larger amounts of power than others. A low score reflects the view that all people should have equal rights;
    (b)   uncertainty avoidance reflects the extent to which a society accepts uncertainty and risk;
    (c)   individualism vs. collectivism – individualism is contrasted with collectivism, and refers to the extent to which people are expected to stand up for themselves, or alternatively act predominantly as a member of the group or organisation;

(d) masculinity vs. femininity – refers to the value placed on traditionally male or female values. Male values, for example, include competitiveness, assertiveness, ambition and the accumulation of wealth and material possessions;

(e) Long-term vs. short-term orientation – this explains the extent to which a society exhibits a pragmatic future-oriented perspective rather than a conventional historic or short-term point of view.

2 Deal and Kennedy (1982) defined organisational culture as 'the way things get done around here'. They measured organisations in respect of:

(a) feedback – quick feedback means an instant response. This could be in monetary terms, but could also be seen in other ways, such as the impact of a great save in a soccer match;

(b) risk – represents the degree of uncertainty in the organisation's activities.

Using these parameters, they were able to suggest four classifications of organisational culture:

(a) the **tough-guy macho culture**. Feedback is quick and the rewards are high. This often applies to fast-moving financial activities such as brokerage, but could also apply to policemen or women, or athletes competing in team sports. This can be a very stressful culture in which to operate;

(b) the **work hard/play hard culture** is characterised by low risks and quick feedback on performance. This is typical in large organisations which strive for high-quality customer service. It is often characterised by team meetings, jargon and buzzwords;

(c) the **bet your company culture**, where big-stakes decisions are made, but it may be years before the results are known. Typically, these might involve development or exploration projects which take years to come to fruition, such as oil prospecting or military aviation;

(d) the **process culture** occurs in organisations where there is little or no feedback. People become bogged down with how things are done not with what is to be achieved. This is often associated with bureaucracies. Whilst it is easy to criticise these cultures for being over cautious or bogged down in red tape, they do produce consistent results (which is regarded as ideal in, for example, public services).

3 Charles Handy (1985) presents four types of culture based on organisational structure. They include:

(a) a **power culture** which concentrates power in a few pairs of hands. Control radiates from the center like a web. Power cultures have few rules and little bureaucracy; swift decisions can ensue. This type of culture is often found in small entrepreneurial firms;

(b) a **role culture**, in which people have clearly delegated authorities within a highly defined structure. Typically, these organisations are large and form hierarchical bureaucracies. Power derives from a person's position and little scope exists for expert power;

(c) a **task culture**, in which teams are formed to solve particular problems. Power derives from expertise as long as a team requires expertise. These cultures often feature the multiple reporting lines of a matrix structure;

(d) a **person culture** exists where all individuals believe themselves superior to the organisation. Survival can become difficult for such organisations, since the concept of an organisation suggests that a group of like-minded individuals pursue the organisational goals. Some professional partnerships can operate as person cultures because each partner brings a particular expertise and clientele to the firm.

Self-assessment question 8.1

Case study: General Motors (GM) – adapting to the environment

In the 1950s, GM dominated the automobile market with a 50% market share. However, by 2000 GM owned only 30% – a dramatic reduction. The company proved slow to make decisions as it possessed a tall hierarchical structure. It also concentrated on low-cost products rather than innovative design. Driven by cost alone, GM's competitors took a hold, creating efficient cars as well as racy sports models.

It was company policy to recruit future executives straight from university. GM then moulded these 'executives-to-be' accordingly. Promotions were mainly in house and ideas were restricted to those at executive level. GM's executives were even encouraged to socialise together.

Abandoning usual company policy, in 2001, GM chief executive Richard Wagner hired former Chrysler Executive Robert Lutz as vice-chairman. He was allocated the task of changing GM's culture. Wagner admitted that the company was entrenched with producing unimaginative cars which were cheap to make. Fortunately, Wagner had a reputation for introducing exciting new products.

Lutz adopted an incremental strategy for instigating change. He encouraged employees to challenge old practices and to test drive their competitors' cars!

(Adapted from Robbins, 2003)

*   Explain GM's old culture.
*   What sort of culture do you think Lutz was trying to create?

Feedback on page 105

8.2 Managing culture

Learning activity 8.2

Should culture be managed? Give two reasons for and two reasons against.

Feedback on page 105

With the rapid changes in the environment, such as globalisation and the sophistication of information technology, it is necessary for an organisation to adapt accordingly, which will involve changing its culture. Mergers and acquisitions, in particular, often require a cultural change. Gilkey (in Bijlsma-Frankema, 2001) stresses, however, that 'mergers often fail as a result of focusing too much on the financial bottom line and neglecting psychological and cultural issues.'

Jones (1994) asks the all-important question: 'Can organisational culture actually be managed?' He contemplates that it would be very difficult, as organisational members, ethics, structure and the property rights system all interact and therefore would require major alterations to change the organisation's values. Schraeder and Self (2003) support Jones' claim believing it to be a feasible but indeed a challenging task. Contrastingly, Meek (in Burnes, 2004) insists:

> 'culture as a whole cannot be manipulated, turned on or off, although it needs to be recognised that some [organisations] are in a better position than others to intentionally influence aspects of it ... culture should be regarded as something an organisation "is", not something it "has": it is not an independent variable nor can it be created, discovered or destroyed by the whims of management.'

In reality, cultures evolve as societies adapt to transitions in the external and internal environment. Therefore, new cultures can be created. Bate (cited in Senior, 2002) observed 'culture can be changed in fact it is changing all the time'. Therefore, the issue is not that culture can or cannot be changed, it is the extent of the changes and the time frame permitted for achieving them.

Nelson and Quick (1996) point out that:

> 'one reason for the difficulty is that assumptions – the deepest level of culture – are often unconscious. As such they are often non-confrontable and non-debatable. Another reason for the difficulty is that culture is deeply ingrained and behavioural norms and rewards are well learned.'

It can be considered that culture is dynamic in nature, as it evolves naturally, can be unpredictable and is an ongoing process. Mabey and White (1993) make the valid point that 'culture emerges over time' therefore, it would be difficult to plan such a task. Burnes (2004) states:

> 'The Culture Excellence proponents argue that there is only one form of culture that matters in today's environment – strong and flexible – and that organisations should adopt it quickly or face the consequences.'

However, the top-down approach to managing culture (that is, planned by management rather than letting it evolve naturally) can be considered unethical. Van Maanen and Kunda (cited in Burnes, 2004) regard management's intentions to change culture as an attempt to manipulate employees' minds. Schein's interpretation (cited in Buchanan and Huczynski, 2004) on the other hand is rather controversial stating 'the unique and essential function of leadership is the manipulation of culture.'

As Nelson and Quick (1996) suggest:

> 'Managers are models who communicate the organisational culture to employees through personal enactment. Their modelled behaviour sets the norms for other employees to follow. Their leadership is essential for developing a culture that values diversity, supports empowerment, fosters innovation in product and service quality and promotes ethical behaviour'.

Self-assessment question 8.2

In the UK in March 2004, the retail supermarket chain Morrisons decided to acquire a competitor, Safeway, to compete with the other three major food retailers, Tesco, Sainsbury's and Asda WalMart. Following this acquisition, Morrisons increased their geographic spread across the UK significantly.

With reference to this acquisition, explain what changes *have* taken place and what changes *need* to take place and give reasons why.

Feedback on page 106

8.3 Managing across cultures

Learning activity 8.3

List seven skills and attributes needed for managing internationally.

Feedback on page 106

It is natural (and perhaps logical) to think that when organisations move their operations overseas (via internationalisation or globalisation) they standardise their procedures and policies throughout the business to enable their geographically dispersed operations to work towards common goals. However, Newman and Nollen (cited in Kessapidou and Varsakelis, 2003) reveal that there is empirical evidence illustrating that 'the variety of national cultures leads to a range of styles of leadership or human resource management'. In support of this, Rodrigues et al (2000) also conclude that national cultures 'develop differing learning styles' and therefore a formalised approach to training is not always appropriate. For these very reasons, it is therefore vitally important for managers to be cognisant of the differing cultures that exist within a multinational business. As Deresky (2006) explains:

> 'An understanding of the local culture and business environment can give managers an advantage in competitive industries. Foreign companies – no matter how big – can ignore those aspects to their peril. Such differences in culture and the way of life in other countries necessitate that managers develop international expertise to manage on a contingency basis according to the host country environment

... A critical skill for managing people in other countries is cultural savvy – that is, a working knowledge of the cultural variables affecting management decisions. Managers have often seriously underestimated the significance of cultural factors. According to numerous accounts, many blunders made in international operations can be attributed to a lack of cultural sensitivity'.

When managing a foreign subsidiary, differences in behaviour are exhibited resulting from the societal variables that relate to the host nation culture, such as religion and language, politics, economic and legal considerations. These cultural differences determine motivation and attitudes to work, which managers should take into consideration, 'materialism, individualism and change' (Deresky, 2006). It is therefore important that managers collate information regarding cultural variables in order to understand different national working environments, behavioural norms and accepted ethical codes. Whilst only a general picture may be built, this will at least help foster good human-relation practices.

8

Self-assessment question 8.3

Case study: Local or expatriate manager?

An important decision for a firm operating in a foreign country is whether to employ a local manager or one from overseas (an expatriate). Unfortunately Harvey's findings (cited in Kessapidou and Varsakelis, 2003) reveal that:

> 'the failure rate of expatriate managers (returning early to the domestic organisation or not meeting performance expectations) exacerbates the already limited number of managers available to relocate for foreign assignments.'

Explain why it may be preferable to employ a local manager.

Feedback on page 107

Revision question

Now try the revision question for this session on page 248.

Summary

Culture is shaped by several factors. An organisation's artefacts such as its physical structure, for example the shape of the building, by its norms such as dress codes and how employees address their superiors. Ethical codes, symbols and slogans all contribute to a company's culture. (Brown, 1995)

An organisation's cultural web comprises: the paradigm; control systems; organisational structures; power structures; symbols; rituals and routines; stories and myths and so on.

Various academics consider that culture:

- is directly related to performance;
- provides stability by having set methods of handling and solving problems; and
- has an impact on organisations at the point of recruitment of staff.

Hofstede's five characteristics of culture (in his study of national influences) are: power distance; uncertainty avoidance; individualism vs. collectivism; masculinity vs. femininity; long-term vs. short-term relationships.

Deal and Kennedy (1982) measured organisations in respect of feedback and risk and suggested four classifications of organisational culture: the tough-guy macho culture; the work hard/play hard culture; the bet your company culture; and the process culture.

Handy (1985) presents four types of culture based on organisational structure: power culture; role culture; task culture; and person culture

Cultures evolve as societies adapt to transitions in the external and internal environment and, as such, new cultures can be created.

Managers communicate organisational culture to employees and set 'norms' for other employees to follow. Leadership is essential for developing cultures that value diversity, support empowerment, foster innovation and service quality and promote ethical behaviour.

National cultures leads to a range of differing styles of leadership or human resource management and, as such, it is important for managers to be aware of the differing cultures that might exist within a multinational business.

National cultural differences resulting from religion and language, politics, economic and legal considerations determine motivation and attitudes to work. Managers must therefore collate information regarding these variables in order to understand different national working environments, behavioural norms and accepted ethical codes.

Suggested further reading

You could read the relevant sections of Dastmalchian, Lee and Ng (2000), Deresky (2006), Herguner and Reeves (2000), Kessapidou and Varsekelis (2003) and Rodrigues, Bu and Min (2000).

Feedback on learning activities and self-assessment questions

Feedback on learning activity 8.1

The following can all influence how culture is manifest.

- History – the reason and manner in which the organisation was formed; its age; its values and the philosophy of its owners.

- Primary function – the nature of the business; the range and quality of its products and services.
- The goals and objectives of the organisation – for example profit, long-term survival, growth and so on.
- The size of the organisation – larger organisations tend to be more formalised and perhaps more bureaucratic.
- Location – a major influence on culture, whether the organisation is multi-domestic, national, international or global.
- Management and staffing – top executives have much influence on the development of culture.
- The environment – organisational responsiveness to external influences requires a culture that is sensitive to change.

You could also include factors such as education systems, the media, political processes and so on.

Feedback on self-assessment question 8.1

GM's old culture was inward looking, narrow minded and stuck in the past. GM was epitomised by low-cost products. Their entire way of working was rigid. For example:

- The company, up until Lutz's tenure, only recruited internally. Sometimes an injection of new blood into a company is needed.
- Future executives arrived straight from university and were moulded for management roles. They had little or no experience to bring to the company.
- Despite their lack of experience, executives were the only ones who contributed new ideas to the company. Ideas were not allowed to filter through to the top. The irony of this is that those with the real experience, for example engineers, designers and particularly sales people, who are familiar with customers' needs, were not allowed to express their ideas.
- Even when socialising, executives were encouraged to stick together rather than talking to others from the automobile industry to gain different perspectives and insights.

Lutz was trying to create an open culture – inspiring and encouraging employees to become involved and contribute their ideas.

Feedback on learning activity 8.2

Culture must be managed because:

- When changes in the external environment occur, organisations should adapt accordingly.
- Mergers fail when attention is not paid to culture.

Culture should not be managed because:

- Culture emerges and evolves over time, it cannot be planned.
- It is unethical to attempt to manipulate employees' value and belief systems.

8

Feedback on self-assessment question 8.2

With this acquisition, the retailers are likely to have relocated jobs, job specifications will have changed and structural changes will be taking place.

With an acquisition/merger, there will often be a clash in corporate cultures. One of the most important aspects of an acquisition, but one that is often neglected, is culture. If an acquisition is to be successful, the cultures of the respective retailers will have to become integrated, so that employees have a common frame of reference to enable them to work towards the same goals. Jay (2004) recognises that 'it is enormously difficult to graft one company's culture onto another'. However, getting the right culture is very important otherwise it will be to Morrisons' detriment. This is supported by Gilkey (cited in Bijlsma-Frankema, 2001) who stresses 'mergers often fail as a result of focusing too much on the financial bottom line and neglecting psychological and cultural issues'. Therefore, cultural change should be of prime concern to Morrisons if they are to succeed with this venture. The higher the cultural fit between the two firms, the less aversion prone the process of cultural integration will be. However, too much cultural fit can reduce the synergetic effects of the two companies.

Feedback on learning activity 8.3

Your answer should include any of the following (or similar feasible alternatives):

- Interpersonal skills – the ability to network and form relationships satisfies the managers' need for friendship and integration into the foreign culture. 'Establishing relationships and building trust allows the expatriate manager to tap into critical information, thus reducing the stressful uncertainties surrounding both work and personal life.' (Schneider and Barsoux, 1997)
- Linguistic ability – whilst the ability to speak the country's language is useful, having total fluency is not always feasible. Making an effort to speak the local language, however, demonstrates an eagerness to communicate and connect with the host country.
- A willingness to live overseas – managers and their families must genuinely want to live overseas and be prepared to adapt to a different way of life. Otherwise, this may strain family and work life.
- Flexibility and tolerance for uncertainty and ambiguity – the behaviour of the employees in different cultures is unlikely to resemble what the manager is already familiar with. When faced with uncertainty, there is a tendency to impose standards and regulations.
- Patience – managers must be patient. Employees may not be familiar with a particular management style and also may have their own learning style.
- Cultural savvy – managers must be sensitive to others' beliefs and values. They should collate information regarding cultural variables in order to understand different national working environments, behavioural norms and accepted ethical codes.
- Self-confidence – international managers must be not be disheartened if they do not achieve immediate results. Schneider and Barsoux (1997)

believe that failure should be treated as a learning experience rather than a narcissistic injury (a blow to their self-image) which can undermine their self-confidence.

Feedback on self-assessment question 8.3

Your answer should include the following points:

- Expatriate managers tend to cost considerably more, for example there are relocation expenses.
- Many blunders made in international operations can be attributed to a lack of cultural sensitivity. Harvey (in Kessapidou and Varsakelis, 2003) insists that '*host country nationals exhibit a relative advantage in terms of cultural and political sensitivity in the host country with respect to expatriate managers.*'
- Kessapidou and Varsakelis (2003) state that it is necessary for expatriate managers to adapt socio-culturally, that is to develop culture-specific skills such as the ability to negotiate in the host country. Rao and Hashimoto (cited in Kessapidou and Varsakelis, 2003) claim that local managers are more effective since they tend to be more assertive with peers of their own collectivistic culture.
- Foreign managers may not be conversant with the country's language and are more likely to encounter language difficulties.
- Overall, a sound understanding of the local culture and business environment can give managers an advantage in competitive industries, therefore employing local managers is most likely to benefit the organisation as they are most familiar with their culture.

8

8

Management decision making

'Effective decision making is crucial to the well-being of the organisation, especially when an increasing number of decisions are being taken further down the organisation.'
Brooks (2003)

Introduction

All organisations must respond to a variety of strategic and operational pressures. These may be internal such as improving efficiency within the firm and the search for gaining competitive advantage. They can also be external such as the nature of competition and legislation. Decision making is therefore a fundamental aspect of the management process. Decisions have to be made at the strategic, administrative and operational level. Regardless of the type of decisions made, Izar (1991) stresses, 'It must be remembered that business decisions affect profits as well as employees, consumers and sometimes the environment'.

Session learning objectives

9

After completing this session you should be able to:

9.1 Use appropriate tools and techniques to 'position' the organisation as the basis for setting objectives (for example SWOT, PEST, balanced scorecard, and so on.).
9.1 Evaluate and apply a range of tools to make effective management choices and decisions.

Unit content coverage

This study session covers the following topic from the official CIPS unit content document:

Learning outcome

Use a range of techniques to support and implement justifiable management decisions.

Learning objectives

3.1 Evaluate and apply a range of tools to make effective management choices and decisions.

Prior knowledge

Study sessions 2, 4 and 6 – 8.

Timing

You should set aside about 6 hours to read and complete this session, including learning activities, self-assessment questions, the suggested further reading (if any) and the revision question.

9.1 Tools for 'positioning' an organisation

To help managers formulate future strategies, they need to be aware of the current position or situation of the organisation in terms of where it is in its competitive environment, and how it can respond to the opportunities and threats that might arise in the future. SWOT analysis is a method of analysing an organisation's competitive situation by assessing organisational strengths (S), weaknesses (W), opportunities (O) and threats (T). Strengths and weaknesses are *internal* strategic factors, and opportunities and threats are *external* strategic factors.

- Strengths – relate to the company's attributes, its core competencies, where the firm's expertise and strengths lie.
- Weaknesses – relate to the company's limitations/negative aspects which require improving/minimising.
- Opportunities – relate to favourable circumstances, often the result of a change in the external environment, which the organisation should take advantage of.
- Threats – relate to hostile conditions, the result of a change in the external environment, which the organisation should be prepared for.

Correctly identifying weaknesses that exist within the company gives rise to opportunities for improvement and development. It is important for a company to develop and build upon its strengths and eliminate weaknesses where possible in order for it to be able to respond appropriately to opportunities and threats in its competitive environment. As Hannagan (2005) asserts: 'a manager's role is to exploit the strengths of a company and to correct or compensate for the weaknesses'.

In order to carry out an accurate positional audit of an organisation, it is important that managers, when conducting a SWOT analysis, evaluate external environmental factors *first* so that they can identify those variables that determine opportunities and threats. This then allows managers to establish their internal position with regard to building appropriate capabilities and competencies which help the organisation respond competitively. The two areas on which managers should focus their attention are:

1   The **task** (or industry) **environment**, which includes those elements or groups that directly affect, or are affected by, an organisation's operations (for example shareholders, governments, suppliers, employee/labour unions, special interest groups, competitors, customers, trade associations, creditors and communities).

2   The **societal** (PEST) **environment**, that is, the more general forces that do not directly affect the short-run activities of the organisation, but that can, and often do, influence its long-run decisions (for

example **p**olitical-legal forces, **e**conomic forces, **s**ocio-cultural forces, **t**echnological forces and Competitive forces).

The frameworks which aid identification of current position in addition to PEST/SWOT are as follows.

Porter's five forces of industry analysis

This framework helps organisations to analyse the nature and intensity of competition in a particular industry, by examining:

1   The intensity of competition – this relates to the number of direct rivals and their ability to maintain their position.
2   The threat of new entrants – this is the ease with which new competitors can enter the same market.
3   The bargaining power of suppliers – this is the extent to which suppliers can exert power over businesses, for example suppliers demanding a particular price for their materials.
4   The bargaining power of buyers – this is determined by the size of the organisation. If they are a major player, then it is likely that they will have a lot of bargaining power.
5   The threat of substitutes – this refers to products or services that can be used as an alternative.
6   Other stakeholders – this is not normally depicted on Porter's model, but also influential nowadays is the level of (potential) intervention from governments, organisational stakeholders and shareholders, and other interested parties.

Figure 9.1: Five forces of industry analysis

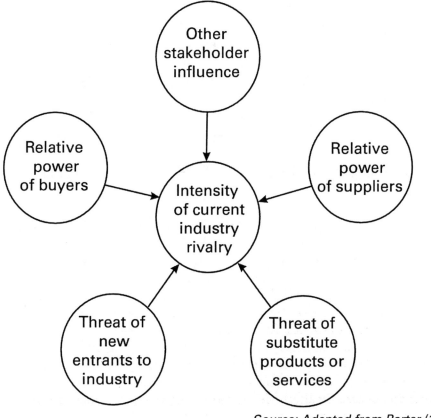

Source: Adapted from Porter (1980)

The Boston Consulting Group (BCG) matrix

This aid to decision making is designed specifically to enhance a multidivisional firm's efforts to formulate strategies, and it graphically portrays differences among product or business divisions in terms of relative market share position and industry growth rate. Primarily, it allows a multidivisional organisation to manage its 'portfolio of businesses' by examining the relative market share position and the industry growth rate of each division relative to all the other divisions in the organisation.

- Relative market share position is the ratio of a division's own market share in a particular industry to the market share held by the largest rival firm in that industry. This is shown on the X axis of the matrix – the mid point set at 0.50 (corresponding to a division having half the market share of the leading firm in the industry).
- Industry growth rate is represented by the Y axis and ranges from –20% to +20%, with 0.0 being the mid point. Here, separate divisions are depicted by circles corresponding to the proportion of corporate revenue generated by that business unit, and the pie slice indicates the proportion of corporate profits generated by that division.

Figure 9.2: The BCG matrix

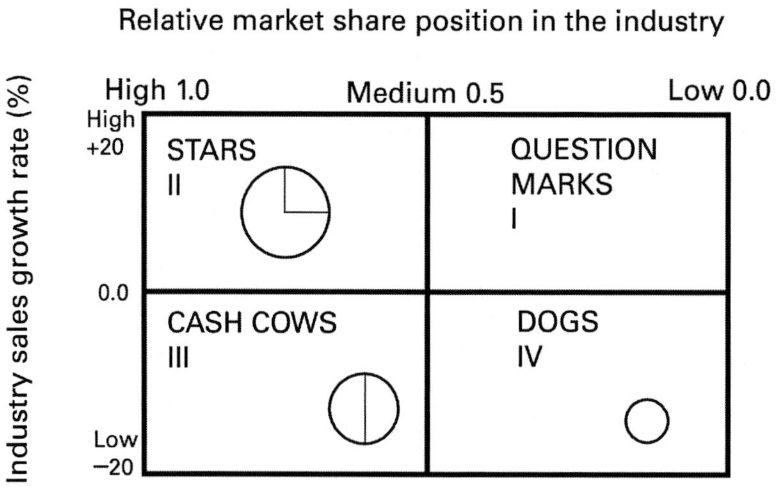

Relative market share position in the industry

Each of the four quadrants of the matrix describes business units or product divisions as:

1   Question marks – product divisions or business units that compete in high-growth industries but with low relative market share position. Their cash needs are high and their cash generation low. Here, the organisation must decide whether to strengthen them by pursuing intensive strategies or sell them off.
2   Stars – those divisions/units that have a high relative market share in high-growth industries, and which are the best long-run opportunities for growth and profitability. As a result, they should receive substantial investment to maintain or strengthen their dominant positions. (Here, intensive and integrative strategies and joint ventures are all appropriate to help the organisation maintain the strong position of these business units or divisions.)

3　Cash cows – these have a high relative market share but compete in low-growth industries. Formerly Stars, they generate cash in excess of their needs and are 'milked'. They should be managed to maintain their strong position for as long as possible. (Appropriate strategies for managing cash cows are product development and/or concentric diversification if they are strong and retrenchment or divestiture if they weaken.)

4　Dogs – divisions or units that have low relative market share in slow or no market-growth industries. They are generally weak internally and externally, and are often liquidated, divested or trimmed down via retrenchment, which is often the first/best strategy to pursue because after asset and cost reduction, some can 'bounce back' to become viable and profitable.

The benefits of the BCG matrix are that it draws attention to the cash flow, investment characteristics, and needs of an organisation's various divisions. It also indicates how divisions of many firms evolve over time where dogs become question marks – question marks become stars – stars become cash cows – cash cows become dogs, in an ongoing counter-clockwise direction (see figure 9.3).

The worst case scenario is when question marks are developed through investment to become stars and then demand and industry or market growth rate falls, resulting in stars becoming dogs (see figure 9.4).

Much less frequently stars become question marks, question marks become dogs, dogs become cash cows and cash cows become stars – in a clockwise motion – but this is rare indeed. (Also, in some organisations, no cyclical motion is apparent.)

Figure 9.3: BCG – ideal portfolio evolution

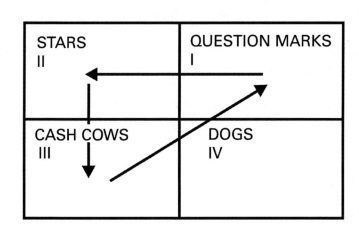

Figure 9.4: BCG – worst case scenario

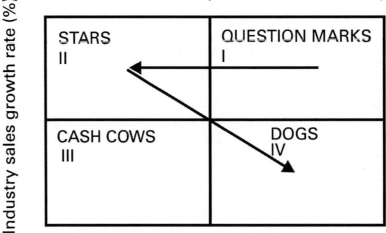

Essentially, over time, organisations should strive for a portfolio of divisions that are stars. However, as Argenti (1993) points out:

'this does not mean that the organisation should treat each business alike. To set all subsidiaries the same ROCE or turnover, or growth target, would be absurd. Alas however, this is exactly what many groups do and it demonstrates an extraordinary lack of understanding of strategy formulation.'

How useful is the BCG?

The BCG is good for telling 'at a glance' how profusely an organisation is blessed with cows and stars, but it does not attend to strategies for people, for computers and management information systems (MIS), for tax, and for all the other elements in a group of businesses that may need attention on a strategic scale. It has also been criticised from many quarters. For example:

- The use of highs/lows to make just four categories is too simplistic.
- The market share/profitability link is not that strong. Low-share businesses can also be profitable (and vice versa).
- The highest growth-rate markets are not necessarily the best.
- It considers the product or strategic business unit (SBU) in relation to only one competitor – the market leader, missing small competitors with fast-growing market shares.
- Growth rate is only *one* aspect of industry attractiveness, and market share is only *one* aspect of overall competitive position.

As Slatter (1990) points out, the common pitfalls associated with using the BCG matrix are related to:

- defining the relative market;
- the validity of the product life cycle;
- the value of market share;
- the effect of market structure;
- market stability;
- inter-relatedness of product-market segments;

- divesting the dogs;
- viewing the portfolio as a closed system.

The balanced scorecard

Kaplan and Norton(1996) introduced the concept of the balanced scorecard to measure performance in organisations. Their theory is useful to managers as it adopts a holistic and an essentially balanced view of the company's performance, rather than just focusing on the company using financial measures. They recognised that decisions should not be made with quantitative data alone, but should consider a great number of issues. Ahmed and Rafiq (2002) assert:

> 'if measurement is narrow, then it drives a very narrow set of behaviours, the risk in this approach is one of gaining in a single area but sub-optimising the totality, especially so if the company ignores critical variables.'

For example, a company may decide to keep their operating costs to a minimum in order to retain as much profit as possible. However, in doing so quality may be compromised. As McLaney and Atrill (2002) emphasise:

> 'it is important to consider qualitative factors carefully. They can seem unimportant because they are virtually impossible to assess in terms of their ultimate economic effect. This effect can nevertheless be very significant.'

Brooks (2003) also states:

> 'recent research (Nutt, 1997) suggests that the quality of management decision making is often poor, primarily because managers rush into decisions or become fixated on aspects of a particular solution, even if it has been shown not to work. Poor decision making is often the result of the decision processes of chief executives who are on fixed-term contracts.'

This illustrates how managers can be short-sighted and opportunistic, concentrating on short-term goals and quick fixes like reducing costs, which can ultimately sacrifice the reputation of the organisation.

The balanced scorecard adopts a broader view looking at performance from four perspectives. They include:

- Financial perspective – this takes into account measures such as profit, overhead expenditure, shareholder wealth and so on.
- Customer perspective – this is likely to include customer retention ratios and feedback from customers regarding how satisfied they are with their product and/or service.
- Internal business perspective – this includes measurement of the percentage of sales from new products; manufacturing costs; manufacturing cycle time; inventory management; quality indicators and technological capabilities.
- Learning and growth perspective – this relates to organisational development – how the organisation has changed for the better. This category can be measured using employee satisfaction surveys and

9

employee retention calculations. Also included in this category is the impact of new technology.

Benefits and drawbacks of balanced scorecard

Benefits:

- it provides a more holistic perspective of an organisation's performance;
- it facilitates the development of robust and hierarchical objectives and strategies;
- it links control to objectives;
- it acts as an aid to achieving 'buy-in' from staff.

Drawbacks:

- it is complex to use;
- it requires investment to use effectively and to embed it in the organisation;
- it needs sustained commitment to avoid any loss of momentum.

Figure 9.5: The balanced scorecard

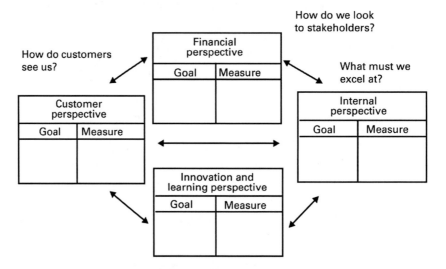

Source: Adapted from Harvard Business Review, July 1, 2005

Learning activity 9.1

A major pharmaceutical company has recently purchased some expensive technology to produce a new medicine. However, looking at the accounts, the company's profits are considerably lower than in previous years. Applying Kaplan's and Norton's balanced scorecard, what advice would you give to the company?

Feedback on page 123

Having completed this activity, now attempt self-assessment question 9.1 below.

Self-assessment question 9.1

Critically evaluate the BCG matrix.

Feedback on page 123

9.2 Tools for decision making

Decision making has been defined as:

- 'a commitment to action' (Mintzberg, cited in Teal et al, 2003);
- 'acts of choice between alternative courses of action designed to produce a specified result, and one made on a review of relevant information guided by explicit criteria' (Rose, cited in Teal et al, 2003).

Learning activity 9.2

What is your decision-making style?

When answering the following questions, select the answer that resembles you most closely.

1   When performing my job, I usually look for:
   (a)   practical results
   (b)   the best solution to problems
   (c)   new ideas or approaches
   (d)   pleasant working conditions.
2   When faced with a problem, I usually:
   (a)   use approaches that have been proved to work before
   (b)   analyse it carefully
   (c)   think of a creative solution
   (d)   rely on my intuition.
3   When making plans, I usually emphasise:
   (a)   the problems I currently have
   (b)   attaining objectives
   (c)   future goals
   (d)   developing my career.
4   The kind of information I usually prefer to use is:
   (a)   specific facts
   (b)   complete and accurate data
   (c)   broad information covering many options
   (d)   a small amount of data that is simple to comprehend.
5   Whenever I am uncertain about what to do, I:
   (a)   rely on my intuition
   (b)   search for facts
   (c)   try to find a compromise
   (d)   wait and decide later.
6   The people with whom I work best are usually:
   (a)   ambitious and enthusiastic
   (b)   self-confident
   (c)   open-minded
   (d)   trusting and polite.

(continued on next page)

Learning activity 9.2 *(continued)*

7   The decisions I make are usually:
   (a)   direct and realistic
   (b)   abstract or systematic
   (c)   broad and flexible
   (d)   sensitive to others' needs.

Look at your scores, did you mainly answer a, b, c or d?

Feedback on page 123

Pareto analysis/80:20 rule

A Pareto analysis is a simple method for separating the major causes ('vital few') of a problem, from the minor ones ('trivial many'). It helps prioritise and focus resources where they are most needed and can also assist in measuring the impact of an improvement by comparing before and after. Pareto diagrams are a visually effective means of displaying the relative importance of causes, problems or other conditions.

Vilfredo Pareto was a 19th-century economist who observed that 80% of Italy's wealth was owned by 20% of its population. This relationship has been found to be true in many other fields, for example 80% of a company's problems are likely to result from 20% of the causes. Although the actual split may not be exactly 80/20, the principle is that only a few causes are usually responsible for most problems that occur. Managers then know where to concentrate their efforts in dealing with these problems.

Pareto analysis is easy to draw conclusions from once you have the information, but it is not always as clear cut as the principle suggests. Sometimes 40% of the causes account for 40% of the overall problems, which could confuse managers on which direction to take. If, however, the ratio was exactly 80:20, managers would be confident that they were making the right decision. It is a very simplistic tool to aid decision making and it does not promote forward thinking.

Figure 9.6 provides a simple example of how the Pareto principle might apply to an analysis of the cost associated with a number of items held in a store or warehouse, where 20% of the items held account for 80% of the total cost of all items.

Figure 9.6: Pareto analysis

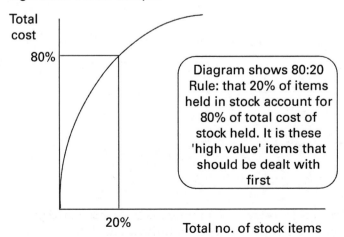

Ishikawa diagram

After using Pareto analysis, the next useful step for management could be to use the Ishikawa diagram to help find a solution to the problem(s). Whilst Pareto analysis proves useful in identifying where the major problems lie, the Ishikawa diagram can be used to help brainstorm the problem to find the underlying/root causes. The diagram begins on the right-hand side (the fish head) with the effect/problem that is currently being experienced. A branch is then labelled with each possible cause. Often the causes can come under five headings: manpower/staffing, materials, machinery, methods and measurement (known as the '5 Ms'). Causes relating to the 5 Ms then branch off further. This allows managers and their teams to help identify all of the possible causes of the problem(s).

In the UK, the Royal Mail once faced a lawsuit for failing to deliver its letters. If the company used the Ishikawa tool, they might be able to identify what is causing this problem. The Ishikawa diagram may look something like the example given in figure 9.7.

Figure 9.7: Ishikawa fishbone diagram

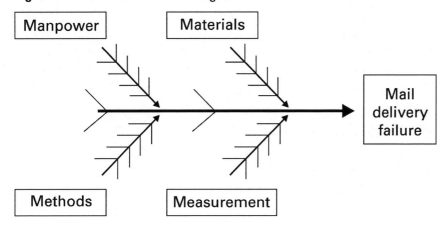

'Mail delivery failure' is on the right-hand side because that is the problem/observed effect.

In this example, some of the causes of the mail delivery problem may be identified as follows.

Manpower:

- understaffed – not enough time;
- staff are absent/sick;
- staff do not understand their role;
- staff are deliberately not delivering the letters – staff want more pay and therefore are on strike.

Methods:

- letters are getting mislaid in the process;
- sorting method is inefficient.

Materials:

- letters do not have correct postage amount/are not weighed correctly;
- letters are not clearly labelled – post code not displayed.

Measurement:

* the cost to Royal Mail to deliver the letter exceeds the price which customers are paying.

The Ishikawa diagram has a number of strengths as it places strong emphasis on the importance of people and their participation in the problem-solving process. It uses statistical and people-orientated techniques and introduces the idea of quality-control circles. However, the Ishikawa diagram is often seen as a too simplistic solution to problem solving and, although quality control circles generate many feasible ideas, the notion of converting these into action is not dealt with adequately (Slack et al. 1995).

Decision trees

Decision tree analysis can be useful to managers when deciding between options. It encourages decision makers to think about alternative approaches and courses of action as well as the future implications of their decisions. Decision trees have branches to illustrate the various decision paths that can be taken. Consider the following scenario.

Company X needs a critical component for the assembly of their finished product. Their choices are to either manufacture the component themselves or outsource it from one of two different suppliers – supplier A or supplier B. So, the decision is based on:

* option 1: carry out the work themselves;
* option 2: outsource the supplies (that is, buy in materials) from supplier A;
* option 3: outsource the supplies from supplier B.

Figure 9.8: Decision tree for company X

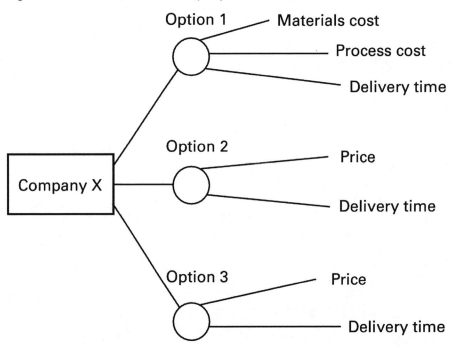

The component will cost £100 to purchase from supplier A and £70 from supplier B. To manufacture the component in-house will cost £150 and this will take one month from raw material to completion. Supplier A can deliver the goods in one month, whereas supplier B can only deliver the goods within three months. However, company X's customer requires the finished goods within two months.

In this case, option 3 is not viable as the customer requires the product within two months, and supplier B cannot deliver for three months. At face value, and based on financial considerations only, option 2 is the most cost effective. However, this simplistic decision tree approach is flawed in that it does not consider other factors such as the reliability of suppliers, the quality of products/components supplied and so on.

Cost-benefit analysis

Cost-benefit analysis is a simple approach used to help decide whether to go ahead with an action or not. Quite simply, the principle is that if the benefits are greater than the costs, then the plan (or investment) will go ahead. If the costs exceed the perceived benefits, then the plan is rejected. Cost-benefit analysis is popular because it is simple and easy to use, but it is subject to much scrutiny. For example, it uses only economic measures and unfortunately does not take into consideration any other variables such as health and safety. For example, if it is perceived that the cost of a minimal safety feature on a car outweighs the benefits, then the company that manufactures the car are likely to not include the safety feature. In addition to this, cost-benefit analysis represents a 'value neutral methodology', yet actual calculations yield efficiency and wealth maximisation results which do not reflect societal values.

9

Self-assessment question 9.2

List and explain three disadvantages to cost-benefit analysis.

Feedback on page 124

Revision question

Now try the revision question for this session on page 248.

Summary

- SWOT analysis is a method of analysing an organisation's competitive situation by assessing organisational strengths (S), weaknesses (W), opportunities (O) and threats (T). Strengths and weaknesses are *internal* strategic factors, and opportunities and threats are *external* strategic factors.
- Evaluating external environmental (PEST) factors *first* helps to identify those variables that determine opportunities and threats. This allows managers to establish their internal position with regard to building appropriate capabilities and competencies to help an organisation respond competitively.
- Porter's five forces of industry analysis helps organisations to analyse the nature and intensity of competition in a particular industry by

examining the intensity of competition; the threat of new entrants; the bargaining power of suppliers and buyers and the threat of substitutes.

- The Boston Consulting Group (BCG) matrix allows a multidivisional organisation to manage its portfolio of businesses by examining the *relative market share* position and the *industry growth rate* of each division relative to all the other divisions in the organisation.

- Each of the four quadrants of the matrix describes business units or product divisions as question marks (product divisions or business units that compete in high-growth industries, but with low relative market share position); stars (those divisions/units that have a high relative market share in high-growth industries); cash cows (divisions/units that have high relative market share but compete in low-growth industries); and dogs (divisions or units that have low relative market share in slow or no-growth industries).

- The benefits of the BCG matrix are that it draws attention to the cash flow, investment characteristics and needs of an organisation's various divisions and it indicates how divisions of many firms evolve over time.

- Kaplan and Norton(1996) introduced the concept of the balanced scorecard to measure performance in organisations. Their theory is useful to managers as it adopts a balanced view of a company's performance rather than just looking at – or focusing on – a company using financial measures.

- The balanced scorecard adopts a broader view looking at performance from four perspectives, that is, the *financial* perspective; the *customer* perspective; the *internal business* perspective and the *learning and growth* perspective.

- Pareto analysis is a simple method for separating the major causes ('vital few') of a problem, from the minor ones ('trivial many') and it helps prioritise and focus resources (or attention). Pareto diagrams are a visually effective means of displaying the relative importance of causes, problems or other conditions.

- Whilst Pareto analysis proves useful in identifying where major problems lie, the Ishikawa fishbone diagram is useful when brainstorming problems to find the underlying causes. This diagram has a number of strengths as it places strong emphasis on the importance of people and their participation in the problem-solving process and uses statistical and people-orientated techniques. It also introduces the idea of quality-control circles. However, it is often seen as a too simplistic approach to problem solving.

- Decision tree analysis can be useful to managers when deciding between options because it encourages decision makers to think about alternative approaches and courses of action as well as the future implications of their decisions. Decision trees have branches to illustrate the various decision paths that can be taken.

- Cost-benefit analysis is a simple approach used to help decide whether to go ahead with an action (or investment) or not. If the benefits are greater than the costs, then the plan (or investment) will go ahead. If the costs exceed the perceived benefits, then the plan is rejected.

Suggested further reading

Greenberg and Baron (2003), chapter 10.

Hannagan (2005) – Chapter 13 is particularly useful.

You could also read the relevant sections of De Wit and Meyer (2004), Harrison (1999), Teale et al (2003), Jennings and Wattam (1994) and Slatter (1990).

Feedback on learning activities and self-assessment questions

Feedback on learning activity 9.1

The purchase of the technology is likely to be needed for the company to be innovative and competitive. It should be viewed as an investment. Whilst currently the company do not score highly with regard to the financial investment, they may reap the rewards at a later date. The company does score highly, however, using the learning and growth perspective as well as the internal business perspective. By looking at the bigger picture, the company has invested in technology, and without it they may have been left in a poor competitive position.

Feedback on self-assessment question 9.1

Whilst the matrix may prove a useful tool for managers, it does contain a number of flaws, which are mainly due to a lack of clarification. For example, the definition of market is ambiguous and can be open to subjective interpretation as it does not identify the model market. Boston Consulting Group could be referring to a niche market or to the whole market. The matrix is unclear with regard to determining what is a high/low-growth market and does not distinguish between which question marks should be invested in and which should be discarded. Therefore, managers may decide to withdraw support from a product, which in fact could have benefited from additional investment.

Using this tool to help manage a company's portfolio also relies heavily on comparisons with competitors, but focusing too intently on the competition could deflect the company from being open to new and innovative ideas. Jobber (2001) states: 'the matrix ignores interdependencies between products'. Despite the fact that dogs and question marks are not viewed in a positive light, retailers may prefer trading with a company that provides a full product portfolio.

The matrix is also based on cash flow rather than what the product is contributing in terms of profits and does not take into consideration risk.

Feedback on learning activity 9.2

- If you answered mainly a's, you adopt the directive style, which is characterised by people who use little information, often relying on traditional rules. These people make decisions quickly and are likely to use their position to achieve the desired outcome.
- If you answered mainly b's, you adopt the analytical style, which is characterised by people who are prepared to investigate solutions thoroughly using as much information as possible.

9

- If you answered mainly c's, you adopt the conceptual style, which is characterised by people who are particularly socially orientated (who prefer working in a team). These people tend to be humanistic and artistic and present creative solutions.
- If you answered mainly d's, you adopt the behavioural style, which is characterised by people who have a great concern for others and are very supportive of their co-workers. They are open to ideas and prefer meetings to make decisions.

(Source: Adapted from Greenberg and Baron (2003))

Feedback on self-assessment question 9.2

The tool utilises only economic measures. Whilst an option may appear to be the best, this is only likely to be in financial terms. In some instances a company may decide to manufacture a specific part themselves despite the fact that it can be outsourced at a cheaper rate. Other aspects need to be taken into consideration. Reputation has its cost too.

Cost-benefit analysis does not take into consideration health and safety. It is just a calculation. When making a decision, much more than figures need to be taken into account, and this requires human judgement. Is it an ethical decision? If it is not, the likelihood is that the company will ultimately pay the price anyway.

Cost-benefit analysis represents a 'value neutral' methodology, yet actual calculations yield efficiency and wealth maximisation results which do not reflect societal values.

9

Operations planning and purchasing

Introduction

By forming collaborative relationships between purchaser and supplier, it is possible for an organisation to achieve a reduction in supplier lead time and transaction costs, as well as a reduction in inventory levels and an improvement in quality of products or services. Van Weele (2005) points out that:

> 'since most companies today spend more than half of their sales turnover on purchased parts or services, efficient and constructive relationships with suppliers are key to the company's short-term financial position and long-term competitive power.'

This session reaffirms the roles and objectives of the purchasing function and explores how it is linked to – and complements – the organisation's operations and planning functions.

'As business is becoming more competitive, purchasing and supply chain management are becoming increasingly recognised as key business drivers by top managers.'
Van Weele (2005)

10

Session learning objectives

After completing this session you should be able to:

10.1 Describe the key objectives of the purchasing function and how this links to operations management and planning.
10.2 State the principal benefits gained from the effective management of the purchasing process.
10.3 Analyse the resource requirements for the implementation of operational plans for the purchasing function.

Unit content coverage

This study session covers the following topic from the official CIPS unit content document:

Learning outcome

Use a range of techniques to support and implement justifiable management decisions.

Learning objective

1.3 Contrast the key roles and functions of managers in the purchasing and supply function.
3.2 Formulate, implement and monitor operational plans for the purchasing and supply function to achieve organisational objectives.

3.3 Assess and deploy the resource requirements for the implementation of operational plans for the purchasing function.

Prior knowledge

Study sessions 2 and 9.

Timing

You should set aside about 6 hours to read and complete this session, including learning activities, self-assessment questions, the suggested further reading (if any) and the revision question.

10.1 The purchasing function: key objectives

Relatively few organisations are self-sufficient, most purchase materials or services from another organisation. According to Waller (2003):

> 'Purchasing is the buying of materials or services from an outside source and thus involves the transfer of goods from one distinct entity to another. The purchasing activity is the upstream part of the supply chain. A client's requirement is negotiated with marketing, this establishes the basis for operating plans and then production decides what needs to be purchased. In order to make an unbroken supply chain, purchasing, marketing and production must work in a team to ensure delivery dates are met.'

Learning activity 10.1

Draw up a list of five key objectives of the purchasing function in your organisation (or one with which you are familiar).

Feedback on page 135

Objectives of the purchasing function

It is the role of purchasing or procurement managers to purchase the correct materials and services of the right specification and quality, at the right time, in the right quantity, from the right source and at the right price. Thus, the key objectives of the purchasing function are to:

- supply the organisation with a steady flow of materials and services to meet its needs;
- ensure continuity of supply;
- obtain efficiently, the best value for every unit of expenditure;

10

- manage inventory so as to give the best service at lowest cost;
- maintain sound cooperative relationships with other departments;
- develop staff policies, procedures and organisation to ensure the achievement of the foregoing;
- link to the operations management and planning functions in order to obtain those items required by the operating system for the efficient and effective production of products or (where appropriate) provision of services.

The purchasing department is responsible for maintaining a supplier database with records of products offered, quality, current price and delivery times. In addition to this, Muhlemann et al (1992) believe that there are a number of other objectives of the purchasing function such as:

> 'providing information on any new products, processes, materials and services. Purchasing should also advise on probable prices, deliveries and performance of products under consideration by the research, design and development functions.'

The ever-changing business environment forces purchasing managers to research the supply market and plan ahead. Stock et al (2001) believe that:

> 'purchasing needs to provide information about supply conditions, such as availability, lead times and technology to different groups within the firm, including top management, engineering and design and manufacturing. This information is important when formulating long-term strategy and making short-term decisions … Strategic planning for purchasing involves materials screening, risk assessment, strategy development, and implementation. It is important to determine whether (1) materials bottlenecks will jeopardise current or future production, (2) new products should be introduced, (3) materials quality may be expected to change, (4) prices are likely to increase or decrease, and (5), forward buying is appropriate. [It is recommended that] management should develop specific plans to ensure that the material supply chain will operate uninterrupted.'

Supply chain management (SCM)

Supply chain management (SCM) is the entire process beginning with raw materials and ending with providing the customer with a finished product. According to Greasley (1999), SCM is concerned with:

> 'the efficient and effective flow of physical items, in the form of materials from suppliers, through the production chain, to the customer, in the form of a finished product. Synergetic relationships between the firm, customers and suppliers, who share information, cooperate in product development and aid in decision making, benefit all parties in the production of a product that enables the supply chain to conform to customer requirements.'

Materials management involves the inbound logistics side, which includes purchasing, inbound transportation (also referred to as traffic), materials handling and warehousing (storage). Alternatively, physical

10

distribution concerns outbound logistics processes which include outbound transportation and distribution to customer.

It was traditional practice for organisations to divide the responsibility for flow of resources between the departments within the firm, such as purchasing, production and distribution (a decentralised approach). Nowadays, however, as shown in figure 10.1, organisational structures have been simplified in order to be more efficient.

Figure 10.1: Evolution of supply chain organisation

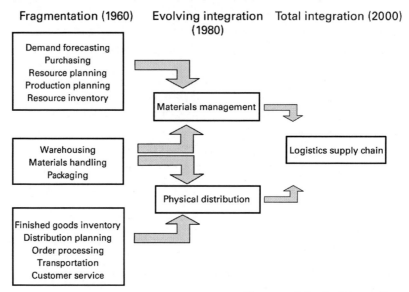

Source: Adapted from Greasley (1999)

The structure of organisations of the 1960s required a lot of communication and information sharing between departments, which often led to a duplication of effort in obtaining and collating the information. If there was a lack of communication or miscommunication, incorrect information would be used. Greasley (1999) states that this 'often leads (unfortunately) to incorrect levels of inventory, poor quality, late deliveries and slow product development'.

During the 1980s, SCM evolved as integration was found to improve company performance. As a result, many activities were integrated into inbound logistics (materials management) and outbound logistics (physical distribution). Today, companies are integrating further (total integration) going as far as involving suppliers in the process, forming a symbiotic relationship. Greasley (1999) found that:

> 'Many companies realise that if they involve their suppliers at an early stage in the business cycle, everyone benefits. Suppliers can help design the product, by advising on suitable materials and production. Suppliers can also help with the design of the logistics systems that will enable rapid delivery of the product in a state fit for use.'

Stock et al (2001) refers to this process of getting suppliers involved in the design process as 'early supplier involvement' (ESI). The end result will be that those suppliers will be favoured by the purchasers and are likely to benefit from a long-term business relationship. The organisation in turn will benefit from an improvement in quality of goods/services, responsiveness and competitiveness.

Self-assessment question 10.1

How is the purchasing function linked with operations management and planning?

Feedback on page 136

10.2 Benefits of effective purchasing

Learning activity 10.2

Large organisations with several sites can have either one main purchasing function or several. One of the major issues facing organisations is the degree to which purchasing should be centralised in order for the organisation to be the most effective. List four advantages of centralised purchasing.

Feedback on page 136

10

The organisation of purchasing

The issues relating to the degree of centralisation of the purchasing function have already been discussed in study session 6, but it is important to remind ourselves of the advantages and disadvantages of centralised purchasing since, in recent years, there has been an increasing trend towards the establishment of centralised purchasing functions. Examples of this can be found in health services and in local and central government supply, as well as in manufacturing.

The advantages of centralised purchasing include:

- the possibility of standardising specifications, establishing common needs namely quality, quantity and so on;
- improved economic purchase through larger batch quantities and so on;
- purchasing in large quantities often means that the supplier is more attentive;
- combining small orders reduces administration costs, the time taken to negotiate orders, billing time, customs procedures where appropriate, and therefore overall cost;
- the possibility of purchase staff specialisation and thus increased knowledge of sources and supplies;
- the use of more effective, detailed and accurate purchasing information and records;

- possibly more detailed and accurate budget and financial control procedures;
- the relationship with suppliers is simplified as there are fewer interlocutors;
- there is a reduction in transportation costs since orders are shipped in larger quantities.

The disadvantages include:

- difficulties with communication within the organisation, perhaps because of geographical separation;
- slower response to new or unusual supply needs from the organisation;
- possible increased dependence on a smaller number of suppliers resulting from increased volume and from standardisation;
- there is a much quicker response than using a centralised function (that is, less bureaucracy);
- the risk associated with currency exchange, quality and delivery is lower.

Whilst centralised purchasing has many merits, in particular the potential financial savings accrued through purchasing large volumes, it unfortunately cannot offer the response times and flexibility associated with decentralised purchasing. When deciding upon the degree to which purchasing should be centralised, therefore, organisations must decide on their priorities.

Overall, according to Wild (2002), the principal benefits of managing the purchasing process, however configured, relate to:

- the organisation procuring materials and items at lower prices;
- a faster inventory turnover;
- ensuring continuity of supply;
- reduced replenishment lead times;
- reduced transport costs;
- reduced materials obsolescence;
- improved relationships with vendors;
- better control of quality;
- more effective administration and hence minimisation of organisational effort;
- the maintenance of adequate records and provision of information for the operations managers.

Self-assessment question 10.2

The total cost of bought-in materials or services forms a large proportion of the final selling price. In some cases the cost of materials and services can account for 65% of an organisation's expenditure or outgoings. The purchasing function can therefore dramatically affect profits and so must be managed effectively.

1   If a company has an annual turnover of £1 million and makes a profit margin of 10%, calculate the potential increase in profit if the procurement manager achieved a 5% saving. Assume the value of purchases amounts to 65% of the annual turnover.

(continued on next page)

10

Self-assessment question 10.2 *(continued)*

2   If the firm wishes to realise the same profit margin as in 1 above, but without any savings being realised on purchases, what increase in turnover is required? What do your calculations tell you?

Feedback on page 137

10.3 Resourcing for purchasing

Learning activity 10.3

List five advantages of integrating the purchasing function into the overall operations planning process.

Feedback on page 137

Although not their sole responsibility, the purchasing or procurement function clearly concerns operations managers, who are responsible for providing goods or services at the right specification and quality, at the right time, in the right quantity and at the right price. In many manufacturing or service situations, the need for resources to be flexible will often dictate that the buyer is part of the production manager's staff, either directly responsible to the production manager or to the production controller, possibly as head of the material control section, where they will undertake duties which include purchasing and procurement of requisite materiel or parts or sub-assemblies for process or manufacture.

To a large extent the resource deployment for the implementation of operational plans for the purchasing department will depend on the nature, size and activities carried out by an organisation and the purchasing organisation structure that exists within the organisation. In turn, this will dictate the range of physical, financial and human resources necessary for the purchasing function to make a cost-effective contribution to the organisation.

Physical resources

Generally, from a purchasing perspective, physical resources are likely to include stores buildings, relevant equipment therein, stockyards (where appropriate) and vehicles (for example transport fleet if not outsourced, and materials moving and handling equipment such as forklifts and so on).

Financial resources

As with any organisation, the purchasing function will require an operating budget. However, it is most likely that this will be centrally controlled (in large organisations) by the finance or accounts department and perhaps also dependent on the overall cost of the production and operations process associated with the production of goods or provision of service.

The purchasing function, like other functions, has a responsibility to manage inventories and service levels appropriate to the needs of

10

the operations function(s). Their aim should therefore be to reduce stockholding to the minimum level compatible with operational requirements and cost effectiveness.

Purchasing organisation structure

Structure and its implications for purchasing and supply have already been discussed in study sessions 5 and 6. However, it is perhaps a good idea to remind ourselves here of the key points in order to put the resourcing issues in perspective. According to Van Weele (2005), 'purchasing structures appear to vary among companies' and, 'a more detailed analysis showed that since 1988, purchasing organisations moved towards hybrid structures (e.g. coordination or combination of centralisation/decentralisation)'.

Van Weele suggests that:

'one of the key factors relating to resource requirements and deployment is the location of purchasing within an organisation. This (organisational location of purchasing) is very much dependent on the view that management holds towards the purchasing function; a view usually related to:

- Purchasing's share in the end-product's cost price
- The financial position of the company
- The extent to which the company depends on the supply market.'

Other factors influencing resource requirements relate to the levels of task, responsibility and authority in the organisation (see study sessions 2 and 11) and the purchasing decisions taken at various levels in an organisation. For example:

- Strategic purchasing decisions, which have a long-term impact on the organisation, relate to the:
  - developing and issuing operational guidelines, procedures and task descriptions, which provide authority to the purchasing department;
  - developing and implementing auditing and review programmes;
  - outsourcing activities and/or functions;
  - establishing long-term contracts with preferred suppliers;
  - adopting a supplier strategy based on multi- versus single sourcing;
  - major investments;
  - deciding on financial participation in suppliers (backward integration);
  - formulating policies concerning transfer pricing and intercompany supplies;
  - formulating policies on reciprocal arrangements, counter-trade and so on.
- Tactical purchasing decisions, which have a medium-term impact, relate to:
  - agreement on corporate and/or annual supplier agreements;
  - preparing and developing value analysis programmes;
  - adopting and conducting quality certification programmes for suppliers;

- selection and contracting of suppliers in general;
- programmes aimed at supply-base reduction.
- Operational purchasing decisions, which have a short-term impact, relate to:
  - the ordering process;
  - expediting activities related to released orders;
  - invoice verification and payment;
  - troubleshooting;
  - monitoring and evaluation of supplier performance.

Organisational structures within purchasing

As discussed in study session 6, structures for purchasing tend to be either decentralised, centralised, a hybrid form of both centralised and decentralised, 'pooled', or based on cross-functional sourcing teams. However, in single-unit organisations the issue of centralised versus decentralised purchasing relates to the extent that purchases need to be made through the purchasing department and, according to Van Weele (2005), this depends on the following variables:

- management's view towards purchasing;
- information technology;
- personal relationships;
- total cost approach.

Based on these variables, purchasing's reporting relationships may take different forms as differentiated in either a fully integrated logistics structure where purchasing reports directly to the logistics manager at the same level as production planning and physical distribution; or a partly integrated logistics structure where purchasing, production planning and physical distribution report to the logistics manager in other ways.

From a human resource perspective, this has a number of consequences for purchasing professionals and the necessary skills and abilities required by the purchasing department. In most large companies, according to Van Weele (2005), the following positions can be found:

- corporate procurement officer (CPO);
- corporate buyer;
- purchasing engineer;
- project buyer;
- MRO buyer;
- materials planner.

Van Weele suggests that:

'compared with ten years ago, these purchasing professionals are:

- Higher educated (business degree, MBA)
- Responsible for more
- More likely to be a woman
- Negotiating more long-term agreements
- Involved in outsourcing decisions

10

- Looking out on a global market shape
- Reducing costs and the number of suppliers.'

Self-assessment question 10.3

Describe and explain what is meant by each of the following:

1 Decentralised purchasing structure.
2 Centralised purchasing structure.
3 Centralised/decentralised purchasing organisation.
4 Pooling structure.
5 Cross-functional sourcing teams.

Feedback on page 138

Revision question

Now try the revision question for this session on page 248.

Summary

- According to Waller (2003):
  'Purchasing is the buying of materials or services from an outside source and thus involves the transfer of goods from one distinct entity to another. The purchasing activity is the upstream part of the supply chain. A client's requirement is negotiated with marketing, this establishes the basis for operating plans and then production decides what needs to be purchased. In order to make an unbroken supply chain, purchasing, marketing and production must work in a team to ensure delivery dates are met.'
- The key objectives of the purchasing function are to:
  - supply the organisation with a steady flow of materials and services to meet its needs;
  - ensure continuity of supply;
  - obtain efficiently, the best value for every unit of expenditure;
  - manage inventory so as to give the best service at the lowest cost;
  - maintain sound cooperative relationships with other departments;
  - develop staff policies, procedures and organisation to ensure the achievement of the foregoing;
  - link to the operations management and planning functions in order to obtain those items required by the operating system for the efficient and effective production of products or (where appropriate) provision of services.
- According to Greasley (1999), SCM (is concerned with:
  'the efficient and effective flow of physical items, in the form of materials from suppliers, through the production chain, to the customer, in the form of a finished product. Synergetic relationships between the firm, customers and suppliers, who share information, cooperate in product development and aid in decision making, benefit

all parties in the production of a product that enables the supply chain to conform to customer requirements.'

- The advantages of centralised purchasing relate to:
  - the possibility of standardising specifications, establishing common needs namely quality, quantity and so on;
  - improved economic purchase through larger batch quantities and so on.
  - purchasing in large quantities often means that the supplier is more attentive;
  - combining small orders reduces administration costs, the time taken to negotiate orders, billing time, customs procedures where appropriate, and therefore overall cost;
  - the possibility of purchase staff specialisation and thus increased knowledge of sources and supplies;
  - the use of more effective, detailed and accurate purchasing information and records;
  - possibly more detailed and accurate budget and financial control procedures;
  - the relationship with suppliers is simplified as there are fewer interlocutors;
  - there is a reduction in transportation costs since orders are shipped in larger quantities.
- The disadvantages include:
  - difficulties with communication within the organisation, perhaps because of geographical separation;
  - slower response to new or unusual supply needs from the organisation;
  - possible increased dependence on a smaller number of suppliers resulting from increased volume and from standardisation;
  - there is a much quicker response than using a centralised function (that is, less bureaucracy);
  - the risk associated with currency exchange, quality and delivery is lower.

Suggested further reading

Waller (2003), chapter 16.

Van Weele (2005), chapter 1.

Feedback on learning activities and self-assessment questions

Feedback on learning activity 10.1

It is expected that your answer should include five of the following points:

- to supply the organisation with a steady flow of materials and services to meet its needs;
- to ensure continuity of supply;
- to obtain efficiently, the best value for every unit of expenditure;

- to manage inventory so as to give the best service at the lowest cost;
- to maintain sound cooperative relationships with other departments;
- to develop staff policies, procedures and organisation to ensure the achievement of the foregoing;
- to link to the operations management and planning functions in order to obtain those items required by the operating system for the efficient and effective production of products or (where appropriate) provision of services.

Feedback on self-assessment question 10.1

The purchasing activity is the early part of the material movement in the supply chain (the upstream part) and is directly tied to manufacturing operations.

According to Wild (2002), 'operations management is concerned with the design and the operation of systems for manufacture, transport, supply or service'. The purchasing manager must converse with the operations manager in order to obtain those items required by the operating system for efficient and effective production of products and provision of services.

According to Waller (2003):

> 'Purchasing is the buying of materials or services from an outside source and thus involves the transfer of goods from one distinct entity to another. The purchasing activity is the upstream part of the supply chain. A client's requirement is negotiated with marketing, this establishes the basis for operating plans and then production decides what needs to be purchased. In order to make an unbroken supply chain, purchasing, marketing and production must work in a team to ensure delivery dates are met.

Feedback on learning activity 10.2

The advantages of centralised purchasing include:

- the possibility of standardising specifications, establishing common needs namely quality, quantity and so on;
- improved economic purchase through larger batch quantities and so on;
- purchasing in large quantities often means that the supplier is more attentive;
- combining small orders reduces administration costs, the time taken to negotiate orders, billing time, customs procedures where appropriate, and therefore overall cost;
- the possibility of purchase staff specialisation and thus increased knowledge of sources and supplies;
- the use of more effective, detailed and accurate purchasing information and records;
- possibly more detailed and accurate budget and financial control procedures;
- the relationship with suppliers is simplified as there are fewer interlocutors;

- there is a reduction in transportation costs since orders are shipped in larger quantities.

The disadvantages include:

- difficulties with communication within the organisation, perhaps because of geographical separation;
- slower response to new or unusual supply needs from the organisation;
- possible increased dependence on a smaller number of suppliers resulting from increased volume and from standardisation;
- there is a much quicker response than using a centralised function (that is, less bureaucracy);
- the risk associated with currency exchange, quality and delivery is lower.

Feedback on self-assessment question 10.2

1   With an annual turnover of £1 million, a profit of 10% (£100,000), and the value of purchases at 65% of turnover (£650,000), if a saving of 5% on the purchases can be achieved this will equate to:
$(5/100 \times 650,000) = £32,500$ increase in profits due to savings on purchases.
This implies that the company will increase its profit margin to 13.25%, calculated thus:
$(132,500/1,000,000 \times 100) = 13.25\%$

2   However, if the profit margin remains at 10%, then in order to achieve the same amount of profit (£132,500) with *no savings* on costs, then turnover must rise to £1,325,500 (£132,500 × 10), a substantial increase of 32.5%, given by:
$(1,325,000 - 1,000,000 = £325,000)/1,000,000 \times 100 = 32.5\%$
However, to achieve a rise in sales, it is likely that the marketing budget will need to increase. Other methods of either generating savings or profits – for example increases in productivity – are slow to be realised. Savings in purchasing costs are immediately visible in the profit margin. Effective purchasing is therefore a crucial activity.

Feedback on learning activity 10.3

Your answer should include any five of the following. It can, however, be supplemented by any specific advantages that relate to your own organisation:

- it avoids problems of divided responsibility;
- it avoids conflicting objectives and priorities;
- it avoids duplication of effort and helps integrate and replicate systems/processes to help achieve synergy;
- it helps improve communication throughout the organisation;
- it provides for better representation of the materials management function at board level;
- there is the possibility of cross-functional career development opportunities;
- in large organisations, where standardised products are mass produced, it helps lead to better economies of scale.

10

137

Feedback on self-assessment question 10.3

Your answer should include the following key points:

1   Decentralised purchasing structure: this structure can be found in companies with a business-unit structure where every business-unit manager is responsible for his own financial results. The management of the business unit is fully responsible for all of its purchasing activities.

2   Centralised purchasing structure: there is a central purchasing department at corporate level where corporate contract specialists operate at the strategic and tactical level. The operating companies conduct the operational purchase activities.

3   Centralised/decentralised purchasing organisation: there is a corporate purchasing department at corporate level but individual business units also conduct strategic and tactical purchasing activities. Often the central department conducts detailed supply-market studies in strategic commodities and it also takes care of coordination issues between divisions or business units.

4   Pooling structure: a combination of 1, 2 and 3 in order to combine common material requirements among two or more operating units with the objective to reduce overall materials costs or improve the service obtained from outside suppliers. Some examples include:
    (a)   voluntary coordination;
    (b)   lead buyership;
    (c)   lead design concept.

5   Cross-functional sourcing teams: cross-functional commodity teams make corporate commodity plans. These teams consist of professionals in product development, R&D, marketing, production, distribution and finance together with purchasing professionals. The leader is a commodity manager and reports to the director or senior manager in charge of purchase and supply. The structure of the teams is thus often virtual.

Authority, delegation and accountability

Introduction

Delegating responsibilities to others increases a managers' available time to carry out important work. Delegation also helps to develop teams which, in turn, increases the effectiveness of operations and improves the chances of achieving departmental or functional goals. Willingness to delegate is one of the marks of leadership, but delegation is difficult to exercise effectively. This is chiefly because it entails getting work done in a way that appropriately balances the quality of the solution with the needs of individuals.

To delegate successfully, managers need to know exactly what task has to be done and what motivates and satisfies their individual members of staff. Effective delegation involves a continued and growing relationship between the manager and those to whom they assign tasks. Managers should delegate *authority* but not responsibility. This means that managers should be prepared to accept responsibility for the actions of their staff. Furthermore, managers should also be prepared to let their staff have the glory when their actions are successful.

This session explores the concepts of authority, delegation and responsibility in more detail.

> It is wrong to say to your subordinates, 'Here is a task, now get on with it', while you sit back and wait for results. Delegate, don't abdicate!
>
> *The Managers Handbook* (1986)

11

Session learning objectives

After completing this session you should be able to:

11.1 Define and evaluate the concepts of authority and power when managing the purchasing function.
11.2 Describe the nature and types of delegation and responsibility.

Unit content coverage

This study session covers the following topic from the official CIPS unit content document:

Learning outcome

Formulate plans to effectively manage work groups and teams.

Learning objective

4.1 Evaluate the concept of authority, delegation and accountability when managing the purchasing function.

Prior knowledge

Study sessions 2, 7, 9 and 10.

Timing

You should set aside about 5 hours to read and complete this session, including learning activities, self-assessment questions, the suggested further reading (if any) and the revision question.

11.1 Authority and power

Learning activity 11.1

Differentiate between the terms 'power' and 'authority'.

Feedback on page 147

The classical theory of authority is based on the hierarchical principle that authority flows down from the top of an organisation and is also dependent on the position held. When removed from this position the individual no longer has the authority associated with it. Opposite to this is the 'acceptance' theory proposed by Follett (1941) and Barnard (1938). Here, a manager's authority depends on their subordinates and whether these do or do not choose to accept the manager's orders. Subordinates have the power to deny authority or to accept it.

Hannigan (2005) makes the point that:

> 'in practice, authority is often a mixture of these theories in that, while managers' positions in an organisation will greatly affect their range and depth of authority, these can only be exerted where they will be accepted. This acceptance may arise out of line management control, because subordinates will depend on their senior line managers for reports and promotion, or out of respect for the judgement and experience of a more senior manager or as a result of consensus. It is important to be aware how authority is exerted so that instructions are not confused, and so that as organisations become more democratic decisions increasingly arise from a consensus of what needs to be done.'

Authority is the power related to each position within the organisation. It involves the right to give orders, make decisions and spend resources. In an organisation, authority provides the right to do these things supported by the structure of the organisation and understood by every employee when they join. The contract or job description will usually describe to whom the employees are responsible and for whom they are responsible. This means that employees accept orders and decisions and expect these to be carried out if they are agreed through an established structure.

11

Power is the ability to carry out an action, whereas authority can be seen as the right to do this. According to Hannigan (2005), 'the power of managers over employees can be described as "social power" because it is derived from the social interaction of leaders and their followers'.

This can be understood better by analysing this 'social power' in more detail. Koontz and Weihrich (1990) assert that:

> 'Power, a much broader concept than authority, is the ability of individuals or groups to induce or influence the beliefs or actions of other persons or groups. Authority in organisations is the right in a position (and, through it, the right of the person occupying the position) to exercise discretion in making decisions affecting others. It is, of course, one type of power, but power in an organisation setting.'

They suggest that there are many different bases of power. However, the power of primary concern here is *legitimate* power, which normally arises from our cultural system of rights, obligations and duties, whereby a 'position' is accepted by people as being 'legitimate'. In privately owned businesses, positions of authority arise primarily from the social institution (a 'bundle of rights') of private property. In government, this authority arises basically from the institution of representative government. A traffic officer who gives you a traffic ticket has the power to do so because we have a system of representative government in which we have elected legislators to make laws and provide for their enforcement.

Also, according to Koontz and Weihrich (1990):

> '[power] may come from the expertness of a person or a group. This is the power of knowledge. Physicians, lawyers, and university lecturers may have considerable influence on others because they are respected for their special knowledge. Power may further exist as *referent* power, that is, influence which people or groups may exercise because people believe in them and their ideas'.

Power also arises from the ability of some people to grant rewards. For example, purchasing agents, with little position power, might be able to exercise considerable influence by their ability to expedite or delay a much-needed component. Likewise, university lecturers have considerable *reward* power because they can grant or withhold high grades.

Another type is **coercive power** – a form of power that is often the main consideration in a general discussion on the subject. It is based on subordinates' fear of the leader and on punishments and threats, and is linked to the most extreme form of autocratic leadership.

While organisation authority is the power to exercise discretion in decision making, it almost invariably arises from the power of position, or **legitimate power**. When people speak of authority in managerial settings, they are usually referring to the power of positions. At the same time, other factors, such as personality and style of dealing with people, are involved in leadership.

11

Splintered authority

Splintered authority exists wherever a problem cannot be solved or a decision made without pooling the authority delegations of two or more managers. For example, a supervisor of Section A may see an opportunity to reduce costs through a minor modification in both their procedures and those in Section B, but their authority cannot encompass the change. However, if the supervisors of both sections can agree upon the change – and it affects no other managers – all they need to do is pool their authority and make the decision. Here, individually, their authority is said to be splintered.

In day-to-day operations of any organisation, there are many cases of splintered authority. For example, many managerial conferences or meetings are held because of the necessity to pool authority to make decisions. Thus, splintered authority cannot be wholly avoided in making decisions. However, recurring decisions on the same matters may be evidence that authority delegations have not been properly made and that some reorganisation is required.

Leadership styles based on use of authority

The various leadership styles and approaches have been discussed in study sessions 1 and 2, but at this point it is perhaps important to remind ourselves of how leadership 'styles' are classified on the basis of how leaders use their authority. Primarily, leaders were seen as applying three basic styles:

- The **autocratic** leader commands and expects compliance, is dogmatic and positive, and leads by the ability to withhold or give rewards and punishment.
- The **democratic**, or **participative**, leader consults with subordinates on proposed actions and decisions and encourages participation from them. (This type of leader ranges from the person who does not take action without subordinates' concurrence, to the one who makes decisions but consults with subordinates before doing so.) Hannigan (2005) believes this style 'works well to generate fresh ideas and where there are confident and competent employees'.
- The **free-rein** leader uses their power very little, if at all, giving subordinates a high degree of independence in their operations. Such leaders depend largely on subordinates to set their own goals and the means of achieving them, and they see their role as one of aiding the operations of followers by furnishing them with information and acting primarily in contact with the group's external environment.

Goleman (cited in Buchanan and Huczynski, 2004) identified six leadership styles which should be used interchangeably depending upon the situation. They relate the styles to an array of golf clubs where a certain club is required in a certain situation. The styles include:

- the **coercive leader** – who demands immediate compliance in order to achieve a goal. Decisions are made at the top (they lie with those in authority). This type of leadership is often used in a crisis situation;

11

- the **authoritative leader** – who has a clear vision and makes it very clear how employees of the organisation will achieve this vision. Performance standards are clear as are the basis for rewards;
- the **affiliative leader** – who attempts to create harmony amongst the workforce. Their intention is to foster loyalty, improve communication and encourage idea generation. This type of leader gives employees the autonomy to carry out their jobs as they see fit. They use a lot of praise and can be useful to bring members of a team together. Hannigan (2005) states:
  'the focus on praise and support may mean that poor performance is tolerated and people may feel that they do not have a guiding sense of direction … On its own it can be seen as a relatively weak form of leadership';
- the **democratic leader** – this leader is considered an equal and decisions are made by consensus. The leader builds trust and encourages others to contribute their ideas to the group. Unfortunately, with this style decisions can take a long time to be reached and in some cases people actually feel that there is a distinct lack of authority and leadership;
- the **pace-setting leader** – who sets high performance standards for all concerned, even themselves (the leader). This type of leader is neurotic with regard to making improvements. Whilst this style works well with those who do not need direction and organisation, it can overwhelm some who do not feel as confident in themselves;
- the **coaching leader** – this is someone who places emphasis on learning and personal development over the actual work tasks themselves. This helps create a strong sense of commitment amongst the workforce.

11

Self-assessment question 11.1

Why are some departments in an organisation considered more powerful (that is, they have the ability to do something) than others?

Feedback on page 147

11.2 Delegation and responsibility

Learning activity 11.2

According to Hannigan (2005) delegation 'refers to the act by which a person or group of persons possessing authority transfers part of that authority to a subordinate person or group'. List four advantages of delegating.

Feedback on page 148

Delegation is the distribution of authority from a manager to a subordinate, and arises because one manager cannot do all the work of the organisation.

By delegating, the managers are able to extend their capability and capacity. They can take on new tasks while monitoring other tasks that are delegated to subordinates. On the other hand, **responsibility** is an obligation to be liable for a task, decision or action.

While authority can be delegated, responsibility cannot, so that a manager can provide a subordinate with the power to make a decision but still retains responsibility for it in the sense of being liable for the result. If the subordinate makes a decision that leads to a success, the manager can accept some of the praise; but if the decision leads to a problem, the manager is obliged to accept the blame. The managers are unable to simply pass all blame on to the subordinates because they have been responsible for the delegation of authority and if this has led to a problem this can be traced back to their decision to delegate.

Delegation can only be successful when the subordinate has the ability, information and willingness to perform a task or make a decision. This can be supported by the organisational structure where clear lines of management and communication can enable the process to operate without difficulty. The position of an individual in the organisation endows that person with a particular type of power, sometimes referred to as legitimate power.

Both power and authority can differ in that authority may arise, for example, out of respect for a person's expertise rather than their position, while power can arise from control over resources. For example, an accountant may have the power to accumulate large amounts of clients' money without having the authority to do so. Managers may have the authority to make decisions in an organisation, but may not have the power to carry them out because their subordinates do not respect their decisions and find ways of ignoring them.

Delegation of authority

Studies have shown that many managers fail because of poor delegation. Delegation is necessary in order for an organisation to exist, since it is impossible, as an organisation grows, for one person to exercise all of the authority for making decisions. There is a limit to the number of people that managers can effectively supervise and make decisions for (see section 7.1) and, once this limit has been passed, authority must be delegated to subordinates, who will then make decisions within the area of their assigned duties.

Authority is delegated when a superior gives a subordinate discretion to make decisions. Clearly, superiors cannot delegate authority they do not have, whether they are board members, chief executives, managers or supervisors. The process of delegation involves:

- determining the results expected from a position;
- assigning tasks to a position;
- delegating authority for accomplishing these tasks; and
- holding the person in that position responsible for the accomplishment of the tasks.

In practice, it is impossible to split this process, since expecting a person to accomplish goals without giving them authority to achieve them is unfair, as is delegating authority without knowing the end purpose for which it will be used. Moreover, since the superior's responsibility cannot be delegated, a boss has no practical alternative but to hold subordinates responsible for completing their assignments.

Barriers or obstacles to delegation

Obstacles to delegation arise from managers' attitudes towards it, or subordinates' reluctance to accept it, or because of factors related to the organisation and its culture. Managers may not want to relinquish authority to a subordinate, or they may feel that 'if you want a job done properly, do it yourself'. They may have a concern either that to delegate may indicate they cannot carry out the job themselves, or that if it is carried out very well by the subordinates they will themselves appear to be less competent.

Most failures in delegation occur not because managers do not understand the nature and principles of delegation, but because they are unable or unwilling to apply them. Delegation is, in a way, an elementary act of managing. However, studies of managerial failures have shown that poor or inept delegation is at the top of the list of causes, and much of the reason lies in personal attitudes towards delegation, for example:

- Receptiveness: an underlying attribute of managers who will delegate authority is a willingness to give other people's ideas a chance.
- Willingness to let go: a manager who will effectively delegate authority must be willing to release to subordinates the right to make decisions.
- Willingness to let others make mistakes: although no responsible manager would sit idly by and let a subordinate make a mistake that might endanger the organisation or the subordinate's position in the organisation, continual checking to ensure that no mistakes are ever made will make true delegation impossible.
- Willingness to trust subordinates: managers have no alternative to trusting their subordinates, for delegation implies a trustful attitude between them.
- Willingness to establish and use broad controls: since managers cannot delegate responsibility for performance, they should not delegate authority unless they are willing to find a means of getting feedback, that is, of assuring themselves that the authority is being used to support enterprise or department goals or plans.

Steps to effective delegation

Successful delegation can be facilitated by managers by following these simple (and practical) steps:

- review and specify tasks and objectives;
- select appropriate person(s) bearing in mind previous experience, ability and availability;
- set parameters, deadlines, resources, considerations about quality, limits of authority and so on;
- check understanding, provide resources and support, ensure commitment;

11

- monitor progress, encourage feedback on regular basis, fix official reporting schedule if appropriate;
- evaluate performance and reward effective delegation and successful assumption of authority (where appropriate);
- apply lessons learned to future tasks.

Self-assessment question 11.2

Describe the main difficulties associated with delegation and suggest possible solutions to overcome them.

Feedback on page 148

Revision question

Now try the revision question for this session on page 248.

Summary

- Delegating responsibilities to others increases a manager's available time to carry out important work and helps increase the effectiveness of operations and achievement of departmental or functional goals.
- Managers should delegate *authority* but not responsibility.
- According to Hannigan (2005), 'in practice, authority is often a mixture of theories in that, while managers' positions in an organisation will greatly affect their range and depth of authority, these can only be exerted where they will be accepted'.
- Authority is the power related to each position within the organisation and involves the right to give orders, make decisions and spend resources.
- The three basic styles of leader are: the autocratic leader; the democratic (or participative) leader; the free-rein leader.
- Goleman (cited in Buchanan and Huczynski, 2004) identified six types of leadership which relate to authority which include: the coercive leader, the authoritative leader, the affiliative leader, the democratic leader, the pace-setting leader and the coaching leader.
- Power is the ability to carry out an action and has various forms, for example coercive power, expert power, referent power, legitimate power and reward power.
- Delegation is the distribution of authority from a manager to a subordinate, and arises because one manager cannot do all the work of the organisation. Delegation can only be successful when the subordinate has the ability, information and willingness to perform a task or make a decision.
- Responsibility is an obligation to be liable for a task, decision or action. While authority can be delegated, responsibility cannot, so that a manager can provide a subordinate with the power to make a decision but still the manager retains responsibility for it in the sense of being liable for the result.

11

- The process of delegation involves: determining the results expected from a position; assigning tasks to a position; delegating authority for accomplishing these tasks; and holding the person in that position responsible for the accomplishment of the tasks.
- Reasons for poor or inept delegation tend to lie in personal attitudes towards delegation, and include a manager's receptiveness; willingness to let go; willingness to let others make mistakes; willingness to trust subordinates; and willingness to establish and use broad controls.
- Effective delegation is based on proper briefing, planning and review.

Suggested further reading

Buchanan and Huczynski (2004), chapter 14.

Koontz and Weihrich (1990), chapters 9 and 16.

You could also read the relevant sections of Hannagan (2005).

Feedback on learning activities and self-assessment questions

Feedback on learning activity 11.1

These terms are similar but are by no means the same. Power refers to the ability to do something. Authority, however, concerns the right/prerogative to do something. For example, Joe has the power to discipline his co-workers, however he does not have the authority to do so. This means that he has the ability but is not permitted to carry out an action – in this case discipline staff. Betts (2000) distinguishes between power and authority:

> 'It [power] is usually defined as the ability to get things done; it implies capability … [whereas authority] is conferred by management. It gives the person the right to require action from others or to take appropriate action within the boundaries of responsibility for undertaking various tasks outlined in a particular job.'

Feedback on self-assessment question 11.1

Some important points to consider include:

- contacts/networks of friends/colleagues – 'it's who you know, not what you know';
- specialist knowledge – the notion that 'knowledge is power';
- employees may have belonged to the organisation for many years, they might have risen up the ranks and are therefore respected;
- the departments' resources may be used more effectively;
- its managers are coercive and use threats;
- its managers are seen as assertive and they communicate effectively;
- the degree of unity within the section (they pull together as a team).

11

Feedback on learning activity 11.2

Your answer should include any four points from the following list:

- it frees up the manager's time;
- the manager cannot effectively conduct all tasks!
- it gives employees an opportunity to demonstrate and improve their skills;
- employees may experience increased job satisfaction, or may feel motivated/empowered;
- it can help build a relationship of 'trust';
- it can help develop a team.

Feedback on self-assessment question 11.2

The main difficulties/solutions include:

- Poor communication between manager and subordinate – the manager must ensure he communicates the duties and what is expected of the subordinate clearly in order to avoid confusion and errors.
- Employee is unskilled and requires training to carry out the task – the manager should be aware of their staff's capabilities and should provide the necessary training.
- The supervisor/manager is reluctant/incapable of delegating responsibility due to low opinion of subordinates, fear of mistakes being made, fear of not having as much to do, not being the sole provider of ideas and/or to avoid more arduous tasks – managers must give subordinates the opportunity to demonstrate and improve on their skills. Managers should acknowledge that mistakes will inevitably be made, but this will help employees to learn. Managers should encourage subordinates to update their superiors on their progress and of any problems in order to avoid any major difficulties. Whilst the task may not be performed of the highest standards, Betts (2000) points out that for effective delegating, managers must 'accept that performance levels may not be ideal'. Managers must accept that they cannot be the sole provider of ideas – more creative solutions may be sought by others. The workforce is a reflection of the manager and his relationship with his subordinates.

11

Sources of conflict in the purchasing and supply function

Introduction

Conflict in the organisation is defined as an incompatibility and a clash/difference of opinions and beliefs. Leat (2003) views conflict in a rather dim light and attributes absenteeism, high stress and anxiety levels and labour turnover to all be symptoms of conflict. However, some conflict can be conducive, helping firms to make improvements. It can also be a sign that employees are passionate about their work. Betts (2000) states: 'Constructively used, conflict may create a more dynamic group which is creative, solves problems more easily, makes better decisions and is generally more productive'. This session explores the nature of conflict, how it is perceived and how it arises.

'While there is much conflict in organisations, all have experienced situations where the absence of conflict is even more worthy of attention.'
Carnall (2003)

Session learning objectives

After completing this session you should be able to:

12.1 Demonstrate an understanding of the main sources of organisational conflict.
12.2 Analyse the sources of conflict which may arise within the purchasing function.

Unit content coverage

This study session covers the following topic from the official CIPS unit content document:

Learning outcome

Formulate plans to effectively manage work groups and teams.

Learning objective

4.3 Manage the sources of conflict which may arise within the purchasing function.

Prior knowledge

Study sessions 1, 2, 6 and 8.

Timing

You should set aside about 5 hours to read and complete this session, including learning activities, self-assessment questions, the suggested further reading (if any) and the revision question.

12

12.1 Organisational conflict

Conflict explained

There are a number of definitions of conflict, and many of them have similar themes. However conflict is defined or manifest, Robbins (2003) argues that 'conflict must be perceived by the parties to it; whether or not conflict exists is a perception issue. If no one is aware of a conflict, then it is generally agreed that no conflict exists'. He defines conflict as:

> 'a process that begins when one party perceives that another party has negatively affected, or is about to negatively affect, something that the first party cares about'.

According to Robbins, this is a broad definition that describes the point in any activity when an interaction crosses over to become an inter-party conflict, and it encompasses the wide range of conflicts that people experience in organisations, that is:

- incompatibility of goals;
- differences over interpretation of facts;
- disagreements based on behavioural expectations.

Also, Robbins suggests, 'this definition is flexible enough to cover the full range of conflict levels – from overt and violent acts to subtle forms of disagreement'. There are a number of different perspectives on conflict, such as:

- The **unitarist** perspective. Unitarism assumes that all employees have common goals. This perspective views conflict as a complication, as unnecessary and unproductive. When it (conflict) does occur, it is thus attributed to poor communication and misunderstandings. Unitarism relates to an autocratic approach (top-down) as management are seen to be the sole source of authority and are responsible for resolving any issues. Here, for example, management do not encourage trade union membership. Instead, they promote an image where 'management will tend to every employee's needs'.
- The **pluralist** perspective. Conversely, pleuralism acknowledges the fact that employees have different interests and that conflict is inevitable. Leat (2003) believes it is common for conflict to exist between different groups and suggests that 'it is not unusual for the finance function within organisations to come into conflict with other functions or departments over issues such as the determination of budgets and expenditure plans'. With this perspective, decisions relating to conflict resolution do not rest entirely in the hands of management, and can involve trade unions or other employees' representative bodies (for example works councils and so on).
- The **radical** perspective. This perspective views the workplace as a war zone, where the controllers of the means of production (managers) exploit the workers (employees) in order to maximise profits by relentlessly driving down the costs of production and controlling the manufacturing (or output) process. This perspective has been likened to extreme Marxism and/or capitalism.

12

Early views and approaches to conflict assumed that all conflict was bad; that it was negative and would adversely affect organisations. The term was generally used associated with terms such as violence, dysfunctionality and irrationality in order to reinforce its negative connotation. Thus it was deemed to be harmful and something to be avoided. However, the human-relations view of conflict believes that it is a 'natural and inevitable outcome in any group'. The interactionist view goes one step further and rather surprisingly, it actively encourages conflict to instigate change. Brooks (2003) stresses:

> 'a group that is harmonious can become static and accepting, blinkered to environmental dynamism and changing priorities and unresponsive to the need for change ... Conflict can, it is argued, enable groups and individuals to maintain a self-critical and creative edge ... Hence, management might use conflict to seek radical change, to alter existing power structures and entrenched attitude.'

Sources of conflict

Conflict arises in organisations for many different reasons. The list of potential sources of conflict could therefore be very long indeed, depending on the nature of the organisation in terms of structure and culture, and the activities it performs. However, some of the more generic sources of conflict include:

- Differences in status or level of authority and responsibility.
- Differences in pay structures for similar job roles.
- Changes in working practices.
- Where something is perceived as unfair.
- Scarcity of resources.
- Unfair or unrealistic allocation of budgets.
- Task interdependence – where the work of one person is dependent on another person having completed their part first. Time delays or bottlenecks may cause conflict.
- Role ambiguity.
- Unfair treatment.
- Differences in opinion/perception.
- Personality clashes.
- Unhealthy rivalry between co-workers. For example, two sales representatives may be so competitive that they pursue personal – rather than organisational – targets.

12

Learning activity 12.1

Having read about the perspectives on conflict, answer the following questions. Provide brief, but suitable, justification/reasons to support each of your answers.

- Which perspective believes conflict is to be expected?
- Which perspective relates to the paternalistic approach to management?
- Which perspective is likely to use collective bargaining?

(continued on next page)

Learning activity 12.1 *(continued)*

- Which perspective is likely to take advantage of its employees?
- Which perspective places profit as the main priority?

Feedback on page 154

Having completed this learning activity, now answer the self-assessment question.

Self-assessment question 12.1

Using your own organisation as the basis for your answer, explain why conflict might be regarded as an inevitable feature of management and organisational behaviour.

Feedback on page 154

12.2 Conflict and the purchasing function

Learning activity 12.2

Make a list of all the potential sources of conflict that exist within your organisation in general.

Feedback on page 155

Potential 'external' conflict

It is important to remember that the purchasing function has a very important role to play in most public and private sector organisations (see study session 2). As such, any internal conflict (functional or cross-organisation) may have a serious impact on both the overall operation of the organisation and its relationships with its supply chain, its distribution channels and ultimately its customers.

Within the purchasing function itself, conflict might arise between senior purchasing managers and purchasing officers (buyers) or between individual buyers in the function. Further, conflict might arise between the purchasing function itself and its suppliers, or with other functional areas within the organisation, for example sales and marketing and/or production. A simple scenario illustrates this:

- The organisation's sales department makes a tight delivery promise to an important customer.
- The production department needs to meet this delivery but does not have the requisite materials to produce the required amount for the customer. This puts pressure on the purchasing staff to procure the necessary materials and/or components or sub-assemblies for the order.
- The suppliers cannot meet the tight delivery deadline at such short notice and cannot prioritise the order at this particular time.

12

- Delays mean that purchasing cannot secure the goods for production, who in turn cannot meet the production and delivery times imposed upon them by the sales department.

As simplistic as this might seem, there will be inevitable conflict between sales, production and purchasing. The sales department, in promising delivery at such short notice creates tension *not only* within and across its own organisation but also between the organisation and its suppliers and customers. The overall effect on the organisation might be that it loses credibility with its customers and they may therefore go elsewhere, or that they sour their relationship with key suppliers on whom they depend.

Potential 'internal' conflict

Within the purchasing function itself conflict may arise because:

- Individual buyers disagree over the best suppliers to use for a particular component or sub-assembly.
- Buyers cannot meet the targets imposed by other functions in terms of procuring required materials on time.
- Buyers cannot meet targets imposed by purchasing managers/directors.
- People differ in terms of experiences, knowledge and skills.
- Individual goals are not always congruent with organisational goals.
- There are differences in goal orientation and evaluation.
- There is an issue of 'self image' and role 'stereotyping'.
- Time perspectives may vary.
- There may be overlapping authority within the function.
- Resources are scarce.

12

Self-assessment question 12.2

Write a short report – around 300–400 words – that identifies sources of potential conflict in your department or function, and explain which of these potential conflict situations may be either positive (functional) or negative (dysfunctional).

Feedback on page 155

Revision question

Now try the revision question for this session on page 249.

Summary

- Betts (2000) suggests that 'constructively used, conflict may create a more dynamic group which is creative, solves problems more easily, makes better decisions and is generally more productive'.
- Robbins (2003) defines conflict as 'a process that begins when one party perceives that another party has negatively affected, or is about to negatively affect, something that the first party cares about'. According

to Robbins, this definition encompasses the wide range of conflicts that people experience in organisations, that is, incompatibility of goals, differences over interpretation of facts and disagreements based on behavioural expectations.

- Three of the key perspectives on conflict are: (a) the unitarist perspective, which assumes that all employees have common goals; (b) the pluralist perspective, which acknowledges the fact that employees have different interests and that conflict is inevitable; and (c) the radical perspective, which views the workplace as a war zone, where the controllers of the means of production (managers) exploit the workers (employees).
- Early views and approaches to conflict assumed that all conflict was bad; that it was negative, and would adversely affect organizations. However, the human relations view of conflict believes that it is a 'natural and inevitable outcome in any group', and the interactionist view goes one step further, actively encouraging conflict to instigate change.
- Some generic sources of conflict include differences in status or level of authority and responsibility; differences in pay structures for similar job roles; changes in working practices; scarcity of resources; role ambiguity; unfair treatment; differences in opinion/perception and so on.
- Within an organisation, conflict can arise externally (between the organisation itself and its customers and suppliers) or internally (between functions or individuals within functions).
- Within the purchasing function itself conflict may arise because individual buyers disagree over the best suppliers to use for a particular component or sub-assembly, buyers cannot meet the targets imposed by other functions in terms of procuring required materials on time, buyers cannot meet targets imposed by purchasing managers/directors.

Suggested further reading

You could read the relevant sections of Brooks (2003) and Buchanan and Huczynski (2004).

Feedback on learning activities and self-assessment questions

Feedback on learning activity 12.1

- Pluralism believes conflict to be expected.
- Unitarism relates to the paternalistic approach.
- Pluralism uses trade unions and therefore they are likely to use collective bargaining.
- Radicalism is where employees are taken advantage of.
- Radicalism places profit as the main priority.

Feedback on self-assessment question 12.1

Here, you should reflect on the behavioural aspects of organisations as discussed in study sessions 1 and 2 and use this as the basis for your answer. There are a number of points you could make, from those relating specifically to management and leadership style and how employees are led, controlled, motivated and so on, to those relating specifically to differences in roles; different levels of experience, skills, knowledge and expertise. Further, since people are all different, they may have different views in terms of how goals/targets might be achieved, if they are achievable. You should also consider how organisational politics creates conflict.

Feedback on learning activity 12.2

Potential sources of conflict might include:

- Differences in status.
- Pay differentials – for example, with the advent of the minimum wage, the lower-paid employees benefited but the other employees did not.
- Changes in working practices.
- Where something is perceived as unfair.
- Availability of resources, for example allocation of budget.
- Where the work of one person is dependent on another person having completed their part first.
- Role ambiguity.
- Unfair treatment.
- Differences in opinion/perception.
- Personality clashes.
- Unhealthy rivalry between co-workers.
- Scarcity of resources.

Feedback on self-assessment question 12.2

You should identify areas of conflict specific to your own organisation and purchasing function. This will provoke a range of disparate points/situations from different students and this is to be expected given your differing cultures, levels of experience, organisations and so on. It is important that you think carefully about where conflict might be beneficial – in that it leads to organisational or departmental progress – and where it might prove to be damaging or detrimental to the well-being of your organisation. Wherever possible, you should provide reasons for your answers.

12

12

Managing conflict

Introduction

Carnall (2003) believes that:

> 'in a world in which resources are finite, there will always be conflicting demands for resources, attention or priority. Moreover, it seems likely that managers and others will conflict over the goals to be pursued and the means of use. Finally, disagreement will have both cognitive and emotional dimensions. While conflict can be a positive force to change, the first point to note about it is that it cannot – and should not – be eliminated.'

Given that this is the case, if conflict cannot (and must not) be eliminated, then it must be managed appropriately to allow organisations to develop and maintain competitiveness. This session examines some of the academic theory that underpins conflict management and the techniques and approaches that can be adopted to manage it effectively.

'A good manager doesn't try to eliminate conflict; he tries to keep it from wasting the energies of his people.'
Townsend (1970)

Session learning objectives

After completing this session you should be able to:

13.1 Apply techniques to deal with conflict within teams and between individuals in the purchasing and supply function.
13.2 Explain some of the strategies and approaches management can adopt to deal with conflict.

Unit content coverage

This study session covers the following topic from the official CIPS unit content document:

Learning outcome

Formulate plans to effectively manage work groups and teams.

Learning objectives

4.3 Manage the sources of conflict which may arise within the purchasing function.
4.4 Manage the lack of integration with the rest of the business, and the perception that purchasing is seen as a process function involved in product design and capital specifications.
4.5 Apply techniques to deal with conflict within teams and between individuals in the purchasing and supply functions.

13

Prior knowledge

Study session 12.

Timing

You should set aside about 4 hours to read and complete this session, including learning activities, self-assessment questions, the suggested further reading (if any) and the revision question.

13.1 Resolving conflict

Learning activity 13.1

Brooks (2003) alleges: 'whereas organisational theory has developed to accept that conflict is inevitable, management theory and practitioner concerns demand that conflict is managed and resolved in the workplace'.

Draw up a list of five bullet points that explain why you consider conflict management to be necessary.

Feedback on page 164

Perspectives on conflict management

Conflict plays a significant role within organisations. However, its effects very much rely upon how it is managed. The management of conflict is primarily dependent upon the political perspective that an organisation adopts. Brooks (2003) states:

> 'managers who recognise that organisations are complex pluralistic entities may seek to understand the nature and causes of conflict, appreciate the divergence of interest and seek compromise or collaboration'.

Alternatively, unitaristic organisations are unlikely to get involved and reach a compromise, but instead they dictate their terms from the top. Conflict, however, will not disappear by denying its existence.

> 'In traditional hierarchical organisations, employees are expected to inform their managers and supervisors of problems and conflicts and abide by their decisions. In teams, employees are supposed to resolve problems and conflicts themselves.' (Cohen and Ledford cited in Chen and Tjosvold, 2002)

The goal of conflict management is essentially to keep conflicts productive. As Zornoza et al (2002) recognises, 'Conflict management operates on the basis that conflict can be positive and thus focuses on directing conflict toward constructive dialogue'.

13

There is much evidence to suggest that conflict, when managed effectively, can enhance decision processes in organisations, leading to improved decision outcomes and the development of a more cohesive approach toward the achievement of functional or organisational objectives. When managed ineffectively, however, conflict results in dysfunctional behaviours and low group productivity.

Conflict resolution between organisations or groups

When conflict or disputes arise between people, organisations or groups with similar (or dissimilar) interests and levels of influence, the approaches adopted within organisations to resolve issues do not necessarily apply. In such circumstances, parties in dispute or conflict (for example employers and employees' representative bodies or trade unions) seek to resolve matters in other ways.

Alternative dispute resolution (ADR) relates to a set of procedures in which the disputing parties work with a neutral party to help resolve their disagreements out of court. It can be in the form of either mediation or arbitration.

Mediation is where a neutral party (called the mediator in mediation) works with both sides to reach an agreement. In mediation both parties are willing to communicate. The mediator will meet with both parties separately and together to find a compromise that will suit both parties. During mediation, the mediator asks each party to state their grievance and to state the other party's view.

The mediator acts as a facilitator, helping the parties to communicate, but has no power to force people to reach a decision. Mediators do not control the agreement but they help the process of resolution to run smoothly. Greenberg and Baron (2003) point out that unfortunately, 'Because it requires voluntary compliance, by the disputing parties, mediation often proves to be ineffective'.

If mediation is unsuccessful, the disputes often go to **arbitration**. Arbitration is a form of dispute resolution where the two parties are unwilling to communicate with one another or to compromise. The neutral party (called the arbitrator in arbitration) will make recommendations, but *has* the power to impose an agreement. As in mediation, the concerned parties state their grievances. However, the neutral party (the arbitrator) behaves more like a judge and is responsible for reaching a decision unless both parties agree between themselves. Buchanan and Huczynski (2004) state: 'on the negative side, [arbitration] rarely results in the parties being committed to a settlement that is imposed on them'.

Buchanan and Huczynski (2004) state: 'with increasing litigation and increasing number of cases log-jammed in the courts, the importance and frequency of alternative dispute resolution (ADR) is increasing'. Greenberg and Baron (2003) report that alternative dispute resolution is very popular nowadays as it not only reaches an agreement relatively quickly, but is inexpensive and keeps people out of the public eye. Mediation, in particular, is very good for parties who wish to maintain a relationship, for example business partners. This informal process helps each party to look at the other

13

party's point of view. It has an emphasis on bringing the parties together, unlike the courtroom where a jury takes sides. With a courtroom, the two parties are more likely to be hostile and have animosity towards each other.

Self-assessment question 13.1

Fill in the missing gaps in the Table.

Table 13.1

Mediation	Arbitration
...	Parties unwilling to communicate
...	Third party intervenes, makes suggestions and recommendations and ultimately has the power to impose a decision which the parties must abide by
Neutral third party is called the mediator	...
Parties likely to be committed to agreement because they reached it	...
Is often ineffective because it requires voluntary compliance	...
...	Parties state their grievances and arbitrator makes their decision
...	Is suitable for those who do not wish to go to court but are both reluctant to reach a compromise

Feedback on page 165

13.2 Dealing with conflict: approaches

Thomas (cited in Brooks, 2003) proposed a conflict-handling model, which depends on:

- the degree of assertiveness in the pursuit of one's interest; and
- the level of cooperation in attempting to satisfy others' concerns.

Thomas also believes that there are five possible styles of handling conflict which are:

- **Avoidance** – where one or more parties either ignore or suppress a conflict, hoping that it will go away or that it will not become too disruptive to their work. A party may resort to referring to a bureaucratic procedure, although this still may not resolve anything.
- **Accommodation** – where one party allows the other party to 'do things their way', putting the other party first to minimise conflict.
- **Compromise** – where the parties involved negotiate and meet each other half way.

- Competition – where the parties concerned are reluctant to cooperate. It creates winners and losers.
- Collaboration – where the parties confront their differences and resolve them together. This is deemed the optimum solution for the good of both parties as well as the organisation.

Learning activity 13.2

Using the following conflict style handling questionnaire, identify your conflict resolution approach (1 = rarely, 5 = always).

1 I try to show the other party the logic and benefits of my position.
1–2–3–4–5
2 I endeavour to satisfy all the needs that I and the other party have.
1–2–3–4–5
3 I give up some points in exchange for others. 1–2–3–4–5
4 I believe that some differences are not worth worrying about.
1–2–3–4–5
5 I avoid hurting the other's feelings. 1–2–3–4–5
6 I seek to convince the other person of the merits of my position.
1–2–3–4–5
7 I strive to get all concerns and issues out on the table, immediately.
1–2–3–4–5
8 I propose a middle ground between us. 1–2–3–4–5
9 I postpone a decision until I have had some time to think it over.
1–2–3–4–5
10 I sacrifice my own wishes for those of the other person. 1–2–3–4–5
11 I am determined when pursuing my goals. 1–2–3–4–5
12 I seek the other person's help in working out a solution. 1–2–3–4–5
13 I try to find a fair combination of gains and losses for both of us.
1–2–3–4–5
14 I refrain from taking positions which would create controversy.
1–2–3–4–5
15 I soothe the other person's feelings in order to preserve our relationship.
1–2–3–4–5

(Adapted from Buchanan and Huczynski, 2004)

Feedback on page 165

Thomas' later work revealed that the conflict management style adopted depended on factors such as:

- The time available to resolve the conflict.
- The importance of the issue(s) giving rise to the conflict.
- The preference of the parties concerned.
- Whether or not a particular style is unacceptable in relation to the circumstances.
- Where contextual variables relating to either party's commitment or motivation is important.
- Where the conflict resolution may create a precedent.

- Where issues relating to a lack of information are important.

Deutsch (cited in Chen and Tjosvold, 2005) also researched conflict management and his findings were similar to the work of Thomas. Deutsch claimed that there were two approaches to conflict management:

- Cooperative conflict management, which relates to Thomas' 'collaboration' where conflict is viewed as a mutual problem that requires a mutual solution. As one party moves toward the achievement of their goals, so does the other party. Both parties recognise that the success of one leads to the success of the other. The emphasis on cooperative goals leads to mutual exchange and an open-minded discussion that in turn helps develop useful, mutually beneficial resolutions that reaffirm the relationship. Therefore, in this instance, conflict is productive. Chen and Tjosvold (2005) stresses that 'the basic steps in cooperative conflict are for team members to express their ideas and feelings directly, take the perspective of the other, communicate the desire to resolve the conflict for mutual benefit, and integrate their ideas to develop new solutions'. However, whilst Tjosvold's recommendations appear sound, conflict can only be a success if the other party is willing to agree to cooperate, which is rarely the case.
- Competitive conflict management relates to Thomas' 'competitive style'. Whereas a cooperative style tends to result in a win-win situation, this approach believes that, as one party moves towards the achievement of their goals, the other party fails (win-lose). Because each party is so compelled to win, discussion is avoided. The consequences tend to lead to weakened relationships and deadlock or imposed solutions. It is likely that the party perceived to be the loser will be frustrated. This kind of conflict management is not very productive.

Friedman et al (cited in Buchanan and Huczynski, 2004) made some interesting observations. Their study revealed that those using a collaborative approach to managing conflict experienced lower levels of task and relationship conflict as well as stress. However, those who used either a competing or avoiding style tended to encounter higher levels of task and therefore relationship conflict as well as a higher level of stress. Friedman et al concluded that the employees' work environment was in fact partly of their own making

Chen and Tjosvold (2005) warn against the use of avoiding conflict.

'Previous research suggests that avoiding conflict is often counter-productive. Studies on groupthink [the tendency for members of highly cohesive groups to conform to group pressures so that they fail to think critically and reject any correcting influences of outsiders] indicate that in their efforts to maintain cohesion, team members may reject those with opposing views. However, this suppression of controversy can result in disastrous decisions ... results suggest that low levels of participation restrict group innovativeness despite strong external pressures to change.'

They concluded that avoiding conflict actually reinforces the competitive approach to conflict.

13

Whilst the competitive approach is generally frowned upon Thomas (in Brooks, 2003), Chen and Tjosvold (2005), Deutsch (in Chen and Tjosvold, 2005) and Townsend (1970) actively encourages it. Townsend argues that:

> 'compromise is usually bad. It should be a last resort. If two departments or divisions have a problem they can't solve and it comes up to you, listen to both sides and then, unlike Solomon, pick one or the other. This places solid accountability on the *winner* to make it work.'

Bottger and Yetton (cited in Zornoza et al, 2002) distinguish between positive and negative conflict-management behaviours. They believe positive conflict management entails an examination of the competing knowledge bases, exploration of alternatives, and a willingness of participants to argue for their points of view. Emphasis is on knowledge and justification of argument. On the contrary, negative conflict management is where differences in opinion are overcome by either giving in, voting or coin tossing, or what Zornoza et al refer to as 'I-win-you-lose' dominance games.

Self-assessment question 13.2

According to Zornoza et al (2002), 'In keeping conflicts constructive, the management of conflict interaction has emerged as an important strategy'. Explain the strategies that management can adopt to prevent conflict from escalating to destructive conflict, using the following headings:

- Resource allocation
- Human resource policies
- Style of management
- Team-building exercises.

Feedback on page 166

13

Revision question

Now try the revision question for this session on page 249.

Summary

- Carnall (2003) suggests that 'while conflict can be a positive force to change, the first point to note about it is that it cannot – and should not – be eliminated'.
- Conflict must be managed appropriately to allow organisations to develop and maintain competitiveness.
- Also, the management of conflict is primarily dependent upon the political perspective that an organisation adopts. Pluralistic entities may seek to understand the nature and causes of conflict, appreciate the divergence of interest and seek compromise or collaboration, whereas unitaristic organisations are unlikely to get involved and reach a compromise, but instead dictate their terms from the top.

- Conflict, when managed effectively, can enhance decision processes, improve decision outcomes and help develop a more cohesive approach toward the achievement of functional or organisational objectives.
- When managed ineffectively, conflict results in dysfunctionality in organisations.
- Where disparate parties are in dispute or conflict, for example dispute between employers and employees' representative bodies or trades unions, resolution is usually via some third-party intervention, for example via arbitration, mediation or conciliation.
- Alternative dispute resolution (ADR) is very popular nowadays as it not only helps to reach agreement relatively quickly, it is also inexpensive and keeps people out of the public eye.
- Thomas (cited in Brooks, 2003) proposed a conflict-handling model, which depends on both 'the degree of assertiveness in the pursuit of one's interest' and 'the level of cooperation in attempting to satisfy others' concerns'.
- Thomas believes that there are five possible styles of handling conflict: avoidance; accommodation; compromise; competition; collaboration.
- Thomas' later work revealed that the conflict-management style adopted depended on factors such as: (a) the time available to resolve the conflict; (b) the importance of the issue(s) giving rise the conflict; (c) the preference of the parties concerned; (d) whether or not a particular style is unacceptable in relation to the circumstances; (e) whether contextual variables relating to either party's commitment or motivation is important; (f) whether the conflict resolution may create precedent; and (g) whether issues relating to a lack of information are important.
- Deutsch (cited in Chen and Tjosvold, 2005) also researched conflict management and his findings were similar to the work of Thomas. He claimed that there were two approaches to conflict management: (a) cooperative conflict management; and (b) competitive conflict management.

Suggested further reading

You could read the relevant sections of Brooks (2003), Chen, Liu and Tjosvold (2005), Chen and Tjosvold (2002), Van Wendel De Joode (2004) and Zornoza, Ripoll and Peiro (2002).

Feedback on learning activities and self-assessment questions

Feedback on learning activity 13.1

Some important points to consider include:

- Research suggests that success in teams is highly dependent on the way they manage conflicts (Van Wendel De Joode, 2004).
- If not managed, conflict can become destructive and spin out of control, causing chaos in the workplace as a result of anxiety, absenteeism and employee turnover.
- If conflict is not resolved, it can get in the way of the achievement of the organisation's goals. For example, if two employees do not get

13

along within the same department and as a result do not communicate properly with one another, mistakes are likely to be made. In extreme cases, they may actually work against each other to their own agendas instead of pulling together as a team.

- Jehn and Mannix (cited in Van Wendel De Joode, 2004) state that 'high levels of conflicts or specific types of conflict can, however, threaten the speed of decision-making and hinder implementation', thus no progress is made.
- 'Conflict can become destructive and produce strong negative feelings, blindness and interdependencies, and uncontrolled escalation of aggressive action and counteraction' (Brown cited in Van Wendel De Joode, 2004).
- Mannix et al (cited in Van Wendel De Joode, 2004) observed that individuals perceive criticism related to a task to be personal criticism which causes affective conflicts (which is emotional and focuses on personal incompatibilities; it is associated with feelings of tension and friction). Conflict management is therefore needed to prevent task conflict from giving rise to affective conflict.
- Conflict management is needed in order to help the organisation to avoid complacency and effectively carry out its tasks.

As Chen and Tjosvold (2005) point out, 'Diversity, when properly harnessed, promotes the "creative abrasion" of dialogue and debate that in turn stimulates innovation'.

Feedback on self-assessment question 13.1

Table 13.2

Mediation	Arbitration
Parties are willing to communicate	Parties unwilling to communicate
Third party acts as a facilitator and encourages parties to communicate, but does not get involved in the actual decision making	Third party intervenes, makes suggestions and recommendations and ultimately has the power to impose a decision which the parties must abide by
Neutral third party is called the mediator	Neutral party is called the arbitrator
Parties likely to be committed to agreement because they reached it	Parties unlikely to be committed to a settlement that is imposed on them
Is often ineffective because it requires voluntary compliance	Arbitration is often effective because it makes an award to one party
Parties state their grievances and the other party's point of view	Parties state their grievances and arbitrator makes their decision
Is most suitable for those who wish to maintain a relationship	Is suitable for those who do not wish to go to court but are both reluctant to reach a compromise

Feedback on learning activity 13.2

Enter your score beside each question number and then add up the totals.

Table 13.3

Competing	Avoiding	Compromising	Accommodating	Collaborating
1	4	3	5	2
6	9	8	10	7
11	14	13	15	12
Total:	Total:	Total:	Total:	Total:

The category with the highest total denotes your primary conflict-resolving approach.

Feedback on self-assessment question 13.2

- Resource allocation: although it is highly unusual for managers to increase their budgets/resources, they can diffuse a situation using other tactics. These include the transferring of resources and possible delay in making new staff appointments in one area to provide for another area.
- Human resource policies: attention should be paid to job demarcation, recruitment and selection policies, job evaluation, performance measurement, grievance and disciplinary procedures as well as arbitration and mediation procedures. All human resource policies must be equitable to all concerned. Bragg (cited in Greenberg and Baron, 2003) recommends: 'Make sure everyone knows his or her specific areas of responsibility, authority and accountability. Clarifying these things avoids potential conflicts when people either avoid their responsibilities or over step their authority'.
- Style of management: a participative and supportive style of management is integral to conflict management. Management need to create a culture that fosters open communication, trust and respect for other people's ideas. Management should encourage conflict to be addressed in a mature manner. As Bragg (cited in Greenberg and Baron, 2003) points out: 'Conflicts will not go away by making believe they don't exist; doing so only will make them worse'.
- Team-building exercises: management could help employees understand the nature of conflict by using team-building and training. Developing employee's interpersonal skills will help them to gain an understanding of other people's points of view. Training could be in the form of seminars and so on which promote collaborative working.

13

Recruitment, training, development and appraisal

'The manager's quintessential responsibility is to help his people realise their own highest potential.'
Maisonrouge (2006)

Introduction

Throughout management literature, the notion that 'employees are an organisation's most valuable asset' is a common occurrence. Whilst products can be easily imitated, employees are unique and should therefore be considered as a prime source of competitive advantage. Recruiting and retaining talented employees is a key issue for organisations.

Session learning objectives

After completing this session you should be able to:

14.1 Explain the process of recruitment and selection of staff.
14.2 Explain the importance of training as a major influence on the success of an organisation.
14.3 Compare and contrast different types and methods of employee appraisal.

Unit content coverage

This study session covers the following topic from the official CIPS unit content document:

Learning outcome

Formulate plans to effectively manage work groups and teams.

Learning objective

4.6 Assess the benefits of a systematic approach to recruitment, appraisal, training and development.

Prior knowledge

Study sessions 2 and 5 – 7.

Timing

You should set aside about 6 hours to read and complete this session, including learning activities, self-assessment questions, the suggested further reading (if any) and the revision question.

14.1 Recruitment and selection

Any recruitment and selection system should be based on three fundamental principles: efficiency, effectiveness and fairness (ACAS, 1983).

14

Mayo (1995) states:

> 'Effectiveness is concerned with distinguishing accurately between suitable and unsuitable candidates. Efficiency is concerned more with the cost of the exercise and measures here may include average cost per recruit, average time lapsed between various stages, percentage of offers made and offer acceptance rate.'

Human resource planning

Human resource planning is traditionally referred to as manpower planning, although some argue that the two things are very different. Mullins (2005) defines human resource planning as 'a strategy for the acquisition, utilisation, improvement and retention of an enterprise's human resources'.

Essentially, both terms refer to a critical process that ensures that the organisation has a sufficient number of staff with the necessary skills and experience. Its purpose is to maintain stability within the organisation. It is also an ongoing process due to a number of factors including employees resigning, retiring or being sacked, or even the organisation's goals altering. HR planning is even more complicated in a firm with seasonal demand.

Pre-recruitment

Authorisation

Firstly management and the human resources (HR) department must agree if they are to recruit. HR must be authorised to recruit new members of staff. Prior to recruiting, alternatives to recruitment should be discussed. It may be decided that it is necessary to restructure staff duties and responsibilities. If the decision is made to recruit new staff, then a realistic budget should be agreed. Having such discussions with departmental managers in advance of any recruitment procedures proves to be both time and cost effective.

Traditionally in large organisations, recruitment was undertaken by the personnel department. However, it is more common today for line managers to carry out the recruiting and selection process.

Guest (1997) recognised that there was a shift in management strategies from personnel management to human resource management (HRM). Personnel management operated using the pluralist perspective, which meant traditionally that recruitment was undertaken by the specialised personnel department. HRM, which is mainly used today, works using the unitarist perspective. This is where line managers are expected to be involved in recruitment. This is known as decentralisation, where responsibility is devolved down the line.

However, some important issues need to be considered, for example is it effective and efficient to devolve the recruiting responsibility to line managers? Are the line managers qualified to recruit and have they got the time to do it? Cully et al (1999) recorded that 80% of managers had responsibility for employment relations matters. Responsibility for recruitment depends on the perspective that the organisation adopts.

14

Recruitment methods

Staff can be recruited via:

- Adverts (in the national and local press, specialist publications (for example *The Grocer* for business-related jobs, *New Scientist* for technicians, research scientists) and on the radio, TV and the internet.
- Formal personal contacts – career fairs, open days, leaflet drops.
- Informal personal contacts – word of mouth, speculative applications (people writing letters to the company).
- Adverts on notice boards that are accessible to everyone inside the organisation.
- External assistance – job centres, employment agencies, head hunters.

Learning activity 14.1

You are the manager of an organisation. Other than cost, what might be the advantages and disadvantages of each of the following recruitment methods? Complete table 14.1.

Table 14.1

Recruitment method	Advantage	Disadvantage
Advertising (specialist publication)		
Career fairs		
Personal contact (word of mouth)		
Notice boards within firm		
Employment agencies		

Feedback on page 175

14

The recruitment method chosen must be appropriate for the position, for example it is a waste of time and money advertising a cleaning position in the *Financial Times* as the main audience of the *FT* are usually business people. Before recruiting, criteria must be decided such as the period of employment, the marketing needed to appeal to the required audience and the recruiting budget.

Short-listing

The job applications are sorted into most likely, possible and unacceptable by comparing the job design and personnel specification with the curriculum vitae (CV).

Selection techniques

Interviewing is the most popular selection technique. The type and number of stages in an interview will depend on the nature of the position.

The use of tests for selection attempts to achieve objectivity. These include ability, aptitude, intelligence and personality questionnaires. The type of tests depends on the nature of vacancy. They must be the same for all of the candidates in order to avoid discrimination. Personality tests can be inefficient as they do not always represent a true reflection of the candidate because they are subjective to how that person feels when they fill in the questionnaire. Candidates may try to answer the questionnaire in accordance with what they think you want to hear. Therefore the personality on paper may be totally different to that of the individual.

An 'assessment centre' is a place where applicants take part in a number of activities whilst being watched and assessed.

The recruiting and selection team must decide on the most appropriate selection techniques for the position. However, the chosen selection techniques alone will not necessarily find the perfect candidate. A more accurate method for selecting an applicant would be the use of both assessment centres and tests.

Cost of selection techniques

Recruitment and selection can be expensive. The costs involved in some selection techniques means that they are not viable for some companies.

Conclusion

Has the recruitment been effective, fair and efficient? A manager who recruits on a large scale can check the efficiency of recruiting procedures by calculating some of the following ratios:

1   Average time during which a vacancy remains unfilled.
2   Number of candidates replying to an advertisement/Number of candidates called for the interview.
3   Total value of wages and salaries offered/Cost of recruitment and selection for those vacancies.

A downward trend in any of these ratios except 3 shows that an improvement is taking place in the efficiency of recruitment and selection.

However carefully an applicant is recruited and selected, a manager will not know the suitability of the candidate until the person has settled in to the organisation. To begin with it should be expected that productivity may drop slightly. However, after an initial period of three months, the successful applicant should become accustomed to the firm's working practices.

Self-assessment question 14.1

Human resource planning allows an organisation to assess its future recruitment needs. List six other reasons why human resource planning is so important.

Feedback on page 176

14

14.2 The importance of training

Learning activity 14.2

Training is necessary to ensure employees are competent at their job. List six other reasons why training is important.

Feedback on page 176

It is strongly recommended that firms provide their workforce with continual training to update their skills, as Stovel and Bontis (2002) concluded that 'the results of employee training include higher productivity, enhanced creativity and increased employee confidence'. Furthermore, Fitz-enz (cited in Stovel and Bontis, 2002) is of the opinion that training contributes more than just the obvious benefits; it actually increases employee loyalty as the employees recognise that the company is helping them to realise their career aspirations.

Continuous training is particularly important to keep up with the ever-increasing pace of change. Up-to-date skills and knowledge are necessary for a firm to maintain and increase their competitive position within the marketplace. However, training must be relevant to the requirements of the organisation and be suitable for the employee's capabilities. An appropriate appraisal system should also be adopted to monitor the effectiveness of the training scheme.

Mullins (2005) contends that:

> 'the general movement towards flexible structures of organisation and the nature of management moving towards the devolution of power to the workforce give increasing emphasis to an environment of coaching and support.'

However, it is highly unlikely that managers will have the time to devote to training their subordinates, otherwise they would probably have retained the power.

Whilst Fitz-enz makes a convincing argument, many organisations only train employees with 'firm-specific' skills and not transferable ones. This is designed to benefit the organisation but not the employees within that organisation. Stovel and Bontis (2002) refer to this as 'low behaviour', where the firm incorporates training schemes but solely to meet industry standards. Rainbird and Maguire's survey (cited in Beardwell and Holden, 2001) revealed that:

> 'much of the training reported was for organisational rather than individual development, suggesting that many employees would not regard the training they receive as training at all, since it neither imparts transferable skills nor contributes to personal and educational development.'

Mullins (2005) states that 'few would argue against the importance of training as a major influence on the success of an organisation', and yet

14

companies remain reluctant to provide it. This is due to management having reservations regarding the cost of training and the extent of its tangible business returns. However, it is essential for the company to acquire new skills in order for it to develop and sustain its competitiveness. Therefore, training should not be viewed as a cost but as an investment in the business. Taylor (2004) considers that 'spending money on training managers to make more considered and less hasty recruitment decisions is likely to prove a good investment, leading to long-term savings'.

Beardwell and Holden (2001) found that in reality, however:

> 'The growing awareness of the importance of training over the past decade was also supported by reports that employers were spending more in aggregate terms on training activities (Training Agency, 1989). However, the measurement of training expenditure is still controversial, and those figures that do exist are open to question, interpretation and political manipulation (Finegold, 1991; Ryan, 1991). Thus there seems to be a gap between the perceived importance of training and the willingness to do something about it. The view strongly persists in the commercial and industrial culture of the UK that training is a "cost" and not an "investment".'

Self-assessment question 14.2

Prepare a list of five important points to consider when designing/considering a training scheme.

Feedback on page 177

14.3 Employee appraisal

14

Appraisals can also be referred to as staff development reviews, development needs assessments and performance reviews. According to Betts (2000) an appraisal is 'a periodic review of a person's performance by conducting a formal documented interview, by referring to informal records, or operating an established system'.

However, this is not strictly true as appraisals are more often than not informal, where the two parties discuss the performance of the appraisee rather than conduct an interview as such. This could be the reason why ACAS (2001) refer to the role of the appraiser as that of a counsellor. The purpose of performance appraisal is to improve the performance of individuals in order to improve the performance of the organisation as a whole.

Appraisals can also provide an opportunity to:

- Identify an employee's strengths and weaknesses.
- Formulate job improvement plans.

- Formulate objectives and goals.
- Resolve problems which may prevent progress and cause inefficient work practices. They therefore encourage consistent performance.
- Identify opportunities related to the job.
- Provide a rationale for salary reviews.
- Highlight potential opportunities for promotion/transfer.
- Identify training and development requirements.
- Identify aspects of the job that are or are not satisfying and why.
- Allow the employee to make suggestions.
- Discuss issues that are of concern to the appraisee (employee).
- Help management allocate duties and decide what level of supervision is appropriate.
- Help human resources with manpower planning.
- Demonstrate commitment to employees.
- Improve communication between managers and employees.

Appraisal approaches include:

- Downward appraisal: where a manager, usually the appraisee's superior but in some cases someone from the HR department, carries out an appraisal on an employee.
- Upward feedback or upward appraisal: where employees give their opinion of their superior/manager. Betts (2000) is of the belief that this technique 'gives employees more empowerment, the opportunity to participate in an appraisal process which before was only one-way, and provides a feeling that subordinates' views are valued'.

Recently some companies have chosen to use an appraisal method called the 'multi-sided appraisal' or '360 degree feedback' whereby employees are judged by other employees as well as customers. This is intended to give a more rounded, truthful view of the individual. However, this type of appraisal is not always constructive and can turn into a popularity contest. 'Peers should be treated with caution because there might be some vindictiveness or jealousy' points out Betts (2000). The effectiveness of this form of appraisal is therefore debatable.

14

With appraisals, it is important that employees know exactly what is expected of them and the yardstick by which their performance and results will be measured. Mullins (2005) suggests that appraisals can encourage a greater degree of consistency through regular feedback on performance. The process of appraisal can also improve the quality of working life by increasing mutual understanding between managers and employees.

Mullins (2005) is of the belief that appraisals held on an annual basis are not sufficient, and that they should be a continuous monitoring process.

Maier (cited in Cole, 1996) identified three main appraisal styles:

- 'Tell and sell' is an autocratic style where the manager informs the team members of their performance and tries to influence them to accept the manager's decisions regarding improvements.
- 'Tell and listen', where the manager informs the team members of their performance and listens to their feedback.

- 'Problem solving' is a fully participative style, where the manager and the team members reflect upon the team members' performance and mutually discuss the way forward.

If employees are unhappy with their appraisal they can appeal. Appeals are usually held by a manager, a superior to the appraiser or by someone in the HR department.

Learning activity 14.3

Identify and explain five potential problems associated with employee appraisals. Make suggestions as to how the problems can be overcome.

Feedback on page 177

Now answer the self-assessment question.

Self-assessment question 14.3

Identify and explain five key features of an effective staff appraisal process.

Feedback on page 178

Revision question

Now try the revision question for this session on page 249.

Summary

- Mullins (2005) defines human resource planning as 'a strategy for the acquisition, utilisation, improvement and retention of an enterprise's human resources'.
- Essentially, human resource planning (HRM) is a critical process that ensures an organisation has a sufficient number of staff with the necessary skills and experience, and its overall purpose is to maintain stability within the organisation.
- Any recruitment and selection system should be based on three fundamental principles: efficiency, effectiveness and fairness.
- Traditionally, in large organisations recruitment was always undertaken by the personnel department. However, today it is more common for line managers to carry out the recruiting and selection process, usually under guidance from an HRM function.
- The main method of recruitment is via advertising. Other methods include informal/formal personal contacts, use of notice boards and external help such as employment centres and agencies.
- Training is necessary to ensure that employees are competent at their job. Furthermore, it can also be beneficial by helping employees to feel involved. It creates a sense of belonging and ownership, which can bring about commitment and loyalty to the firm.

14

- Training can also be rewarding as employees feel a sense of achievement, leading to increased job satisfaction and motivation. It also helps employees take on additional responsibility, which helps the firm's productivity.
- Training also helps employees to become more knowledgeable and competent at their job, increasing their efficiency and effectiveness.
- Training should not be viewed as a cost but as an investment in the business. As Taylor (2004) argues, 'spending money on training managers to make more considered and less hasty recruitment decisions is likely to prove a good investment, leading to long-term savings'.
- An appraisal is 'a periodic review of a person's performance by conducting a formal documented interview, by referring to informal records, or operating an established system'. (Betts, 2000)
- The purpose of performance appraisal is to improve the performance of individuals in order to improve the performance of the organisation as a whole.
- Appraisal approaches include downward appraisal (where a manager, usually the appraisee's superior, carries out an appraisal on an employee) and upward appraisal (where employees give their opinion of their superior/manager).
- In recent times, some companies have chosen to use an appraisal method called 'multi-sided appraisal' or '360 degree feedback' whereby employees are judged by other employees as well as customers. This approach is intended to give a more rounded, truthful view of the individual. However, it is not always constructive and its effectiveness is somewhat debatable.
- Mullins (2005) suggests that appraisals can encourage a greater degree of consistency through regular feedback on performance, and the process of appraisal can also improve the quality of working life by increasing mutual understanding between managers and employees.

Suggested further reading

You could read the relevant sections of Mullins (2005).

Feedback on learning activities and self-assessment questions

Feedback on learning activity 14.1

Table 14.2

Recruitment method	Advantage	Disadvantage
Advertising (specialist publication)	Can specifically target an audience	Job may not be appropriate for the specialist publication
Career fairs	Promote the company brand whilst talking to a large audience	A lot more time consuming than other methods
Personal contact (word of mouth)	You are likely to have some background information about the applicant	Person making the recommendation may feel

(continued on next page)

14

Table 14.2 *(continued)*

Recruitment method	Advantage	Disadvantage
		offended if the applicant is unsuitable
Notice boards within firm	You are more likely to know about capabilities of the employee. Also, in-house recruitment promotes a good company image	May want to bring in 'fresh blood'. Also will have to re-advertise the employee's job
Employment agencies	Can find applicants quickly	Often give a false impression of the job. Also indirect – employment agency's opinion of suitability may differ from manager's view

Feedback on self-assessment question 14.1

Human resource planning allows the organisation to:

- Assess what future skills are required, therefore helping to formulate training programmes.
- Avoid redundancies by relocating people within the firm (redeployment).
- Develop a flexible workforce to meet the changing needs of the organisation, in other words reconciling the demand of work with the supply of employees. For example, the organisation may be overloaded with work and therefore HR will recruit some temporary employees.
- Retain control regarding the costs involved. For example, if the company's budget does not allow for the recruitment of additional staff, then changes will have to be made elsewhere. Employees may have to take on additional work.
- Identify where it is suitable for employees to be promoted.
- Keep salaries competitive, which may help retain staff.

Feedback on learning activity 14.2

- Helping employees to feel involved. It can create a sense of belonging and ownership, which in turn can bring about commitment and loyalty to the firm.
- Training can be rewarding as employees may feel a sense of achievement which can lead to increased job satisfaction and motivation.
- Training can mean that employees may be able to take on additional responsibility, thus the firm can become more productive.
- With training, employees can become more knowledgeable and competent at their job, thus making them more efficient and effective.
- It helps employees understand their role within the organisation. Gilbert (1996) considers role ambiguity to be a stimulus for employee turnover. Reduced turnover will help to lower the costs of the organisation.
- Helping to smooth out the turnover process. For example, if the workforce are trained to be multiskilled this will help to provide cover for holidays, sickness or if people leave the organisation.

14

Feedback on self-assessment question 14.2

Your answers will vary. However, the most important points to consider include:

- Has the organisation the resources (time and money) it needs for the training scheme? Can the organisation afford it?
- The capability of the employees. Can the employees selected for training cope with the level of training?
- What training is necessary? Is it relevant to the job?
- Are the employees willing to participate in a training scheme? What if they are reluctant?
- Will it motivate staff?
- How will the company know if the training is worthwhile?
- How will it benefit (a) the organisation, and (b) the employee?
- Who will conduct the training – external consultants or managers? Have they got the time and ability?

Feedback on learning activity 14.3

A good answer will include the following points:

- The reliability of the assessment; risk of favouritism or nepotism. The appraiser may be biased. Tackey (cited in Mullins, 2005) states that 'the evaluation of the performance of individuals in the workplace is fraught with difficulties even at the best of times. The difficulties are compounded when there are allegations of bias in such evaluation'. Appraisals are subjective, but it may be possible to get a more rounded view of the employee by 360 degree feedback.
- Mullins (2005) asserts 'appraisals should not be limited to a formal event occurring once or twice a year but should be a continuous process of monitoring, feedback and review'. It could be viewed that constantly monitoring staff can stifle creativity and irritate employees.
- Despite many academics' recommendations, the appraiser cannot constantly monitor everyone's performance. Therefore, the appraiser may not always see the employee in their true light. To overcome this, it is suggested that employees build a portfolio of evidence to prove their competence, to enable them to expand their horizons and/or to be eligible for promotion and/or increase in salary.
- The style of the appraiser may not be appropriate. For example, the tell-and-sell style may be adopted, where the manager is dictatorial and sets objectives instead of agreeing them with the employee. In this instance, appraisals can prove futile as the objectives set may be unrealistic and therefore improvements in performance are not made. It is recommended that the appraiser should adopt a more suitable style.
- According to Betts (2000), 'an effective (appraisal) system is expensive in investment, time and effort'. These costs are likely to be recouped by the improvements that are made in performance.
- Appraiser and appraisee may not agree on issues, for example intended action or salary rise. If the appraisee feels that the appraiser was unjust then they should appeal.
- The appraiser is poor at conducting interviews. The appraiser must receive thorough training.

14

- Employees have no faith in the system. They may agree on intended action, but really ignore anything that has been discussed. This is a difficult one to overcome!

Feedback on self-assessment question 14.3

A good answer will include the following points:

- Employees must have a clearly defined job description so that they know exactly what is expected of them. The appraisal is based around the job description. Using the job description, the employee can point out what aspects of the job they find easy/difficult, enjoyable/unpleasant. Strengths and weaknesses can be identified as can areas for improvement. On this basis, targets can be set.
- Changes to the job description might be discussed. The appraisal process is a good opportunity to get feedback from an employee. The employee may make suggestions about where efficiencies can be made. The employee may feel unhappy and stifled in their current job role. The appraisal provides a good opportunity for employees to discuss possible changes to their current role and any potential chances for a role change.
- An effective appraisal process should be constructive to the extent that it sets realistic goals for the employee for the forthcoming year.
- The work carried out must be measurable and have clearly defined performance measures, for example key performance indicators (KPIs), to enable the employee and appraiser to judge if the employee has met the targets set.
- To avoid creating jealousy and resentment amongst the workforce, the staff appraisal process must be consistent and fair to all employees concerned.
- An effective appraisal process will discuss any training/staff development requirements to help the employee carry out their job more effectively and for personal development.

14

Managing team performance

'No one's perfect,
but a team can be.'
Belbin (1981)

Introduction

Over the past decade there has been a huge increase in academic and industrial interest in the subject of teamwork. The classical approach to organisation ignored the importance of teams and the social elements they bring, but the work of Mayo (1995) stimulated a shift in mindset. Japanese companies in particular have sparked interest as a result of their resounding success with teamwork, motivating other companies to readdress their working practices. Teams are very useful when performing a complex task, especially when deadlines are tight. Through teamwork and collaboration an individual's limitations can be overcome. It can also be argued that teams create synergy, where the outcome is greater than its counterparts.

Session learning objectives

After completing this session you should be able to:

15.1 Develop procedures and measurements of control for monitoring team performance, designed to ensure good performance.
15.2 Explain the nature and importance of control as an integral part of the process of management.
15.3 Monitor and control individual and team performance.
15.4 Analyse reasons for poor team performance.

Unit content coverage

This study session covers the following topic from the official CIPS unit content document:

Learning outcome

Formulate plans to effectively manage work groups and teams.

Learning objective

4.2 Apply techniques for building, motivating and managing successful teams within the purchasing and supply function.
4.5 Apply techniques to deal with conflict within teams and between individuals in the purchasing and supply functions.

Prior knowledge

Study session 14.

15

Timing

You should set aside about 6 hours to read and complete this session, including learning activities, self-assessment questions, the suggested further reading (if any) and the revision question.

15.1 Teams and groups

Traditionally, employees worked individually to achieve the organisation's objectives. However, today organisations increasingly use teams (which are not to be confused with groups). Cook and Goff (2002) state 'it is important to differentiate between teams and working groups since these two terms are often used synonymously, albeit incorrectly'.

Learning activity 15.1

Write two paragraphs clearly distinguishing between the terms 'groups' and 'teams'.

Feedback on page 186

Cook and Goff (2002) assert that:

> 'While groups focus on individual performance and goals, teams come together to 1) share information, perspectives and insights; 2) make decisions that help each person do his or her job better; and/or 3) reinforce each other's individual performance standards.'

Katzenbach and Smith (cited in Cook and Goff, 2002) state:

> 'By definition, a team is a small number of people with complementary skills who are committed to a common purpose, performance goals, an approach for which they hold themselves mutually accountable.'

Senior and Swailes (2004) distinguish between groups and teams stating that:

> 'work groups have no need or opportunity to engage in collective work that requires collective effort … their performance is merely the summation of each group member's individual contribution. There is no positive synergy that would create an overall level of performance greater than the sum of inputs.'

Therefore, it would appear that a team is much more than just a group.

Team size

Betts (2000) makes the point that team size is an important consideration, and that:

> 'effective teams tend to be small – with fewer than 10 people. They have members who fill **role** demands, are flexible, and who prefer to be part of a group. They also have adequate resources, effective leadership, a

15

climate of trust and a performance evaluation and reward system that reflect team contributions.'

Optimum group size is generally regarded as six members. With large teams of eight or more, communication problems can arise and the team will require more organising. With a group of this size, sub-groups tend to form, social loafing is very likely to occur and members generally do not feel involved. Conversely, with small teams of four or less, communication will be easier but the team is vulnerable whenever a member is absent.

Team development

Tuckman (in Brooks, 2003) proposed a model to illustrate team development, initially with four stages: forming, storming, norming and performing. A fifth stage, adjourning, was added later in 1977 by Tuckman and Jensen. These stages can be explained as follows:

- Forming – involves a number of people being brought together. People at this stage tend to feel anxious and cautious as they are meeting other members as well as trying to create an impression. At the beginning Tuckman believes that people are sceptical, hesitant, defensive and therefore are likely to scapegoat.
- Storming – this is a stage where people feel more confident and are willing to express themselves and challenge others. As a result disagreement and conflict tend to occur, which is not necessarily a negative outcome – it can be productive! Also, during this stage people's **roles** begin to establish, for example the leader.
- Norming – the team establishes its norms such as team roles, standards of performance and working procedures. It is suggested at this stage that management should become involved to influence desired behaviours. Otherwise, dysfunctional groups can develop ingrained attitudes and norms which are difficult to reverse.
- Performing – this is where the group is working towards its desired goals, some actual results are produced here!
- Adjourning – this is a time for reflection on the task undertaken. The team then splits, either because the task is completed or because the team members have left.

This model provides a useful insight into team development. In reality though, a team is unlikely to go through all of these stages in a linear fashion. Teams tend to jump from stage to stage. For example, the team may be at the storming stage and regress to the forming stage. this should still be viewed as progress since it can bring about creativity. Alternatively, some groups never reach the performing stage at all as they are too preoccupied with trivialities.

Team roles

Dr R Meredith Belbin (1993), one of the world's leading gurus on team building, is renowned for identifying the roles that individuals adopt when they are in a team. His nine roles include:

- The **chairman** (CH): a leader, who coordinates the efforts of the team, who acknowledges their talents, but is not threatened by them. Chairmen tend to be concerned with what is feasible over what is

15

creative. The chairman clarifies goals, promotes decision making and delegates well.

- The **shaper** (SH): a leader, but unlike the chairman this person is persuasive and shapes the decisions of the team. This person is challenging, dynamic, thrives on pressure and has the drive and courage to overcome obstacles.
- The **monitor/evaluator** (ME): this person is objective and has sound analytical and judgement skills. They are sober, strategic and discerning.
- The **plant** (PL): creative, imaginative and unorthodox, this person generates lots of ideas and tires of routine and conformity. They are good at solving difficult problems.
- The **company worker/implementer** (CW): this person translates plans into action and is disciplined, reliable, conservative and efficient.
- The **team worker** (TW): this is a supportive role. This person is responsible for keeping the group functioning together, for cohesiveness and collaboration. They are perceptive and attentive to the team's needs. Team workers are cooperative, mild and diplomatic.
- The **resource investigator** (RI): this is a supportive role. This individual is mainly concerned with finding the necessary resources to carry out the task. They are extrovert, enthusiastic and communicative; they explore opportunities and develop contacts.
- The **completer/finisher** (CF): this individual is concerned with getting the job done and to a high standard. They are painstaking, conscientious and anxious; they search out errors and omissions and deliver on time.
- The **specialist** (S): this individual is single minded, self-starting and dedicated, and provides knowledge and skills in rare supply.

Belbin emphasises that it is important to build a balanced team of people with complementary skills and traits. He developed a 'Self-perception inventory questionnaire' whereby individual team members could assess themselves against his (team) role 'types'. He makes the point that 'not all teams consist of nine people each taking one of the roles', but he also states that 'effective and successful teams should be based on these nine roles'.

Self-assessment question 15.1

Drawing on Belbin's nine team roles (and other references herein) as the basis for your answer, critically evaluate each of the following in terms of their relative importance to the development of a team:

1   Interpersonal processes.
2   Roles.
3   Norms.
4   Cohesion.

Feedback on page 186

15.2 Self-managed teams

According to Baron and Armstrong (cited in Beardwell & Holden, 2001) performance management is:

'a strategic and integrated approach to increasing the effectiveness of organisations by improving the performance of the people who work in them and by developing the capabilities of teams and individual contributors'.

However, managing team performance is particularly difficult. Whilst the literature is well documented regarding the distinction between groups and teams and the roles that team members can play, it lacks any real evidence concerning how (and if) the team's performance should be managed.

Buchanan (cited in Brooks, 2003) defines self-managed teams as 'a work group allocated an overall task and given discretion over how the work is to be done'. Self-managed teams (SMTs) (also referred to as autonomous work groups, self-directed teams, high-performance teams or empowered teams) have grown in popularity over the past decade. This is due to documented increases in organisations' profitability, improvements in productivity, more efficient use of resources, better problem solving and increased innovation.

Self-managed teams make decisions that were once reserved for, or were the prerogative of, managers. Moravec (cited in Cook and Goff, 2002) believes 'these teams are a most powerful and proven management strategy that accelerates productivity and quality and enhances human competencies and commitment'. Along with the emphasis on using teams, management style has shifted from an autocratic approach to a more participative one.

Learning activity 15.2

List five advantages of an organisation forming autonomous workgroups.

Feedback on page 187

The role of the manager today is seen more as that of a coach and facilitator rather than as a director and controller (Nelson and Quick, 1996; Cook and Goff, 2002; Brooks, 2003). Brooks (2003) warns that 'managers may resist such a new role, supposing that the self-organising team structure will be a threat to their position'. However, Cook and Goff (2002) reassure that:

'certainly, managers still have a role with SMTs. They assist in the composition of the team and do the training necessary for the team to succeed. Beyond that, they continue to be present, observing what is happening and lending support hopefully without unduly interfering with the process itself. Still, the primary responsibility for managing the SMT lies with the team members themselves … The manager's role in all this is to be a resource to the team and to be supportive of decisions made by the team.'

Conversely, Hales and Knowles (2003) contest this view, believing 'the function of managers, including first-line managers, is seen as preventative rather than facilitative and therefore are primarily concerned with monitoring and control'. This is supported by Buchanan and Huczynski (2004) who state:

15

'several researchers have highlighted the contradictions between management desire for control and attempts to increase team autonomy. Anna Pollert (1996) studied the imposition of team-working on a repetitive, low-skill assembly line manufacturing chocolate. She described how the managers sought to gain employee commitment to the company in a situation in which the work intensification and job rationalisation engendered feelings of alienation, and where management values stressed cost control.'

Self-assessment question 15.2

Under the headings 'Building a successful team', 'Motivating a successful team' and 'Managing a successful team', list the important points to consider.

Feedback on page 187

15.3 Managing poor team performance

Learning activity 15.3

List eight reasons why team performance could be poor.

Feedback on page 188

Greenberg and Baron (2003) state that 'teams are no places for hot shots who want to make their individual marks – rather, teams require "team players"'. They recommend that the 'organisation should reward employees for their team's successes' and that the more often they reward team success, the stronger the team spirit will be. A team member may be reluctant to share their ideas in case someone else gets the credit for them. Larsen (cited in Cook and Goff, 2002) describes these individuals as 'co-dependents' who 'have a tendency to hoard information, seeing it as something to be controlled, rather than shared', viewing it as a valuable commodity in short supply. However, Betts (2000) stresses:

'to achieve effectiveness, it is often argued that some team members who do not conform to rigid group requirements are equally essential. These people may be wayward to some extent. However, they are often enthusiastic and creative, so they have to be tolerated'.

Some teams/groups will contain members who have conflicting interests and are unwilling to cooperate and compromise. Cawthray (1984) refers to such people as 'wreckers' who have a 'high capacity for spontaneous action combined with a disinclination to consult others'.

Betts also suggests that 'management should try to select individuals with the interpersonal skills to be effective team players, provide training to

15

develop teamwork skills and reward individuals for cooperative efforts'. He emphasises that:

> 'once teams are mature and performing effectively, management's job isn't over. Mature teams can become stagnant and complacent. Managers need to support mature teams with advice, guidance, and training if these teams are to continue to improve.'

Self-assessment question 15.3

Explain how poor team performance can be overcome.

Feedback on page 189

Revision question

Now try the revision question for this session on page 249.

Summary

Cook and Goff (2002) explain:

> 'While groups focus on individual performance and goals, teams come together to 1) share information, perspectives and insights; 2) make decisions that help each person do his or her job better; and/or 3) reinforce each other's individual performance standards.'

Katzenbach and Smith (cited in Cook and Goff, 2002) define a team as 'a small number of people with complementary skills who are committed to a common purpose, performance goals, an approach for which they hold themselves mutually accountable'.

Optimum group size is generally regarded as being six members. Larger teams have communication problems, for example where sub-groups are formed members may not feel 'involved'. With small teams of four or less, communication will be easier, but the team is vulnerable whenever a member is absent.

Tuckman (in Brooks, 2003) proposed a model to illustrate team development, with four stages: forming, storming, norming and performing. A fifth stage, adjourning, was added later by Tuckman and Jensen.

Dr R Meredith Belbin emphasises that it is important to build a balanced team of people with complementary skills and traits. He developed a 'Self-perception inventory questionnaire' whereby individual team members could assess themselves against his (team) role 'types'. His nine roles are: chairman, shaper, specialist, monitor/evaluator, plant, company worker, team worker, resource investigator and completer/finisher.

15

Self-managed teams have grown in popularity due to documented increases in organisations' profitability, improvements in productivity, more efficient use of resources, better problem solving and increased innovation. Buchanan (cited in Brooks, 2003) defines self-managed groups as 'work groups allocated an overall task and given discretion over how the work is to be done'.

Self-managed teams make decisions that were once reserved for, or the prerogative of, managers. Moravec (cited in Cook and Goff, 2002) believes 'these teams are a most powerful and proven management strategy that accelerates productivity and quality and enhances human competencies and commitment'.

In relation to team performance, Greenberg and Baron (2003) argue that 'teams are no places for hot shots who want to make their individual marks – rather, teams require "team players"'. They recommend that 'organisations should reward employees for their teams' successes' and that the more often they reward team success, the stronger the team spirit will be.

Suggested further reading

You could read the relevant sections of Belbin (1981), Brooks (2003), Nelson and Quick (1996), Swailes and Swailes (2004), Cook and Goff (2002), Sisaye (2004), Mendibil and Macbryde (2005) and Mullins (2005).

Feedback on learning activities and self-assessment questions

Feedback on learning activity 15.1

- A **team** is a small collection of people with complementary skills who are committed to a common goal and approach for which they all hold themselves mutually accountable. Teams tend to be cohesive, they are tightly knitted together, have strong social interaction and they support each other. Teams work together, collaborate and share information. They integrate their efforts and therefore are capable of achieving synergy.
- Conversely, **groups** emphasise individuality, often working to their own agenda with each member being accountable solely for their own accomplishments. They may bring their individual efforts to the group, but they do not achieve synergy.

As Betts (2000) observed, 'all teams are groups, but not all groups are teams'.

Feedback on self-assessment question 15.1

You should be able to identify the following important points:

1   Interpersonal processes – groups of individuals move through a series of stages (group 'process') before achieving effective performance at the performing stage. Tuckman and Jensen's (1977) model describes

15

the characteristics of each stage – storming, forming, norming and performing.

2   Roles – are a defining feature of a team (refer Belbin), and the role of a leader is much documented. Points of discussion or consideration here are whether the required member roles are being performed given the group's tasks, and whether or not the task and interpersonal aspects of the leadership role are being fulfilled.

3   Norms – discussion about whether or not the norms and rules of behaviour which are agreed on by group members are supportive of – or in conflict with – effective performance. You should make reference here also to whether or not organisational culture can be used to modify team norms and behaviour.

4   Cohesion - team cohesion can engender mutual co-operation, generosity and helping behaviour, thus motivating team members to contribute fully. However, it can also stifle creative thinking as individuals seek to 'fit in' and not 'rock the boat' as it were. Small group size, similar attitudes and physical proximity of workspace have all been found to encourage cohesion. One question that might be worthy of further discussion here is whether or not the level of cohesion aids or impedes a team's effectiveness.

(Source: Huczynski and Buchanan (2004).)

Feedback on learning activity 15.2

Important points to consider include:

- Autonomous workgroups take the onus off management.
- They have been proven to increase profits in organisations.
- They allow employees to decipher which direction they wish to go, rather than being directed by management. This can empower employees and increase job satisfaction.
- They foster close relationships.
- They allow employees to be more creative.
- Autonomous workgroups can brainstorm, generating different ideas (two heads are better than one). They can achieve synergy and increased productivity.
- They can reach decisions quicker than an individual can.
- Absenteeism and labour turnover is reduced.
- There is increased flexibility in working practices.

Feedback on self-assessment question 15.2

Building a successful team

- When composing a team, management should try to select individuals with the interpersonal skills to be effective team players who can be flexible.
- Management should be careful with the size of the team. If the team is too large there may be communication problems, social loafing may be encouraged and it will require more organising. However, small groups can be vulnerable when a team member is absent.

15

- Management should select members who are complementary (they can bring something different to the team and have different perspectives and strengths), who fill Belbin's roles in order to create a balanced team.

Motivating a successful team

- Management should provide training to develop teamwork and other skills.
- Management should facilitate the group by providing adequate resources.
- A reward system should be used that reflects *team* contributions and not individuals. This in turn will bring the group closer (group cohesion) and create a healthy team spirit.
- Management should be available to support teams with advice and guidance but not interfere. As Cook and Goff (2002) stress, 'while it may be difficult for managers to assume a hands-off policy, intervening will destroy the group process, and place the team in the position of relying upon the manager to solve future problems'.

Managing a successful team

- Managers should reinforce desired behaviours through their own actions and by associating them with rewards.
- Management must be equitable.

As Nelson and Quick (1996) suggest:

'the manager is responsible for creating a receptive organisational environment for work groups and teams. This requires that the manager achieve a balance between setting limits (so that individuals and teams do not go too far afield) and removing barriers (so that empowered individuals and self-managed teams can accomplish their work).'

Feedback on learning activity 15.3

A good answer is likely to include the following points:

- Team members have conflicting interests, are unwilling to cooperate and compromise.
- Lack of support from top management.
- Management is reluctant to relinquish control.
- A particular team member is dictatorial and does not permit/dismisses any suggestions made.
- Team members dislike each other and are reluctant to communicate and/or they create conflict within the team.
- Goal/objective is not SMART (specific, measurable, attainable, realistic and time related).
- The team is too big, causing communication problems.
- Team members lack the necessary interpersonal skills, for example leadership skills, and therefore the team does not really make any progress.
- Team members may prefer to work alone as opposed to in a team.

15

- A team member may be reluctant to share their ideas in case someone else gets the credit for them.
- The team/certain members lack interest in their work.
- Pressure from within the group. For example, the other group members may already be familiar with one another, but you may not be. Thus, you may feel pressurised.

Feedback on self-assessment question 15.3

To begin with a manager needs to know and understand each individual who belongs to the team. It is suggested that to overcome poor performance it is necessary to:

- Provide training in team skills.
- Reward good team performance where necessary in order to build 'team spirit'.
- Provide managerial support and guidance as well as promote employee support.

Managers should review the objectives set for the team and ensure all team members understand and agree with them.

15

15

Study session 16
Drivers of change

Introduction

'Innovation – the successful exploitation of new ideas is essential for sustained competitiveness and wealth creation. A country aiming to keep ahead of its competitors needs companies which innovate. Successful innovation requires good management, appropriate finance, skills and a supportive overall climate.'

UK Government White Paper on Competitiveness (cited in King and Anderson, 1995)

Session learning objectives

After completing this session you should be able to:

16.1 Analyse the causes (or drivers) of organisational change.
16.2 Describe the managerial skills required for successful change.

Unit content coverage

This study session covers the following topic from the official CIPS unit content document:

Learning outcome

Propose processes and systems to enable the successful implementation of change programmes to maximise purchasing efficiency and effectiveness.

Learning objective

5.1 Evaluate the causes of organisational change.

16

Prior knowledge

Study sessions 1, 2, 6 and 8.

Timing

You should set aside about 4 hours to read and complete this session, including learning activities, self-assessment questions, the suggested further reading (if any) and the revision question.

16.1 Drivers of change

Learning activity 16.1

Drivers of change can be described as the forces, pressures or triggers that cause change. For example, new legislation and government policies/intervention force companies to change their existing procedures. List five other drivers of change.

Feedback on page 198

The competitive market (that is, the social, political, economic and technical environmental factors) strongly influences the way organisations operate today. Drivers for change include:

- advances in technology;
- globalisation;
- Japanisation;
- changing consumer tastes; and
- legislation and government policies.

Changing labour demographics, the composition of the workforce, changing domestic and global economic trading conditions and dynamic competition also instigate change.

As Waterfield (cited in Osborne and Brown, 2005) posits: 'financial cutbacks, restructuring on a global scale, increasing technological advances and changing labour demographics and higher expectations of services on the part of citizens have fuelled the agenda for change'. O'Neil (cited in Osborne and Brown, 2005) believes that 'Demographic changes wrought by the increasing proportion of older workers, greater longevity and increased cultural diversity also drove change'.

De-industrialisation

In the UK during the 1960s an important trend developed where the focus on agriculture and manufacturing shifted to a more service-based economy. Buchanan (2004) comments:

> 'Whole industries collapsed and almost disappeared (coal mining, steel making) in the twentieth century whilst others blossomed (computer software, mobile telephony). Many of the technologies that shape the nature of medicine, communications and home entertainment, for example, were not available five years ago. These technologies potentially affect the design of jobs, the experience of work, the progress of individual careers and organisation structures.'

'Japanisation'

The Japanese are renowned for their employee participation practices, especially large corporations such as Toyota and Nissan. Research into Japanese organisations has been carried out in order to find out the secrets of their economic success, and their teamworking techniques were found to be a contributory factor.

16

The Japanese style operates using quality circles and teamwork when problem solving, which encourages employees to become involved and is meant to empower employees. The system seeks to make every worker a quality inspector, to be responsible for continuous change and improvement. However, even though everyone may be included in decision making, the ultimate decision is made by management and all employees do not receive the same remuneration.

The Japanese attitude towards staff is that employees are seen as a resource which must be cherished and made best use of. It sees the employee as an actual and potential return on investment, which ultimately strengthens the company.

In recent years the move to ever-increasing globalisation has driven economies, governments and organisations to constantly make changes in order for countries and industries to compete successfully. This shift towards a more integrated and interdependent world economy has had two main components:

1   *The globalisation of markets*, that is, the merging of distinctly separate national markets into a global marketplace; tastes and preferences converging onto a global norm and firms offering standardised products worldwide thus creating a world market. Significant differences still exist between national markets on many relevant dimensions, and these differences require that marketing and operating strategies and product features be customised to best match conditions in a particular country, because:
    (a) countries are different;
    (b) the range of problems is wider and more complex;
    (c) government intervention in trade and investment creates problems;
    (d) international investment is impacted by different currencies.
2   *The globalisation of production*, which refers to sourcing of goods and services from locations around the world to take advantage of differences in the cost or quality of the factors of production (that is, labour, land and capital).

Further, globalisation has created the need for institutions to help manage, regulate and police the global marketplace, for example:

- The General Agreement on Tariffs and Trade (GATT);
- The World Trade Organization (WTO);
- The International Monetary Fund (IMF);
- The World Bank;
- The United Nations.

Global drivers

There are a number of (macro) factors that underlie the trend towards greater globalisation such as:

- a reduction in trade barriers and removal of restrictions to foreign direct investment;
- technological change – increased use of microprocessors and telecommunications, the internet and world wide web etc.;

16

- improved transportation technology resulting in a 'shrinking' globe;
- changing demographics of the world economy in terms of world output and world trade;
- changing foreign direct investment patterns: the changing nature of multinationals, the increase of 'mini' multinationals, more non-US multinationals and the national origin of largest multinational corporations.

Globalisation debate – pro

- Lower prices for goods and services.
- Economic growth stimulation.
- Increase in consumer income.
- Creation of jobs.
- Countries specialise in production of goods and services that are produced most efficiently.
- Environmental performance and income.

Globalisation debate – con

- Destroys manufacturing jobs in wealthy, advanced countries.
- Wage rates of unskilled workers in advanced countries decline.
- Companies move to countries with fewer labour and environment regulations.
- Loss of sovereignty.

Self-assessment question 16.1

Using your own organisation as the basis for your answer, briefly describe the factors that are driving change in your industry.

Feedback on page 198

16.2 Managerial skills for successful change

Learning activity 16.2

Managing change requires much more skill than just the ability to plan, organise, direct and control. Draw up a list of skills that you think a manager should possess for successful change.

Feedback on page 199

As we discussed in study session 1 in relation to management roles, managers need leadership skills, just as leaders need management skills. In the context of change it could be argued that all managers will need to be able to exercise proactive leadership skills. As Adair (1984) points out:

'Good management is both art and science: it involves analysis and emotion. People respond to other people, not just to arguments in favour of a proposal; this is why leadership is important. Managers in times of change need to be leaders as well as good managers: indeed, if they are good leaders others will forgive their failings and seek to compensate for them. A Leader is someone who believes in what he or she is trying to accomplish and is able to get others to believe it too. Managers have subordinates: leaders have followers because people believe in them, trust them and admire them. The chief executive has a key leadership role to play in major restructuring and cultural changes. Other managers also have to be able to lead their staff if the changes are to succeed.'

In order to be effective change *agents*, managers must have a sound understanding of their business, understand and genuinely believe in the need for change, and understand the tools and techniques for implementing the proposed changes. With regard to organisational change, Kirkpatrick and Locke's (cited in Senior, 2002) 'identification of drive, leadership, motivation, honesty and integrity, self-confidence, cognitive ability and knowledge of the business' seem most relevant. Buchanan and Huczynski (2004) observed that 'the effective change agent seems to be someone with a broad and well-developed range of skills and qualities'. Kanter (cited in Buchanan and Huczynski 2004) identifies seven change-agency skills. They include:

- the ability to work independently;
- to collaborate effectively;
- the ability to develop high-trust relationships, based on high moral and ethical standards;
- self-confidence, tempered with humility;
- respect for the process of change;
- ability to work across business functions and units, 'multifaceted and ambidextrous';
- the willingness to stake reward on results and gain satisfaction from success.

Balogun and Hope Hailey (2004) recognise that for successful change, managers must possess a combination of:

- analytical skills (the ability to understand employees' motives and the culture of the organisation);
- judgemental skills (to monitor and assess the change process and take corrective action where necessary);
- implementation skills (the ability to put plans into action.)

For successful change, managers must be able to create a vision and exhibit sound *interpersonal skills* in order to communicate this effectively to their employees, in particular, the underlying reasons for the change. Additionally, they must have the ability to *influence, persuade* and thus '*sell*' the benefits associated with any change in order to gain the workforce's full commitment to the project.

Managers must be able to relinquish control and *delegate responsibility* in order for the change initiative to be sustained. They should encourage others to participate so that employees feel a real sense of involvement and responsibility.

16

It is also important that managers are sensitive and receptive to employee's needs and concerns. As Balogun and Hope Hailey (2004) emphasise, 'People need help to cope with the stress, anxiety and uncertainties of change'. They maintain that 'Managers need coaching and counselling skills to help members of their team cope with change'. Furthermore, Kirkpatrick and Locke (cited in Senior, 2002) perceive the ability to *empathise and sympathise* with employees as 'one of the key skills for managing change'.

It is imperative that managers have the ability to understand what motivates their staff and take action accordingly. Without this, their intentions will *remain* as plans. Balogun and Hope Hailey (2004) believe that:

> 'It can be necessary to inject some energy, emotion and direction into the process. Otherwise, an awareness of the need for change may be developed, but this awareness will not translate into a commitment to doing something about it, especially if there is no onus on senior managers to take note of ideas that arise and act on them.'

McCaskey (cited in Randall, 1992) deems charisma (the ability to stir enthusiasm, confidence and commitment in others) as an important skill for the change agent to possess. Although, implicit in this assumption is that managers must have a personal enthusiasm to begin with if they are to stir it within others.

Managers must be approachable and personable, so employees can ask questions or seek advice without feeling awkward. They must possess the necessary *negotiation skills* in order to resolve issues and conflict that may occur. As Balogun and Hope Hailey (2004) stress, they 'need well-honed political skills to help them manage the power relations in any change situation'.

Buchanan and Boddy (cited in Randall, 1992) briefly mention the 'helicopter perspective', and it is assumed that they are referring to the ability to take a step back and look at the bigger picture. Adopting a more holistic view can be useful for managers as they tend to become preoccupied/too involved with trivialities.

McCaskey (cited in Randall, 1992) talks about the 'humour that oils' as in laughter to ease the tension and raise morale. Although this may be helpful during a transitional period, it is doubtful that this can be considered as a skill. Above all, managers must remain a stable figure throughout the transformation process, even when things are not going according to plan, for they should act as a role model for the employees to follow.

Self-assessment question 16.2

Which in your opinion are most important when managing change: process or technical skills? Give reasons to support your answer.

Feedback on page 199

Revision question

Now try the revision question for this session on page 249.

Summary

- Drivers for change include:
    - advances in technology;
    - globalisation;
    - Japanisation;
    - changing consumer tastes; and
    - legislation and government policies.
- The 'globalising' shift towards a more integrated and interdependent world economy has had two main components:
    - the globalisation of markets (the merging of distinctly separate national markets into a global marketplace); and
    - the globalisation of production (sourcing goods and services from locations around the world to take advantage of differences in the cost or quality of the factors of production).
- Further, globalisation has created the need for institutions to help manage, regulate and police the global marketplace (for example GATT, WTO, IMF, The World Bank and the United Nations).
- There are a number of (macro) factors that underlie the trend towards greater globalisation such as:
    - reduction in trade barriers;
    - removal of restrictions to foreign direct investment;
    - technological change;
    - improved transportation technology;
    - changing levels of world output and world trade; and
    - changing foreign direct investment patterns.
- Arguments FOR globalisation include the following:
    - lower prices for goods and services;
    - economic growth stimulation;
    - increase in consumer income;
    - creation of jobs;
    - countries specialise in production of goods and services that are produced most efficiently;
    - environmental performance; and
    - income
- Arguments AGAINST globalisation include:
    - it destroys manufacturing jobs in wealthy, advanced countries;
    - wage rates of unskilled workers in advanced countries decline;
    - companies move to countries with fewer labour and environment regulations;
    - loss of sovereignty.
- In order to be effective change *agents*, managers must have a sound understanding of their business, believe in the need for change, and understand the tools and techniques for implementing proposed changes.
- Kanter (2004) identifies seven change agency skills including:
    - the ability to work independently;
    - the ability to collaborate effectively;

16

- the ability to develop high-trust relationships;
- self confidence;
- respect for the process of change;
- ability to work across business functions and units; and
- willingness to stake reward on results and gain satisfaction from success.
- For successful change, managers must possess a combination of analytical skills, judgemental skills and implementation skills.

Suggested further reading

You could read the relevant sections of Osborne and Brown (2005) and Strachan (1996).

Feedback on learning activities and self-assessment questions

Feedback on learning activity 16.1

Choose any five points from the following:

- competition/globalisation;
- advances in technology;
- changes in consumer tastes;
- changing labour demographics;
- cultural diversity;
- shift in economy; for example, in the UK there was an emphasis on agriculture and manufacturing which shifted to a more service-based economy;
- Japanisation;
- trading conditions;
- availability of resources.

Feedback on self-assessment question 16.1

Your answer here is likely to be quite subjective, but some of the generic driving factors for change in most industry situations will relate directly to:

- national culture and political/government influence or intervention;
- the buoyancy (or otherwise) of the economy;
- socio-cultural factors relating to supply and demand and markets/customers;
- the pace of change of technology generally and industry specifically.
- the degree of internationalisation or globalisation in the industry;
- the degree of competition from existing and emerging markets and economies;
- the degree of specialisation that exists in the particular industry;
- patterns of both inward and outward Foreign Direct Investment (FDI);
- patterns of trade and the existence or otherwise of emerging tariff and non-tariff barriers (in some command economies for example);
- the degree of backward/forward integration that exists in the industry – which strengthens the competitive position of the larger or main players or competitors.

16

Feedback on learning activity 16.2

Important points to consider include:

- interpersonal skills – to communicate the need for change;
- persuasive/influencing skills – to communicate the benefits of the changes;
- being able to delegate responsibility – a manager cannot achieve results alone;
- coaching and counselling skills – to help employees cope with change;
- the ability to motivate staff – so plans turn into action;
- negotiation skills – to resolve any problems or conflict;
- the ability to remain stable throughout the transitional period.

Feedback on self-assessment question 16.2

Whilst both sets of skills are needed, it could be argued that process skills are more important than technical skills when managing change. Much depends on the nature and the circumstances relating to both the organisation and the change itself.

Whereas process skills refer to 'people skills' such as interpersonal skills, managing politics and motivating employees, technical skills relate more to 'control techniques' such as planning, organising and resourcing of the organisation. This is not to say that technical skills are not important, but managing change involves more than conventional project management. Here, you may wish to refer to the differences between leaders and managers as discussed in study session 1. Technical skills relate more to managers, whereas process skills relate more to the leadership and behavioural aspects of managing human resources.

Whilst technical skills are integral to the manager's role, it is the process skills that enable these plans to be put into action.

16

16

Planning change

Introduction

Many authors on the subject of change now agree that organisations are changing at an unprecedented rate. The frequency and magnitude of change depends upon the preferences of the organisation and the context, for example the competitive environment in which it operates. In the change literature, there are two dominant approaches to planning change. Generally, change is regarded as either evolutionary (gradually evolving out of the current state or situation) or revolutionary (a radical departure from the past). That is, it is either *continuous* or *transformational*. This session explores both of these approaches in detail.

'Firms which don't recognise the need for change, simply disappear – whilst those who recognise that "we must change" can use this to build new and growing businesses.'
Brown et al (2000)

Session learning objectives

After completing this session you should be able to:

17.1 Distinguish between the need for fundamental and incremental change in organisations.

Unit content coverage

This study session covers the following topic from the official CIPS unit content document:

Learning outcome

Propose processes and systems to enable the successful implementation of change programmes to maximise purchasing efficiency and effectiveness.

Learning objective

5.2 Differentiate between the need for fundamental and incremental change in organisations.

Prior knowledge

Study session 16.

Timing

You should set aside about 5 hours to read and complete this session, including learning activities, self-assessment questions, the suggested further reading (if any) and the revision question.

17.1 Perspectives on change

Evolutionary (continuous) change

The evolutionary (or *incremental*) approach to planning change is where strategy evolves through an accumulation of relatively small changes over time. It proposes that one problem should be dealt with at a time. Japanese companies in particular are renowned for their success using this approach. Dunphy and Stace (cited in Burnes, 2004) prefer this approach and oppose rapid transformations (*punctuated equilibrium*) believing them to be 'brutal'. They argue that the evolutionary or incremental perspective is useful in preventing stagnation by gently fine-tuning the organisation, in small step (incremental) changes, over time. (See figure 17.1.)

De Wit and Meyer (2004) define **evolutionary change** to be:

> 'the process whereby a constant stream of moderate changes gradually accumulates over a longer period of time. Each change in itself is small, but the cumulative result can be large. Evolutionary change processes take the current firm as a starting point, constantly modifying aspects through extension and adaptation. Some "mutations" to the firm prove valuable and are retained, while other changes are discarded as dysfunctional. Thus a new business system and/or organisational system can steadily evolve out of the old, as if the organisation were shedding its old skin to grow a new one (e.g. Aldrich, 1999; Kagono et al, 1985).'

More simplistically, Johnson and Scholes (1999) suggest that evolutionary change is 'transformational change implemented gradually through different stages and interrelated activities' (implying that collectively the small changes that take place can result in a substantial change overall). They maintain that evolution 'is likely to be planned, proactive transformation, in which change is undertaken by managers in response to anticipation of the need for future change'. Brown et al (2000) also make the point that:

> 'changes do not always have to be great leaps forward or involve radical new ideas. Most of the time, change is more gradual, moving incrementally forward with a sequence of little, cumulative improvements … In recent times the dramatic growth and success of the Japanese car manufacturing industry is primarily the result of a forty-year programme of systematic and continuous improvement of product and process design.'

When it is necessary for organisations to develop new skills, the evolutionary approach to planning change is most appropriate. This is because in-depth knowledge cannot be acquired quickly. It is a slow process where repetition and reinforcement is necessary. As De Wit and Meyer (2004) stipulate, 'when groups of people in a firm need to develop new routines, new competencies, new processes as well as new ways of understanding the world, time is needed to experiment, reflect, discuss, test and internalise'. Moreover, the combination of knowledge and skills that employees acquire or already possess are unique. For this very reason, Greasley (1999) is of the belief that evolutionary change can deliver improvements that are difficult for competitors to imitate.

17

Evolutionary change is therefore based on the organisation using permanent learning and constant upgrading to achieve cumulative improvements (that is, making small incremental changes that take place slowly but continuously). This approach to change is far more proactive than reactive in nature; the organisation is constantly scanning its external environment and making changes as and when required. Furthermore, it is much more likely to involve employees at all levels and stages of the change process.

Revolutionary (transformational) change

The revolutionary (or *punctuated equilibrium*) approach to planning change, according to Romanelli and Tushman (cited in Burnes, 2004) depicts organisations as:

> 'evolving through relatively long periods of stability (equilibrium periods) in their basic patterns of activity that are punctuated by relatively short bursts of fundamental change (revolutionary periods). Revolutionary periods substantively disrupt established patterns and install the basis of new equilibrium periods.'

In contrast to their definition of evolutionary change, De Wit and Meyer (2004) define **revolutionary change** as:

> 'a process whereby an abrupt and radical change takes place within a short period of time. Revolutionary change processes are those that do not build on the status quo, but overthrow it. "Revolutionaries" revolt against the existing business system and organisational system, and attempt to push through changes that will reinvent the firm. This revolution leads to a clear break with the past – a discontinuity in the firm's development path [as change cannot be handled with the existing paradigm]'.

Johnson and Scholes (1999) argue that revolutionary change is:

> 'fundamental transformational change that occurs by simultaneous initiatives in many forms, and often in a relatively short space of time. It is more likely to be a forced, reactive transformation, due to the changing competitive conditions the organisation is facing'.

Revolutionary (or transformational) change is particularly suitable for companies that are stuck in a rut and have become rigid, complacent and stagnant and therefore are in need of a new (strategic) direction. For example, employees can become set in their ways and narrow minded. They become conditioned to particular ways of doing things and opt to maintain the status quo rather than work to improve existing processes and develop new ways of doing things for the organisation. This closed mind-set stifles creativity and innovation and prevents the company from moving forward and progressing. For some organisations it is therefore necessary to suddenly shock and shake up the organisation to break away from these cultural norms and ingrained behaviours so that the company can make improvements. Thus, when an organisation is in crisis, under-performing and under serious threat by its competition, the only option remaining is revolutionary (or transformational) change to bring it back in line with its objectives. (See figure 17.1.)

17

203

Figure 17.1: Revolutionary and evolutionary change

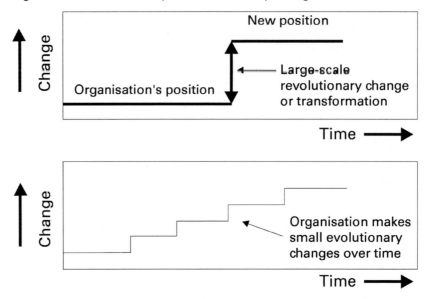

Furthermore, by adopting a revolutionary approach to change, an organisation can be proactive and innovative, that is, it can be the first company to bring a new product or service to the market. For example, a previous chairman of Nestlé prescribed that for successful change and growth it is important to 'be first, be daring and be different' (Carnall, 2003).

Revolutionary change can help the organisation shift from a stable and predictable way of operating to one which is more creative, flexible and unconventional approach. It helps organisations to challenge existing and well-established working practices. Brown et al (2000) distinguishes between successful, flexible firms and those that have not survived: 'New firms moved into the new technology and exploited the new opportunities emerging; older firms often failed to see the change coming or to respond quickly enough'. Furthermore, Markrides (cited in Carnall, 2003) is clear about how distinctive strategic positions are identified: 'it's about breaking out of the existing mental model, about creating a questioning culture, organising diverse inputs to the strategic planning process, and it requires experimentation and learning'.

Fiercely competitive, dynamic industries such as the retail sector and technology-based organisations are constantly having to look for ways to reinvent themselves. Brown and Eisenhardt (cited in Burnes, 2004) state that: 'for firms such as Intel, Wal-Mart, Hewlett-Packard and Gillette, the ability to change rapidly and continuously, especially by developing new products, is not only a core competence, it is also at the heart of their cultures'. They maintain that 'in high-velocity industries with short product lifecycles and rapidly shifting competitive landscapes, the ability to engage in rapid and relentless continuous change is a crucial capability for survival'.

Whilst a lot can be gained from revolutionary change in a relatively short space of time, it does require heavy investment and is associated with a high failure rate. Some academics also feel that revolutionary change places *too much* emphasis on planning. For example, Clarke (in Carnall, 2003) is of

17

the opinion that organisations which operate in uncertain and complex environments, where knowledge is at a premium, cannot be managed alone by planning, command and control. Clarke favours the Japanese approach where 'simultaneous, cheap explorations of multiple options evolve via a "bottom-up" approach rather that being imposed "top-down" via some grand strategy'.

In summary, according to Brown et al (2000):

> 'At one end of the spectrum we have tiny, incremental changes which take place every day and which represent minor improvements – doing what we've always done a little bit better. But at the other end of the spectrum we have innovations which are major changes, often representing significant shifts in what we offer or how we create that. At the limit there is discontinuous change where innovation involves a jump to something completely different and rewrites the rules of the game.'

Thus, it would appear that the evolutionary and revolutionary approaches to managing change are at opposite ends of a spectrum, that they are mutually exclusive. However, Duncan (cited in De Wit, 2004) emphasises that 'some authors suggest that organisations should be "ambidextrous", using both revolution and evolution, contingent upon internal and external conditions'. This may in turn counteract and overcome the limitations that each approach possesses.

Learning activity 17.1

Fill in the missing spaces.

Table 17.1

Evolutionary	Revolutionary
...	Also called fundamental, ground/frame breaking and disruptive change
Tends to be a proactive approach	...
Builds on the status quo	...
...	Occurs over a relatively short space of time
Is bottom-up	...
...	Requires heavy investment and carries a high element of risk
...	Relates to business process re-engineering (BPR)
...	Can offer a vast improvement
...	Is particularly suitable for realigning processes throughout the organisation that would remove non-value adding activities and speed up process times. For example, implementing a new IT system requires a radical approach. It must be implemented throughout the organisation for it to be effective

Feedback on page 207

17

Now answer the self-assessment question.

Self-assessment question 17.1

Discuss the importance of organisations needing to balance the need for continuous change against the need to conserve their core values.

Feedback on page 207

Revision question

Now try the revision question for this session on page 249.

Summary

Evolutionary change

The evolutionary approach to change (also called continuous or incremental change) is a strategy that builds upon the current state of the organisation, making continuous minor changes which, collectively, can produce a major change in the long run.

Benefits of evolutionary change include the following:

- It introduces change gently, therefore it tends to be more readily accepted.
- It is bottom up. It encourages empowerment and ownership.
- It is necessary for learning to occur.
- It is cost effective.

Criticisms include:

- Significant changes take a long time to be visible.

Revolutionary change

The revolutionary approach to change (also called frame/ground breaking, transformational, punctuated equilibrium, disruptive, transformational fundamental change, big bang/clean sheet approach) is a strategy which starts from scratch, ignoring the current state of the organisation and any rules in the industry that may exist. It is an approach where a major, sudden change occurs, followed by a period of stability (no change).

Benefits of revolutionary change include the following:

- It can produce a vast turnaround for the organisation.
- It provides for new innovation and development.

Criticisms are:

- It can be considered brutal as in 'too much change all at once'.

17

- It is management lead – imposed by management.
- The success rate is low and it requires heavy investment

Suggested further reading

You could read the relevant sections of Brown, Lamming, Bessent and Jones (2000), Carnall (2003) and De Wit and Meyer (2004).

Feedback on learning activities and self-assessment questions

Feedback on learning activity 17.1

Table 17.2

Evolutionary	Revolutionary
Also called continuous, incremental change	Also called fundamental, ground/frame breaking and disruptive change
Tends to be a proactive approach	Tends to be a reactive approach
Builds on the status quo	Overthrows the status quo, starts with a clean sheet and innovates
Occurs over a long period of time	Occurs over a relatively short space of time
Is bottom-up	Is top-down (management lead)
Is slow to produce a considerable change	Requires heavy investment and carries a high element of risk
Relates to Kaizen and total quality management (TQM) philosophy	Relates to business process re-engineering (BPR)
Improvements are small but over a long period can amount to a considerable change	Can offer a vast improvement
Allows the company to build and develop its core competencies, knowledge and expertise. In other words, continuous improvement is suitable for learning. For example, if the company decides it needs to alter its culture, this must be learnt, which is a gradual process	Is particularly suitable for realigning processes throughout the organisation that would remove non-value adding activities and speed up process times. For example, implementing a new IT system requires a radical approach. It must be implemented throughout the organisation for it to be effective

Feedback on self-assessment question 17.1

This question is basically addressing the paradox of the importance of staying competitive versus retaining the skills and capabilities of the company. What should dominate: a company's strengths or a company's opportunities? This relates to the 'outside in' and 'inside out' perspectives proposed by De Wit and Meyer (2004). The 'outside in' perspective refers to taking advantage of the external environment, that is, attractive market opportunities where the company adapts its resources accordingly.

17

Advocates of this perspective believe that successful companies are market driven and that companies should be prompted by their competitors and customers.

The 'inside out' perspective concentrates on its core competencies. 'Successful companies, it is argued, build up a strong resource base over an extended period of time, which offers them access to unfolding market opportunities in the short and medium term' (De Wit and Meyer, 2004). Proponents of this perspective believe strategies should be formulated around the organisation's capabilities, not solely based upon attractive opportunities in the marketplace. One particular advantage of this approach is that core competencies are difficult to imitate unlike physical processes.

Prahalad and Hamel (cited in De Wit and Meyer, 2004) stipulate that 'companies that judge competitiveness, their own and their competitors', are primarily in terms of the price/performance of end products courting the erosion of core competencies'. They illustrate this point with the company General Electric (GE). GE felt that the television industry was mature and that competition was too strong. As a result, GE retired from the television industry. Unfortunately, this is where GE's strengths lay.

Whilst companies must change with the times, it is also critical for companies to conserve their strengths (that is, use their knowledge and the expertise gained over the years to their advantage). In the case of GE, the company based its change of direction on its assessment of its competitive environment. However, its core competencies were vested in the television industry and as a result they chose the wrong option. Companies can also do what they do best, but not offer what the market wants! Therefore, they must achieve a balance between the two extremes.

Consider the example of a company whose real competence was in the design and production of themed screens for pinball game machines. With market demand dwindling because of the advent of electronic hand-held game consoles, the company was facing bankruptcy. With the help of an external consultant, the company realised that its competencies lay not in production of the machines but in the design. As a result, they stopped manufacturing games machines and focused on the design and development of electronic games. This change in strategy proved to be successful.

17

Study session 18
Managing the change process

'Managers cannot control all change, nor prevent it from occurring. They can however, influence its outcome.'
Blockley (2006)

Introduction

In an ideal world, a manager could assess the environment for changes and then collaborate with their employees to develop appropriate strategies in response. They would have time to prepare and adapt accordingly. However, this is rarely the case. Change is often thrust upon an organisation and it can neither control nor predict it. On top of this, managers have the tricky task of gaining their employee's commitment to these changes. Managers cannot control all change or prevent it from occurring, but they can influence its outcome. As Benjamin and Mabey (cited in Burnes, 2004) point out, 'while the primary stimulus for change remains those forces in the external environment, the primary motivator for how change is accomplished resides within the organisation'.

Session learning objectives

After completing this session you should be able to:

18.1 Describe the importance of the successful management of change.
18.2 Formulate plans to overcome human resistance to change and to implement change successfully within the purchasing and supply function.

Unit content coverage

This study session covers the following topic from the official CIPS unit content document:

Learning outcome

Propose processes and systems to enable the successful implementation of change programmes.

Learning objective

5.3 Formulate plans to overcome human resistance to change and to implement change successfully within the purchasing and supply function.

18

Prior knowledge

Study sessions 16 and 17.

Timing

You should set aside about 5 hours to read and complete this session, including learning activities, self-assessment questions, the suggested further reading (if any) and the revision question.

18.1 Change – planned or emergent?

The **planned** approach to managing change was first coined by Kurt Lewin in 1947. It involves consciously taking steps to form a strategy for implementing change using a systematic, goal-orientated approach. Lewin researched managing change extensively and presents a three-step model for successful change. 'Lewin believed that the stability of human behaviour was based on a quasi-stationary equilibrium supported by a complex field of driving and restraining forces' (cited in Burnes, 2004). The first step of the model is to unfreeze the current behaviour in order to leave people open to change and new ideas. Step two involves learning the new values, and the final stage is refreezing to represent consolidating the new values and habits to ensure that there is no regression.

The **emergent** approach is where change is allowed to evolve naturally, it can be unpredictable and it is an ongoing process. The emergent approach is particularly relevant in today's organisations as it takes into consideration the uncertain nature of the external environment such as competition. Quinn (cited in Thornhill et al, 2000) is of the opinion that developing organisational strategy in such a manner generates employee effort and commitment, although Carnall (2003) favours the planned approach believing that it is impossible to be innovative by 'random mutation, as-it-were'.

According to Garvin (in Bamford and Forrester, 2003), one criticism of planned change is that 'change cannot occur from one stable state to another with the turbulent business environment that exists today'. Dawson and Kanter et al (cited in Hayes, 2002) support Garvin, stressing that 'organisations need to be fluid and adaptable and that the last thing they need is to be frozen into some given way of functioning'. However, Lewin feels that a sense of permanency is needed and is an important goal, even if it is momentary just to take stock before moving on again.

Mabey and White (1993) argue that:

> 'Managers become fixated on the future state and assume all that is needed is to design the most effective organisational arrangements for the future. They think of change from A to B as simply a mechanical or procedural detail.'

Planned change, therefore, has a major flaw in that it ignores the current state of the organisation. During the process of an organisational change such as an acquisition, circumstances may alter and therefore the planning may be rendered useless. Long-term planning can be useful in terms of predicting trends/markets using historical data. However, the plan must be lenient enough to allow for alterations.

The planned approach to change is management led (top down). Wilson (cited in Burnes, 2004) warns that 'this approach is too heavily reliant on the role of managers and assumes that they have a full understanding of the consequences of their actions in advance and that their plans will be understood, accepted and implemented'. This is an unrealistic assumption to make and ignores the possibility of resistance and organisational conflict and politics.

It is indeed possible to adopt both emergent and planned strategies simultaneously. For example, the manager may decide that a specific change must take place, but gives employees the autonomy to decipher how they achieve the desired outcome.

Learning activity 18.1

Complete the table.

Table 18.1

The emergent approach to change	The planned approach to change
...	Involves consciously taking steps to form a strategy for implementing change using a systematic, goal-orientated approach
Is up to date (current)	...
...	Is described as 'frozen'
Is bottom up	...
...	Prepares for the forthcoming period
Is particularly relevant in today's organisations as it takes into consideration the uncertain nature of the external environment such as competition	...

Feedback on page 217

Having completed this learning activity, now answer self-assessment question 18.1 below.

Self-assessment question 18.1

Over the past ten years, a major bank has witnessed significant variations in their level of profit. Under the management of Peter Murray, the bank was the largest and the most profitable one in the country. However, it was a different story when successor Will Sorrel took over the operations. Consequently, Murray was rehired to restore the bank to health, despite the fact that the bank's problems were partly due to Murray's initial tenure. Murray made some radical changes. They included making over 40,000 employees redundant and sacking managers who were not performing.

(continued on next page)

18

Self-assessment question 18.1 *(continued)*

Having read the passage, answer the following questions:

- What is management's approach to change?
- Murray made some drastic changes. Do you think his approach is advisable in the long run? Justify your answer.

Feedback on page 217

18.2 Managing change

Change in organisations is inevitable as businesses strive to stay abreast of their competition. As organisations make changes they are likely to encounter different reactions from their employees. Depending on the type and magnitude of the change, employees are likely to react either positively or negatively. For some, change may be welcomed on the basis that they can see long-term benefits for themselves and the organisation; hence it is seen as an opportunity to experience something new and exciting. Others will perceive change as problematic, as a means of getting rid of what is familiar and replacing it with the unknown and uncertain, hence causing fear and resistance.

Learning activity 18.2

Change is often associated with uncertainty and risk. List five further reasons why employees are resistant to change.

Feedback on page 218

Mullins (2004) makes the point that:

> 'Fears may be expressed over such matters as employment levels and job security, deskilling of work, loss of job satisfaction, wage rate differentials, changes to social structures and working conditions, loss of individual control over work, and greater management control'.

Burnes (2004) stresses that 'one of the major mistakes companies can make when introducing change is to fail to recognise, and deal with, the real and legitimate fears of the managers and staff'.

Mabey and White (1993) shed light on why employees are resistant to change in an organisation. The first point they discuss is the need for stability and security, and they are of the opinion that 'change presents unknowns which cause anxiety'. For example, change can result in employees having less control over their work and their ways of operating can be disrupted. Another reason why resistance is experienced is that employees may not perceive the need for change; they may genuinely believe that their current methods of working are more effective than any other alternative.

According to Carnall (2003), 'Much of what we refer to as resistance to change is really resistance to uncertainty'. Change threatens to move us out

18

of our comfort zone, away from what is familiar and common practice to us. However, Burnes (2004) argues that change is inevitable and is undertaken to 'safeguard rather than threaten' an employee's future.

Change for change's sake?

Many organisations now face turbulent external conditions and therefore they are compelled to continuously improve their performance. Consequently, in some organisations, employees can be subject to too much change. Buchanan and Huczynski (2004) refers to this as '"initiative fatigue", where employees become tired of change, and thus lose enthusiasm and commitment to further change'. Thus, repeat change can be considered as damaging. Abrahamson (cited in Buchanan and Huczynski, 2004) stresses that 'organisations should stop changing all the time, because this generates cynicism (that is, change for change's sake) and burnout.'

Abrahamson's views are consistent with Morgan (2001) who favours an **evolutionary** approach to change, as opposed to a **revolutionary** one. As Buchanan (2003) contends, 'His [Morgan's] solution is to reduce the number of change initiatives, abandon the preoccupation with large-scale transformation, and focus on incremental improvements instead'. Indeed, Carnall (2003) believes that 'if major changes come suddenly and dramatically, then paralysis can often result'.

The Kubler-Ross coping cycle

Dr Elizabeth Kubler-Ross (cited in Buchanan and Huczynski, 2004) extensively researched the emotional states of the terminally ill. She observed that 'we deal with loss by moving through a series of stages, each characterised by a particular emotional response' which she refers to as 'the coping cycle' (see figure 18.1). More recently, it was noticed that these responses are not exclusive to the terminally ill but are typical to those reacting negatively to a change in circumstances.

Figure 18.1: The coping cycle

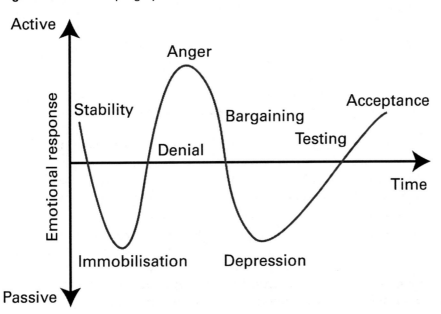

18

213

The various emotional responses relating to each of the stages in this model are:

- The denial stage: reluctance to confront reality, that is, there is still a chance things will return to normal.
- The anger stage: frustrated feelings especially towards scapegoats. Why me reaction.
- The bargaining stage: exert effort to negotiate and to mitigate loss.
- The depression stage: final realisation of what is happening. 'There's nothing that can be done, I'm stuck like this'.
- The testing stage: seeks solutions.
- The acceptance stage: comes to terms with situation and moves forward.

Kubler-Ross's 'coping cycle' is used nowadays to gauge reactions to radical organisational change (revolutionary change). It is applied as a diagnostic tool to detect where in the response cycle an employee may be, to enable management to offer appropriate guidance and support.

Guidelines to managing change

It is essential that management have clearly defined objectives for any transitional period. Any proposed change(s) and how they are to be implemented should be clearly explained. Employees will tend to be defensive and resist change if they do not understand the reasoning behind the change. As an old Chinese proverb says: 'Tell me and I will forget; show me and I may remember; involve me and I will understand'. Thornhill et al (2000) state 'the greater level of understanding and involvement may also, perhaps, be associated with the generation of increased levels of commitments to the goals of the organisation'.

Communication and information sharing using appraisals and team meetings should be used to emphasise benefits to employees and also prevent information from being misinterpreted by use of the grapevine. However, De Wit and Meyer (2004) stipulate that not everyone will benefit from the changes proposed. In such situations, Burnes (2004) comments, 'it is often the case that those who fear they will lose out will vociferously oppose any change, whilst those who believe they will gain from the change will keep quiet for fear of antagonising the losers'. Therefore, management need to be careful when highlighting the benefits.

One of the sources of conflict and resistance within an organisation undergoing change is the balance of power. For example, Salancik (cited in Mabey and White, 1993) asserts that 'all organisations are political systems composed of individuals, groups and coalitions that compete for power'. Mabey and White (1993) also point out that during any transitional period, 'the struggle for power intensifies because the equilibrium could be subject to movement'. De Wit and Meyer (2004) claim that 'even a situation in which a person or department thinks that it might run the risk of losing power to others can be enough to block a change'. They maintain that 'it can be necessary to break through this political resistance by imposing a new business system and reshuffling management positions'. (However, this may be too simplistic a solution. Organisations facing considerable competitive pressures and financial constraints may not be in a position to do this.)

18

It should be noted that employees should not be merely consulted and informed, they should be involved in the process of change. Smith (2003) stresses 'communication throughout the project is critical to developing and maintaining stakeholder support'. Dictatorial, coercive approaches to implementing change tend to generate hostility towards management and are likely to be unsuccessful in producing the required results. Employees tend to fear – and react against – managerially imposed change. Further, they may resist change in this context because they may also be afraid to make mistakes in any new job roles or responsibilities. The true role of management should be to facilitate change and to act as a support mechanism, where they are responsible for reinforcing desired behaviours.

Participation and involvement at every level should be encouraged to allow for openness in negotiations, which in turn allows true opinions to be voiced and problems identified and discussed. Employees should be given the chance to have their own input and to seek and develop solutions. This also takes the burden off management.

During the early stages of any change initiative, some 'quick hits' need to be achieved. Peppard and Rowland (1995) suggest 'early demonstrable successes will help overcome resistance , build momentum and a "can do" attitude and make people feel confident of their abilities'. These quick hits are intended to motivate and empower employees as well as helping to introduce change.

Providing feedback to all concerned is also an important part of the change management process. It aids the monitoring of any change project and can be used as a basis for further improvements. Feedback should be provided regularly, as Burnes (2004) stresses that very little is achieved from yearly reviews.

Walker (cited in Schrader and Self, 2003) suggests that there are seven key areas to be addressed in order for change to be successful. These include:

- Celebrating small wins (to help maintain impetus).
- Acknowledging value in past practices.
- Measuring progress at regular intervals.
- Involving employees in managing the integration process.
- Identifying ingrained behaviours that become obstacles.
- Communicating how integration will be implemented.
- Should be communicated clearly.

Note: although these areas are all important, Walker has overlooked the obligatory provision of any necessary training for employees.

For a change initiative to be successful, management should be careful not to overwhelm employees. As Mabey and White (1993) point out, 'an overload of uncertainty may create dysfunctional effects, as people may begin to panic, engage in extreme defensive behaviour, and become irrationally resistant to any new change proposed'. Organisations must have a strong leader to provide employees with a vision of what the organisation will be like, for support and guidance in order to embrace the changes. Thus, clear lines of authority need to be established to explain the new

18

ground rules and provide employees with somewhere to go should they need advice.

Despite management's efforts and best intentions, it must be acknowledged that not all employees will accept change. It should be pointed out that not all resistance to change is necessarily a hindrance. It can be considered that a unitary culture actually stifles diversity. Some types of resistance can be positive and lead to constructive criticism, whereby further change can lead to improvements.

Self-assessment question 18.2

Write a short report regarding suggestions for overcoming resistance to change. If the suggestions fail, should management resort to coercion?

Feedback on page 218

Revision question

Now try the revision question for this session on page 249.

Summary

* Planned change involves consciously taking steps to form a strategy for implementing change using a systematic, goal-orientated approach. Lewin proposed a three-step model for successful planned change. The steps include unfreezing current behaviour, learning new values and refreezing.
* Emergent change is where change is allowed to evolve naturally, it can be unpredictable and is an ongoing process.
* Planned change criticism:
  - Change does not result in movement from one stable state to another.
  - Circumstances may change and therefore planning may be rendered useless.
  - It is management led.
* Emergent change criticism:
  - Bottom-up change is an emergent process and therefore can be considerably slower to mature than top-down initiatives.
  - Causes for resistance include a lack of understanding, employees may be in agreement with the changes, feel they may lose out or decide to rebel against managerially imposed change. Other reasons relate to uncertainty regarding their future job role and security. Organisations can also subject employees to too much change otherwise known as change fatigue.
* The Kubler-Ross coping cycle has five stages. The stages are denial, anger, bargaining, depression, testing and acceptance.
* Guidelines for managing change:
  - Management should have clearly defined objectives which should be communicated clearly to employees.

18

    – Communication and information sharing by way of appraisals and team meetings should emphasise the benefits to employees.
    – Participation and involvement should be encouraged which allows for problems to be discussed and solutions sought.
    – Managers should facilitate change and act as a support mechanism.
    – Feedback should be provided to inform employees of their performance and to make further improvements.

Suggested further reading

You could read the relevant sections of Burnes (2004), Parker (2005) and Robbins (2003).

Feedback on learning activities and self-assessment questions

Feedback on learning activity 18.1

Table 18.2

The emergent approach to change	The planned approach to change
Is where change is allowed to evolve naturally, can be unpredictable and is an ongoing process	Involves consciously taking steps to form a strategy for implementing change using a systematic, goal-orientated approach.
Is up to date (current)	Plans are usually for a minimum of three months and can become obsolete and therefore may render useless
Is described as 'fluid'	Is described as 'frozen'
Is bottom up	Management led (top down)
Reacts to external environment	Prepares for the forthcoming period
Is particularly relevant in today's organisations as it takes into consideration the uncertain nature of the external environment such as competition	Is particularly suitable for innovation and research and development. You have to plan to bring a product to market

Feedback on self-assessment question 18.1

- Top management's approach is reflective of the emergent approach, it is reactive to the external environment. However, the board were slow to react as they did not replace Sorrel until the bank had gone from being the most profitable in the country to the least profitable. The bank suffered from being too reliant upon the emergent approach to change. They were also very narrow minded and concentrated on their immediate profits. Whilst the financial industry is very unpredictable, the emergent approach is appropriate. However, the bank may have benefited in the long term if they had made more use of the planned approach to change.
- Murray's approach involved co-option, which is often referred to as 'explicit and implicit coercion'. Whilst this method may prove quick

18

and effective in the short run, it does not come highly recommended. It seems to be a harsh remedy, which in the long run will demoralise staff and earn the company an unseemly reputation.

Feedback on learning activity 18.2

Besides the fact that change offers uncertainty and is associated with risk, employees resist change because:

- They do not comprehend the reasoning behind the changes.
- They may not be in agreement with the proposed changes. They may be happy with their current situation and therefore not perceive the need for change.
- They may feel that they are 'losing out', for example the new change may undermine their role, removing the power they once had.
- They tend to rebel against what is imposed upon them, making them feel like a child – not responsible and having to be told what to do.
- They are afraid to make mistakes in their new job role.
- If faced with a substantial amount of change they may be overwhelmed and feel unable to cope and adapt.
- They may feel that the changes are yet another management fad.
- They may be tired of change and therefore lack enthusiasm and commitment to the project.
- They may feel that if they make too many improvements too quickly, management will continually force them to be more efficient.

Feedback on self-assessment question 18.2

There are many methods to help management overcome the barriers to change and facilitate unfreezing. They include training and communication to provide understanding. Participation and involvement should also be encouraged. This not only provides an outlet to more creative solutions, but ultimately increases employees' commitments to the new changes. Support and guidance should be given to those having adjustment difficulties. Negotiation may be used when employees feel that they are losing out, especially if it concerns an entire group which retain a lot of power. Shah (1998) believes manipulation may be used if alternatives are exhausted or prove to be too expensive. He recommends that explicit and implicit coercion be used when either speed is a priority or when the change initiators possess considerable power. However, this is not advisable as this is likely to create resentment and hostility, which eventually results in employee absence and turnover.

Study session 19
Employment legislation

Introduction

Since the early 1970s to the present day, employment law in the UK has been changing radically. It is essential for an organisation to be aware of the rights of an employee as well as the employer's obligations as both parties are protected in UK and European Union (EU) law. Equality in working practices, salaries, and health and safety are major factors which contribute to the successful running of present-day organisations.

As members of the EU, the UK and other member states are required to make EU directives law within three years of the directive being issued.

'The world is not going to be saved by legislation.'
Taft, WH, 27th President of the USA (1909–1913)

Session learning objectives

After completing this session you should be able to:

19.1 Assess the importance of changes in employment and equal opportunities legislation on organisations.

Unit content coverage

This study session covers the following topic from the official CIPS unit content document:

Learning outcome

Propose processes and systems to enable the successful implementation of change programmes to maximise purchasing efficiency and effectiveness.

Learning objective

5.4 Assess the importance of changes in employment and equal opportunities legislation on organisations.

Prior knowledge

Sessions study sessions 16 – 18.

Timing

You should set aside about 5 hours to read and complete this session, including learning activities, self-assessment questions, the suggested further reading (if any) and the revision question.

19.1 Employment legislation and the effects on organisations

This study session reviews the employment legislation as it applies in the UK. If you are based outside the UK then you should familiarise yourself with the employment legislation that applies to your own organisation or within your own country. You might usefully compare your findings with that of the UK.

In the UK there are six key major legislative acts (or EU directives) that employers need to be fully aware of when employing staff. Each different act or law covers a specific area and should be fully enshrined in an organisation's policy of employment and code of conduct.

These six acts/directives are:

- Equal Pay Act 1970.
- Employment Act 2000 (including TUPE).
- Health and Safety at Work Act 1974.
- Freedom of Information Act 2000.
- EU employment directives.
- Disability Discrimination Act 1995.

Learning activity 19.1

For your own organisation obtain a copy of each of the following (if you do not already have them):

- Your own contract of employment.
- Policy on flexible working.
- Policy on equality and diversity.
- Health and safety policy.
- Discipline and grievance policies.
- Equal opportunity policy.
- Confidentiality policy (including data protection).

If you do not currently work for an organisation, search the internet to find examples of these.

Feedback on page 230

Equal Pay Act 1970

This Act governs the provision of equality between men and women but only came into force on 29 December 1975. (See also the Sex Discrimination Act 1975.) It established the right of men and women to equal treatment as regards terms and conditions of employment when employed on the same or broadly similar work or work which has been given equal value. It applies to full- or part-time employment. Since 1975 the Act has been further amended by the Equal Pay (Amendment) Regulations 1983 (SI 1983/1794) and the Sex Discrimination Act 1986.

What the law says

The purpose of the Equal Pay Act 1970 is to eliminate discrimination between men and women in terms of their pay and contracts of employment where they are doing:

- work that is the same or broadly similar;
- work rated as equivalent under job evaluation or work study;
- work of equal value in terms of the demands made on them under headings such as effort, skill and decision making.

What is covered under the Equal Pay Act 1970

The Act gives men and women the right to equality in the terms of their contract of employment. It covers both pay and other terms and conditions such as piecework, output and bonus, payments, holidays and sick leave.

European law has extended the concept to cover redundancy payments, travel concessions, employers' pension contributions and occupational pension benefits.

The Equal Pay Act 1970 applies to pay or benefits provided by the contract of employment. The Sex Discrimination Act 1986 covers non-contractual arrangements including benefits such as access to a workplace nursery or travel concessions.

Who is comparable?

In order to bring a claim, a person must compare themselves with actual people of the opposite sex who are treated more favourably and are shown to be employed on equal work. The person is their 'comparator'. They can compare themselves to a predecessor or successor in the job.

When employing staff, employers must take care to ensure that value and pay factors have been determined. These factors can be determined by way of a job evaluation exercise and by the use of market rate surveys within a similar industry and geographic area. Output should be linked to pay structure and salary rating.

Implications of the Equal Pay Act 1970

Despite the fact that the Act has been in place for a generation, the pay gap between men and women has not disappeared. After a period of fairly rapid improvement in the first decade after the Act, further progress has been very slow. Research in 2005 revealed that there was still a difference of over 17% in the mean hourly earnings of men and women in full-time employment. While some of this can be explained by differences in taking on family responsibilities and by variations in the jobs typically taken on by men and women, a substantial element could still be blamed on organisations that continue to deploy payment practices that directly or indirectly discriminate against women.

Currently organisations are encouraged to conduct pay reviews voluntarily to iron out these differences. However, a substantial number (especially

19

among smaller organisations) have failed to do this, leading to calls that this should become a statutory obligation.

This issue is a ticking time bomb beneath many organisations given that a group of employees who can prove a case of discrimination under the Act can claim up to six years' back pay. Just what this can mean was revealed in 2006 when 1,500 health workers at two hospitals in Cumbria were awarded £300 million in compensation. In this case individual rates of compensation ranged from £35,000 to £200,000.

You might like to consider how well your organisation could survive a proportional financial hit.

Sources of information and advice include the Equal Opportunities Commission, ACAS and the Employment Tribunal Service.

Employment Act 2000 (including TUPE)

As an update to the Employment Act 1994 and 1996, this Act covers all aspects of employment law including pensions, statutory working hours, pay and so on, and it also covers the Transfer of Undertakings (Protection of Employment) Regulations 1981 (TUPE)). TUPE details the employee's rights when the organisation they are employed by is taken over by another organisation. The Act benefits both parties. The Employment Act 2000 is amended/updated on a regular basis by European directives.

Prior to TUPE, which was updated with the Employment Act of 1994/1996 and 2000, it was deemed an automatic termination of contract of employment for all employees when a business changed ownership. It was at the discretion of the new owners whether or not to employ all or any of the employees of the original business. All that the employees were entitled to was a redundancy payment. When TUPE came into force it changed entirely.

If there is a 'relevant transfer' under the regulations then the new purchaser automatically takes over the contractual rights and obligations of the employees.

A dismissal connected with the transfer is unfair unless linked to economic, technical or organisational (ETO) reasons .

What is a transfer?

A transfer can take place where there is a change of ownership as a result of the sale or merger of companies. A business has to be transferred in its entirety and not by simple acquisition of shares.

In *Suzen* v *Zehnaker Gebuadereingung Krankenhausservice and Lefarth GmbH* [1997] the European Court of Justice ruled that it is not a transfer when there is simply a change in contractor. There must also be a transfer of some tangible asset.

Therefore, an outsourcing of the right to provide catering facilities is not caught by the regulations unless there is also a transfer of the right to use the kitchens and other facilities or the staff.

Implications of TUPE

New TUPE regulations came into effect in April 2006. These tightened up many points in the previous regulations.

From the point of view of organisations, some of the most significant implications relate to the scope of TUPE – outsourcing and insourcing changes are now definitely covered by TUPE regulations – and obligations relating to consultation with affected employees and the provision of adequate information to those potentially affected are made clearer and tougher.

Failure to comply with TUPE can lead to substantial compensation payouts for both the organisation divesting itself of the employees and the organisation taking them on. Each employee can claim up to 13 weeks' pay in compensation. This can very quickly add up – a claim could cost an organisation over £9,000 per employee.

The complications around the application of TUPE in situations where employees' contracts of employment are being changed means that organisations need to take great care in order to avoid falling foul of TUPE and probably need to take specialist legal advice. For example, any organisation considering outsourcing or insourcing any aspects of its purchasing and supply function will need to consider carefully the implications of TUPE.

Health and Safety at Work Act (HASAWA) 1974

Before the introduction of this Act in 1974, approximately 8 million employees had no safety protection at work.

HASAWA 1974 provides the legal framework to promote, stimulate and encourage high standards of health and safety in places of work. Everyone has a duty to comply with the Act, including employers, employees, trainees, the self-employed, manufacturers, suppliers, designers and importers of work equipment.

The employer's responsibilities

This Act states that it is the duty of the employer to ensure the health, safety and welfare of their employees without prejudice to their duties, including:

- The provision and maintenance of plant and systems to ensure they are safe and without risks to the employees.
- Ensuring as far as reasonably practical the absence of risk to health in connection with handling, storage and transport of items associated with the organisation.
- The provision of instruction, training and supervision to ensure as reasonably practical the health and safety of all employees.
- The maintenance of any place of work to ensure where reasonably practical the health and safety of employees.
- The provision and maintenance of a working environment for employees that is, so far as reasonably practicable, safe and without risk to health and safety.

19

The phrase 'so far as reasonably practicable, safe and without risk' means that a computation must be made as to the risk and the sacrifice involved in instituting the measures necessary for alleviating risk.

The employer is forbidden to charge the employees for any measures which the employer is required to provide in the interests of health and safety, for example provision of personal protective equipment.

The employee's responsibilities

Employees have specific responsibilities too. They:

- Must take care of their own health and safety and that of other persons. In the event of an accident, employees may be held liable.
- Must cooperate with their employers.
- Must not interfere with anything provided in the interest of health and safety.

Enforcement of health and safety legislation

Depending on the type of business the local authority Environmental Health Officer (EHO) for local authorities and Health and Safety Executive (HSE) for large manufacturing/construction or industrial sites have the power to enforce the legislation contained in the Act.

Powers of an enforcement officer

The enforcement officer has a right:

- of entry at reasonable times, without an appointment;
- to investigate and examine;
- to dismantle equipment, take substances/equipment;
- to see documents, take copies;
- to assistance (from colleagues or the police);
- to ask questions under caution;
- to seize articles/substances in cases of imminent danger.

Enforcement action

Both the HSE (Health and Safety Executive) and the EHO (Enviromental Health Officer) have certain enforcement powers/tools available to them:

- *Legal notices*: These require a person or organisation to do/stop doing something and can be issued to any organisation with a stated deadline. Failure to comply with the instructions contained in the notice puts the organisation/person liable to prosecution.
- *Improvement*: An officer can state where they believe improvement could take place and how corrective action should be undertaken. An example of this would be a shop which falls below the standard required to sell/operate. A notice would be given with instructions of how to bring the conditions up to the legal standard within a set timescale.
- *Prohibition*: Prohibits use of equipment/unsafe practices immediately. Again if an organisation has equipment which falls below the legal

standard it can be deemed too unsafe for use and a prohibition order would be issued by the officer. Prosecution would follow if the equipment or practices were not discontinued.

- *Prosecution*: Who faces prosecution? Both the employer and the employees are liable to prosecution. These can take the following form:
  - Maximum £5,000 fine via Magistrates Court.
  - Unlimited fine and jail in Crown Court.

Enforcement officers will give advice and explain the rules but also have the power to enforce the legislation.

Implications of the Health and Safety at Work Act 1974

Accidents and injuries at work currently cause the loss of about 40 million days of work to the UK economy. In financial terms this loss is put at between £3.3 billion and £6.5 billion per year. This roughly equates to every single person at work in the UK losing two days of work a year due to accident or injury. The objective of the Health and Safety at Work Act 1974 is to reduce this figure.

The costs to organisations go well beyond the immediate cost of the accident or injury. There is:

- the downtime and disruption caused by the accident to the individual and to those who come to assist and administer first aid;
- the cost of the person's absence from work – including the need to find a temporary replacement or pay other staff overtime;
- the impact on the organisation's ability to deliver on time, meet contractual obligations and so on (for example, late delivery penalties);
- the time taken up in meetings and investigations to determine the cause of the accident;
- potentially substantial intangible losses due to loss of reputation and loss of morale among the workforce.

Added to all this is the potential for a fine if the organisation is found to be at fault and in breach of the legislation. In 2004/2005, the average fine imposed by the HSE was approximately £19,000.

Many organisations fail to recognise that a lot of these costs will not be covered by their insurance. Estimates indicated that the ratio of insured to uninsured losses runs at about 1:3.3. In other words, for every £1 of loss that can be reclaimed, £3.30 will not be.

All this should provide a very sound incentive for organisations to ensure the highest practicable standards of health and safety at work. Depressingly, however, between 1997 and 2004 there were about 2,000 deaths and over 200,000 serious injuries to workers and the public due to accidents at work in the UK.

The aspect of the Act that is perhaps of particular relevance to the purchasing and supply function is that relating to the handling, storage and transport of items associated with the organisation. You might like to consider what steps your own purchasing and supply function takes to

19

ensure the health and safety of employees, employees of other organisations and the public.

Freedom of Information Act 2000

This Act is an amendment to the Data Protection Act 1998 and the Public Records Act 1952. It governs the provision of disclosure of information.

In essence it enhances the rights of employees to access personal data held on them by employers, public authorities or relevant third parties which may include credit reference agencies, banks, unions, political organisations, mail order companies, examining bodies and so on. It encompasses both computer records and all paper records.

Who can make a request for information?

Any person can make a request under the Act – there are no restrictions on your age, nationality or where you live.

All that is required is written communication to the authority that you think holds the information including the following information:

- your name;
- an address where you can be contacted;
- a description of the information you want.

Public authorities must comply with your request promptly, and should provide the information within 20 working days (approximately one month); if they require more time they must write to you and confirm when they will be able to respond.

Who can you ask and what can you ask for?

The Freedom of Information Act 2000 applies to all 'public authorities'. This includes:

- central and local government;
- the health service;
- schools, colleges and universities;
- the police;
- lots of other non-departmental public bodies, committees and advisory bodies.

You can ask for any information at all, but some information might be withheld to protect various interests, as permitted by the Act. However, in these instances the authority must tell you that they have withheld information and why.

If you ask for information about yourself, then your request is handled under the Data Protection Act 1984 instead of the Freedom of Information Act 2000. Your rights differ, different fees apply and public authorities have longer to respond.

Data Protection Act 1984

Implications of the Data Protection Act 1984

The Data Protection Act 1984 has implications for every organisation in terms of putting policies and procedures in place to ensure its employees comply with the requirements of the Act.

In particular, organisations need to pay attention to ensure that employees understand their responsibilities in terms of handling, for example, customer data; that is, keeping it secure, only using it for the purposes for which it was collected and keeping it for as long as necessary.

Abuses of data can lead to substantial fines.

You might like to consider how your own organisation ensures that the data it holds on its customers is protected and is only used appropriately.

EU employment directives

Employees and other workers have a wide variety of different rights, some of which are based on the Acts and legislation described above and further enhanced by additions and legislative directives made by the EU, specifically:

- employment rights (the Employment Rights Act 1996);
- rights and working hours (Working Time Regulations 1998);
- National Minimum Wage Act 1998;
- Public Interest Disclosure Act 1998;
- Trade Union and Labour Relations Act 1992;
- Part-time Workers Regulations 2000.

Implications of EU employment directives

All of this legislation, deriving from EU directives, has implications for organisations in the UK.

The Employment Rights Act 1996 covers issues relating to contracts of employment, disciplinary and grievance procedures, pensions and so on – all those things that govern the day-to-day interaction between the employee and employer.

The Working Time Regulations 1998 cover the maximum hours and periods that people can work, time off, rest breaks and annual leave entitlements. It also covers the special requirements for working at night and the health implications of night working.

The National Minimum Wage Act 1998 stipulates in the UK the minimum hourly rate of pay for adult workers and younger workers. In addition it specifies workers' rights in relation to access to their own pay records and provides protection against dismissal for enforcing their right to receive the minimum wage. It is a criminal offence for employers to violate the Act.

The Public Interest Disclosure Act 1998 is sometimes known as the whistleblower's charter. This sets out to protect employees from unfair

19

action by their employer for making certain public disclosures which are in the public interest. An employee may be protected under the Act for disclosing an event that has happened or is likely to happen in the future that constitutes a criminal offence, a breach of a legal obligation, a miscarriage of justice, a danger to health and safety, damage to the environment or an action to cover up one of these instances.

The employee must act in good faith in believing that a 'qualifying' event has taken place, they must not act maliciously and must have attempted to bring the issue to the attention of the employer in the first instance via the appropriate internal procedures.

The Trade Union and Labour Relations Act 1992 is concerned with union recognition and derecognition procedures to ensure fair play by trade unions and employers (with regard to collective bargaining procedures), provision of information, as well as providing some protection to individuals whose rights might be signed away for a financial inducement.

The Part-time Workers Regulations 2000 give part-time male and female workers a right to the same pay and terms and conditions of employment (contractual and non-contractual) on a pro-rata basis as full-time workers with a similar contract, doing the same or broadly similar work, unless any difference in treatment can be objectively justified. In addition, full-time workers who become part time are entitled to retain pro-rata terms and conditions.

Disability Discrimination Act 1995

This Act aims to protect disabled people against discrimination – both in employment and when using a service facility.

The government has implemented legislation in three phases:

- Phase 1 (1996) made it illegal to treat disabled people less favourably because of their disability.
- Phase 2 (1999) obliged organisations to make reasonable adjustments for disabled staff, which include changes in the way services for disabled customers are provided, for example large-print documents like bank statements.
- Phase 3 (from October 2004) – organisations have to make alterations to their premises to overcome access barriers, for example providing wheelchair ramps.

Organisations employing staff should refer to the above and implement required legislative action to their organisation, its working practices and identified methods of employment.

Implications of the Disability Discrimination Act (DDA) 1995

From the point of view of organisations, much of the concern has been about the cost implications of what constitutes 'reasonable adjustments' in making it possible for disabled employees to function and disabled customers to make use of an organisation's goods and services.

19

In reality, the costs of such adjustments for employees have usually been much less than feared.

If you have a colleague with a recognised disability under the DDA 1995, you might like to discuss with them what adjustments have been made to enable them to carry out their job.

Self-assessment question 19.1

Answer the following questions.

1   Which of the following are covered under the equal pay legislation?
    (a)   Redundancy payments.
    (b)   Holiday entitlements.
    (c)   Travel concessions.
    (d)   Sick leave.
    (e)   Holiday entitlement.
    (f)   Pension contributions.

2   What does TUPE stand for?

3   Under TUPE both the transferee and transferor are liable for ensuring the adequate transfer of employee information and employee consultation.
    Is this statement true or false?

4   Employers have the main responsibility for ensuring health and safety at work.
    Is this statement true or false?

5   An enforcement officer under health and safety legislation has the right to do which of the following?
    (a)   Enter premises at any time without an appointment.
    (b)   Dismantle equipment.
    (c)   Seize articles.

6   It is a criminal offence to disregard the requirements of the National Minimum Wage Act 1998.
    Is this statement true or false?

7   The following are reasons for which an employee could be justified in making a public disclosure and be protected from adverse action from his or her employer:
    •   Danger to health and safety.
    •   Miscarriage of justice.
    •   A criminal offence.
    What are the other two reasons?.

8   The Disability Discrimination Act 1995 only applies to people who have a physical disability or are visually impaired or hearing impaired.

(continued on next page)

19

Self-assessment question 19.1 *(continued)*

Is this statement true or false?

Feedback on page 230

Revision question

Now try the revision question for this session on page 249.

Summary

This session has covered the major pieces of legislation in the UK that govern the relationship between employers and employees and which have attempted to ensure an equitable, safe, healthy and fair working environment for all and to stamp out unfair discrimination on the grounds of sex and disability.

As we have seen, such legislation has some way to go in achieving its aim, although much progress has been made over the last 30 years.

The UK's membership of the EU has extended the range and depth of employment legislation.

Suggested further reading

You should read the relevant sections of Mullins (2005).

Feedback on learning activities and self-assessment questions

Feedback on learning activity 19.1

If you work in the UK you should reasonably have expected to receive copies of all these policies and more when you joined the organisation as they set out the terms of the relationship between you, the organisation, your colleagues and those you interact with outside the organisation as part of your job. If you have not been able to obtain a copy of any of these policies, you should check this with your personnel or human resources department. If any of these policies do not exist, you should be asking why.

Keep these policies by you as you work through the rest of this session and see how the requirements of the various pieces of employment legislation have been in covered by them.

Feedback on self-assessment question 19.1

1   All of these are covered under the Equal Pay Act 1970.
2   TUPE stands for Transfer of Undertakings (Protection of Employment).
3   This statement is true. The obligations are now shared.

4   This statement is false. While it is true that employers have a major responsibility, this is shared with employees, who also carry very definite responsibilities.

5   The correct answer is (b) and (c). Enforcement officers cannot enter at *any* time without an appointment, but they can enter at any *reasonable* time without an appointment.

6   This statement is true.

7   The other two reasons for legitimate disclosure are:
    *   Damage to the environment.
    *   Covering up any of the other offences.

8   This statement is completely false. The DDA 1995 covers a whole range of physical and cognitive disabilities both permanent and temporary.

Study session 20
Impact of e-commerce and technology

Introduction

Globalisation and increasing pressures from customers, competitors and dynamically volatile markets has meant that many organisations are rethinking their strategies in order to maintain their competitiveness. The internet has led to organisations differentiating their approaches to business in terms of how they reach and serve their customers. As a result, more and more organisations are turning to e-commerce, the basis for which is a robust management information system.

Session learning objectives

After completing this session you should be able to:

20.1 Evaluate the impact of e-commerce and technology on the management of organisations and people.
20.2 Evaluate the impact of intranets and electronic business.
20.3 Explain the specific benefits of using e-commerce and technology in the purchasing and supply function.

Unit content coverage

This study session covers the following topic from the official CIPS unit content document:

Learning outcome

Propose processes and systems to enable the successful implementation of change programmes to maximise purchasing efficiency and effectiveness.

Learning objective

5.5 Evaluate the impact of e-commerce and technology on the management of organisations and people, and in particular the benefit to the purchasing function.

Prior knowledge

Study sessions 16 – 18.

Timing

You should set aside about 6 hours to read and complete this session, including learning activities, self-assessment questions, the suggested further reading (if any) and the revision question.

20.1 E-commerce and technology in organisations

The role of information systems

Management information systems (MIS) are typically computer-based systems that are used within an organisation. *WordNet* describes an information system as 'a system consisting of the network of all communication channels used within an organisation', and a management information system as 'a system that collects and processes data (information) and provides it to managers at all levels who use it for decision making, planning, programme implementation and control' (see http://en.wikipedia.org/wiki/WordNet). An information system comprises all the components that collect, manipulate and disseminate data or information. It usually includes hardware, software, people, communications systems such as telephone lines, and the data itself. The activities involved include inputting data, processing of data into information, storage of data and information, and the production of outputs such as management reports.

As an area of study it is commonly referred to as **information technology management**. The study of information systems is usually a commerce and business administration discipline, and frequently involves software engineering, but also distinguishes itself by concentrating on the integration of computer systems with the aims of the organisation. The importance for business is that management information systems support business processes and operations, decision making and competitive strategies that are essential for organisations to be dynamically reponsive to ever-changing competitive environments.

E-commerce

Traditionally **e-commerce** applications were originally limited to electronically mediated buying and selling. Nowadays, however, e-commerce encompasses a much broader spectrum and thus it has many definitions, for example:

- Cawsey and Dewar (2004) suggest that e-commerce 'describes the buying and selling of products, services and information via the internet'.

- Van Weele (2005) describes e-commerce as:

  'the whole of business actions carried out electronically to improve the efficiency and effectiveness of market and business processes. In practice, however, e-commerce is usually understood to be marketing, sales and purchasing of products and services via the internet and/or other open electronic information networks.'

- Zwass (cited in Tassabehji, 2003) places the emphasis more on business-to-business relationships by defining e-commerce as 'sharing business information, maintaining business relationships and conducting business transactions by means of telecommunications networks'.

- Bocij et al (2003) explain it as:

  'all electronically mediated transactions between organisations and any third party it deals with. In this definition, non-financial transactions such as customer requests for further information would also be considered to be part of e-commerce.'

However it is defined, e-commerce is a technological medium that can help increase revenues, reduce overhead costs and improve customer service in addition to corporate image. According to Chaffey et al (2003), 'a key factor driving e-marketing and e-business strategy objectives is the current level and future projections of customer demand for e-commerce services in different market segments'.

Implementing e-commerce

There are three distinct ways in which organisations can implement e-commerce:

- Brick and mortar: an organisation that has an internet site which (re)directs customers to a specific location or telephone number.
- Click and mortar: an organisation that has a location that the customer can visit, as well as an internet site where the customer can browse products online and complete a transaction online. (In the UK, for example, this includes organisations such as Marks and Spencer and Tesco.)
- Pure play: an organisation that has no physical presence but does have an internet site which allows customers to browse and complete transactions online. Examples include eBay and Dell Computers.

The impact of e-commerce and technology

Whilst the sophistication of information technology such as e-commerce has proven to make efficiencies within organisations, one of the unfortunate consequences has been the removal of layers of (usually *middle*) management. As a result, in some cases, employees have become resistant to the introduction of new technology as a means of driving organisational change as they fear the loss of their jobs. Mabey and White (1993) shed some light on why employees can be reluctant to accept change in an organisation, maintaining that 'employees need stability and security … and … change presents unknowns which cause anxiety'.

The following extract from Betts (2000) provides a wider explanation of the impact of information technology in general:

'Information technology (IT) can seldom eliminate all the wide range of supervisory roles. Certainly IT is effective in improving communication, and in improving and increasing operating data, but its use in attempting to modify employee behaviour is debatable. Clearly, IT applications change the emphasis on some supervisory roles, others may disappear, and new ones may emerge. However, the strong need for supervising remains.'

20

Betts continues by arguing that:

> 'information technology is the prime mover of change and practically
> every job will be affected eventually. Computers (especially personal
> computers) have revolutionised systems and organisational structures,
> and have created new skills. Managerial and supervisory roles are
> changing as networks provide direct access to massive information stores
> … Drucker stresses that computers only hold quantifiable data but
> accuracy still depends on the human being inputting the information.

> 'In industry the poor management of IT resources is well known.
> Measuring intangible benefits like competitive advantage and quality
> is often ignored. According to some surveys, companies even now
> remain reluctant to install comprehensive systems and they do not
> value IT highly. Nevertheless, IT has dramatically changed the way
> information is made available, processed and distributed within a
> company. Consequently, if IT is to be properly applied, the quality,
> access and delivery of information can improve problem solving and
> decision making, which is a distinct advantage in any organisation.'

Learning activity 20.1

The internet is a marketing tool for organisations, but has different
variations of importance depending on the nature of the business.
E-commerce can benefit organisations in a number of ways, describe two.

Feedback on page 244

Knowledge management

Knowledge management (KM) can refer to the technology, techniques or
social practices for organising and collecting knowledge so that it is applied
at an appropriate time or place. Generally, corporate KM emphasises the
technology of databases and software applications collecting information.

Definitions of knowledge management

There is nothing essentially new in the basic concept of managing
knowledge, even though as a new discipline it has emerged only recently
and, given its newness, is still developing its theoretical foundations.
Knowledge management has always been conducted in one way or another,
for example via apprenticeships, colleagues chatting or a parent handing
over their business to their children. The essential difference today is the
pace of the environment we live and work in and the demands it puts on the
flow of knowledge.

Organisational knowledge management (OKM) is the creation,
organisation, sharing and flow of knowledge in organisations. Knowledge
management seeks to make the best use of the knowledge that is available
to an organisation, creating new knowledge, increasing awareness and
understanding in the process. Knowledge management can also be defined
as the capturing, organising and storing of knowledge and experiences of

individual workers and groups within an organisation and making this information available to others in the organisation.

Several types of knowledge are relevant to an organisation. Nonaka and Takeuchi (1995) suggest separating the concepts of data, information, tacit knowledge and explicit knowledge:

- **Data** is factual, raw material and therefore without information attached.
- **Information** is refined into a structural form, for example client databases.
- **Explicit – or codified or articulated – knowledge** relates to 'knowing about' and can be written and easily transferred. This category of knowledge may include manuals, specialised databases or collections of case law, or may even be in the form of standardised techniques of investigation or templates for documents. A key attribute of explicit knowledge is the possibility to store it. Explicit knowledge is 'knowing about', and few disagree that it can be stored and shared using manuals and databases.
- **Tacit knowledge** relates to 'knowing how' or 'understanding' and cannot be transferred directly between individuals; it is transferred through application, practice and social interaction.

Related definitions

- **Personal knowledge management** (PKM) pays attention to the organisation of information, thoughts and beliefs. In this approach, the responsibility for knowledge creation lies with the individual who is charged to learn, connect and share personal insights.
- **Enterprise knowledge management** (EKM) is concerned with strategy, process and technologies to acquire, store, share and secure organisational understanding, insights and core distinctions. KM at this level is closely tied to competitive advantage, innovation and agility.

Self-assessment question 20.1

Evaluate the impact of e-commerce and information technology in your own organisation or an organisation of your choice.

Feedback on page 244

20.2 Intranets, extranets and the purchasing function

Intranets

Tassabehji (2003) defines an intranet as:

> 'a private network that is contained within an enterprise. It may consist of many interlinked local area networks and also use private leased lines in a wide area network. Typically, an intranet uses internet technology and other internet protocols and includes connections through one or more secure gateways to the outside internet.'

20

Essentially, an **intranet** is a private, corporate internet designed to improve communication and access to information. It should encourage the workforce to collaborate, and thus make the company more efficient. The main function of an intranet is to promote knowledge sharing by means of publishing information such as company news, events, training courses and product information. Chaffey et al (1998) suggests that 'the intranet also enables shared document authoring, text and video conferencing, electronic meetings as well as email'.

Additionally, intranets enable users to create hyperlinks to speed up the process of checking inventory levels, to test software from their desks, as well as being used to support marketing activities. Standing (2000) comments, 'Intranets are being used for a whole range of organisational applications that are revolutionising internal communication and information processing'.

The intranet is also beneficial to the purchasing function because it allows purchasing staff to:

- Check inventory levels (availability, price, quantity and value of goods in stock).
- Look up questions and answers using a frequently asked questions (FAQ) option.
- Search for products and specific information regarding the product, for example product suitability.

Extranets

Tassabehji (2003) defines an **extranet** as something that 'extends intranets and links several intranets in different locations using secure hardware and software'.

An extranet can be used by selected suppliers, distributors, vendors, partners, customers and businesses. An extranet is often comprised of intranets, web servers, firewalls and interface software to guarantee effective communication between authorised users only.

According to Tassabehji, the security and privacy of extranets is ensured by 'encryption of messages and virtual private networks (VPN) that use tunnelling to use the public network securely'. (In this context 'tunnelling' means that data transmissions across the internet can be made secure by authenticating and encrypting all internet provider (IP) packets. The tunnelling principle is the basic concept that makes the extranet possible.)

Extranets enable effective communication between the purchasing function and its suppliers. Furthermore, they allow an organisation to collaborate with other companies to lower design, supply and production costs whilst simultaneously improving the development process and reducing lead times. This allows the organisation to be more responsive to its customers' requirements and maintain its level of competitiveness.

Self-assessment question 20.2

'The great debate within almost every organisation is who has ultimate control of intranet development' (Bickerton et al, 2001). Consider the suitability of end users (that is, the people who use information systems but are non-IT specialists) being responsible for the maintenance and development of intranets.

Feedback on page 245

20.3 The benefits of e-commerce for purchasing and supply

E-procurement (electronic procurement), also referred to as supplier exchange, is the business-to-business (B2B) purchase and sale of supplies and services via the internet as well as other information and networking systems such as electronic data interchange (EDI and enterprise resource planning (ERP).

According to Bocij et al (2003), e-procurement is 'The electronic integration and management of all procurement activities including purchase request, authorisation, ordering, delivery and payment between a purchaser and a supplier'.

E-procurement (also known as 'buy-side e-commerce') is expected to be integrated with the current trend towards more integrated computerised supply chain management, and has been more formally defined as:

- 'The electronic tendering and procurement of goods and services'. (Timmers, cited in Chaffey et al, 2003)
- Entailing 'information technology solutions for ordering, logistics and handling systems, as well as payment systems. Examples include electronic ordering systems and catalogue systems'. (Van Weele, 2005)

Typically, e-procurement websites allow qualified and registered users to look for buyers or sellers of goods and services. Depending on the approach, buyers or sellers may specify prices or invite bids. Transactions can be initiated and completed. Ongoing purchases may qualify customers for volume discounts or special offers. E-procurement software can make it possible to automate some buying and selling.

There are six main types of e-procurement:

- Web-based **electronic resource planning** (ERP): creating and approving purchasing requisitions, placing purchase orders and receiving goods and services by using a software system based on internet technology.
- **E-MRO** (maintenance, repair and operating): The same as web-based ERP except that the goods and services ordered are non-product related MRO supplies.

20

- **E-sourcing**: identifying new suppliers for a specific category of purchasing requirements using internet technology.
- **E-tendering**: sending requests for information and prices to suppliers and receiving the responses of suppliers using internet technology.
- **E-reverse auctioning**: using internet technology to buy goods and services from a number of known or unknown suppliers.
- **E-informing**: gathering and distributing purchasing information both from and to internal and external parties using internet technology.

According to Bailey et al (cited in Bocij et al, 2003), e-procurement is designed to improve performance in the five 'rights' of purchasing, which are:

- at the *right* price
- delivered at the *right* time
- of the *right* quality
- of the *right* quantity
- from the *right* source.

E-procurement and the purchasing cycle

In many cases, for non-critical purchases (for example, consumable items), the procurement process tends to be highly manual, involving an employee's submission of a purchase requisition to a purchasing department or a head of department, where all requisitions are then aggregated into purchase orders and sent to contracted suppliers to fulfil. The purchasing cycle tends to be drawn out by the control and approval process. (This is known as 'indirect' procurement and is illustrated in figure 20.1.)

Figure 20.1: The purchasing cycle without e-procurement

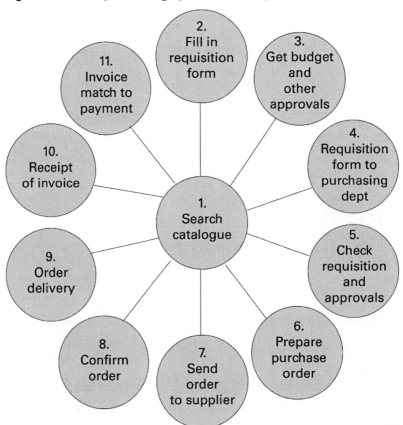

Where purchasing requirements are core to the business (for example, major materials supplies or critical components), very often orders are automatically generated by core planning and transaction processes, such as material requirements planning (MRP) systems and manufacturing. Here, delivery, receipt and quality of direct materials are more closely monitored and managed to ensure that dependent manufacturing schedules are not compromised. An e-procurement system allows the facilitation of this more direct procurement approach, where the purchasing cycle is more condensed, as in figure 20.2.

Figure 20.2: The purchasing cycle using an e-procurement system

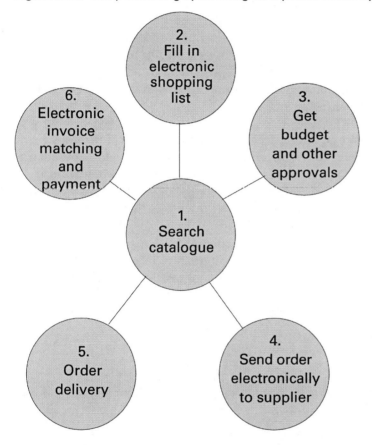

Figure 20.2 illustrates that, with e-procurement, the purchasing cycle is much more condensed and hence more efficient.

Benefits of e-procurement

E-procurement can also provide significant savings and other benefits for an organisation which, in turn, can be delivered to customers.

Learning activity 20.3

Cost reduction is the predominant reason for organisations shifting to electronic procurement. List three further advantages of e-procurement.

Feedback on page 246

Apart from the obvious saving from cutting out the use of specially printed paper order forms, the *real* savings are a result of the efficiencies in the procurement process (see figures 20.1 and 20.2) such as:

- Purchasers' time spent searching and ordering products and reconciling deliveries with invoices is reduced. E-procurement systems enable electronic invoicing, invoice matching and payment.
- Savings occur through the automated validation of pre-approved spending budgets for individuals or departments, leading to fewer people processing each order, and in less time. E-procurement systems permit employees to order directly from an electronic catalogue without interference from the purchasing department. Employees can also enquire about delivery times without having to ask the purchasing department, thus cutting out/removing the middle man.
- Cycle times between order and use of supplies can be reduced. By using integrated ordering and goods-handling systems, transaction costs can be reduced substantially.

According to Van Weele (2005), e-procurement systems represent 'an important productivity tool for both purchasing managers and departments, since these will lead to a significant reduction of administrative workload'. With the advent of e-procurement the role of the purchaser shifts from an administrative role to one that more closely resembles that of a key account manager. A benefit often overlooked but very important, is the fact that with e-procurement, purchasers can actually spend more time maintaining and building relationships with suppliers in order to improve product delivery and costs – or analysis and control – of purchasing behaviour.

Self-assessment question 20.3

Despite the fact that e-procurement can offer considerable savings to organisations and hence their customers, adoption of e-procurement is low. This is because there are number of risks associated with it. Describe three risks in detail:

Feedback on page 246

Revision question

Now try the revision question for this session on page 250.

Summary

A management information system is a system that collects and processes data and provides it to managers at all levels who use it for decision making, planning, programme implementation and control.

E-commerce is more than just electronically mediated buying and selling. It also includes non-financial transactions such as customer requests for further information.

There are three ways that an organisation can implement e-commerce:

- Brick and mortar is where an organisation has a website, but it only directs you to the store. You cannot purchase items from the site.
- Click and mortar is where the organisation has a store that the customer can visit as well as a website which enables customers to purchase products.
- Pure play is where the organisation operates entirely using the web. You cannot visit the shop, all transactions are conducted online.

Positive impacts of e-commerce include the following:

- It can makes processes more efficient – leading to long-term savings.
- It is likely to improve communication.

Negative impacts of e-commerce include the following:

- Efficiencies made may result in redundancies.
- E-commerce costs a lot initially to install.

Benefits of e-commerce include the following:

- It enables organisations to reach a wide audience.
- It allows firms to reduce their advertising costs.
- It has made market research more efficient.
- It means that organisations can exist without the expensive overheads of a store.

An intranet is a private, corporate internet designed to improve communication and access to information. It should encourage the workforce to collaborate, and thus make the company more efficient. The main function of an intranet is to promote knowledge sharing by means of publishing information such as company news, events, training courses and product information.

An extranet is a network of intranets (that is, involving several companies) that enables suppliers, vendors, selected businesses and customers to communicate.

E-procurement (supplier exchange/buy-side e-commerce) uses the internet for tasks such as raising a purchase requisition, authorisation, ordering, delivery and payment.

Benefits of e-procurement include the following:

- Purchaser's time carrying out administrative tasks is reduced.
- E-procurement systems allow employees to order directly from an electronic catalogue without having to converse with the purchasing department.
- Cycle times between order and use of supplies can be reduced.

Risks and disadvantages of using e-commerce include the following:

- Because employees do not get their orders pre-approved, there is a risk that employees may order inventory that is not necessary and is too expensive.

20

- Security concerns and lack of trust between trading partners.
- The e-commerce system between supplier and vendor must be compatible.
- E-commerce can be very expensive to set up.

Further reading

You could read the relevant sections of Bradley (2005), Deresky (2006) and Porter (2001).

Feedback on learning activities and self-assessment questions

Feedback on learning activity 20.1

- It captivates a wider audience. For example, customers from the other side of the world are able to purchase a product that otherwise they would not have been able to buy unless they travelled to the point of sale.
- Using e-commerce allows firms to reduce their advertising costs. This can be beneficial to smaller organisations in particular, allowing them to compete with larger organisations for market share.
- Organisations can trade online rather than bear the cost of setting up operations. As Griffen and Pustay (2003) explain: 'Today a well-developed website can draw consumers without the need to establish a physical presence in each country'.
- E-commerce has made market research more efficient by increasing the opportunities to identify and address customer trends and target these accordingly (Aldin et al, 2004). With the increased use of email and knowledge of individual customers' buying habits, target marketing of goods and services is now more easily achievable.

Thus, e-commerce is now an important and integral part of organisational life and, as Cronin (1995) stresses, 'those organisations who do not embrace the internet will be increasingly isolated as managers become increasingly dependent on information to operate and control their business'.

Feedback on self-assessment question 20.1

You should identify where information technology is used in your organisation, for example within and across functional areas, the systems used to support such approaches and the benefits accrued in the organisation. Your evaluation should relate to how technology has affected (positively and/or negatively) or impacted the changing job roles.

Some points to consider are as follows

- Has the introduction of information technology meant that levels of management have been removed and this has therefore placed increasing pressure on other levels of management?
- Is the organisation more efficient?
- Has the level of customer service improved?

20

- Was the old method just as good?
- How have job roles changed – are they easier or more complicated?

Feedback on learning activity 20.2

The intranet is beneficial to the purchasing function because:

- It allows the user to check inventory levels.
- It allows the user to search for answers to questions.
- It allows the user to search for specific information.

Overall, intranets can improve communication and information sharing throughout the business. Whilst intranets can prove very useful, the intranet does not take the place of someone with expert knowledge. For example, a customer may ask a specific question regarding a toxic product; it would not be wise for someone who lacks experience to use the intranet to provide the customer with information.

Feedback on self-assessment question 20.2

Reasons why end users should maintain and develop intranets include the following:

- End users understand their own business processes better than technology orientated staff, therefore systems can be tailored to end-users' needs. Laudon (2003) states, 'allowing users to specify their own business needs improves requirements gathering and often leads to a higher level of user involvement and satisfaction with the system'.
- Having responsibility for the maintenance and control of intranets can empower employees, as it involves them in decision making and gives them added responsibility.

  'End-user computing can lead to the empowerment of staff in functional areas of an organisation to follow through creative ideas for information systems to improve the efficiency of their work. Innovated ideas may be fostered in this way when they would otherwise be stifled if there were no mechanism for their being implemented.' (Bocij et al, 2003)

  With end users maintaining and controlling their part of the intranet, it allows the end user to develop their skills. It encourages creativity and adds variety to their everyday work schedule. Meanwhile, the IT specialists can concentrate on activities requiring their expertise, such as programming.
- By using end users, fewer IT programmers or independent consultants are required.

Reasons why IT specialists should maintain and develop intranets include the following:

- Creating intranets can be quite complex and requires the expertise of the IT department. Otherwise there is the expense of training end users.

20

- End users might demand expensive hardware which may not be necessary.
- Developing and maintaining the intranet distracts end users from their core work. It could be argued that employees carrying out their usual duties may generate more profit for the company than the money that would be saved by employing fewer IT specialists.
- If training is inadequate, end users may fail to produce anything useful, or the intranet may appear to function properly but actually produce inaccurate data, which could influence end users to make the wrong decisions. There is also the concern of security as end users may not be able to safeguard confidential data.
- End users tend to duplicate each other's efforts as they work in isolation rather than consulting each other.

Feedback on learning activity 20.3

E-procurement can:

- Control parts inventories more effectively.
- Reduce the overheads associated with using purchasing agents.
- Improve manufacturing cycles.

Feedback on self-assessment question 20.3

- Since the cost savings of e-procurement are achieved through empowerment of originators throughout the business to directly purchase their own items rather than through purchasing, there is a risk that some originators may take advantage of this. This is known as maverick purchasing where items are ordered that are unnecessary or too expensive. Van Weele (2005) points out that 'by using electronic catalogue systems, more purchasing transactions can be contracted so that the percentage of maverick buying can be drastically reduced'.

- Security concerns and lack of trust between trading partners. Some businesses could see e-procurement as risky. However, as Deise et al (2000) argue, 'if companies do not take advantage of opportunities (such as utilising e-procurement), they will not flourish in the world of twenty-first century business'.

- The difficulties associated with the integration of systems. Van Weele (2005) stresses:

  'Implementation of e-procurement systems is far from a simple matter. It requires a high level of purchasing professionalism, clearly spelled out purchasing procedures and a seamless integration with the general ledger system and other systems within the company. Next, these systems need to match with the administrative systems of supplier, which in many cases is a big problem!'

- The likelihood of redundancies. If the organisation becomes more efficient it may not require as many employees. Employees will be resistant to the introduction of e-procurement if they feel their jobs may be at risk.

Revision questions

Revision question for study session 1

According to Knight and Willmott (1992), 'Established methodologies of leadership have placed unnecessary constraints upon our capacity to examine creatively actual leadership practices and generate fresh insight into their dynamics.' Discuss.

Feedback on page 251

Revision question for study session 2

Using available electronic databases, list the basic EC Directives on public procurement and explain in detail the key elements of each of them.

Feedback on page 254

Revision question for study session 3

In the context of purchasing, under what circumstances would you allow the following?

- Accepting gifts from a supplier.
- Accepting an invitation for dinner.
- Engaging in a personal friendship with a supplier sales representative.
- Extending the deadline for a competitive bid to one of your suppliers.
- Giving the right of first refusal to your current supplier.

Feedback on page 254

Revision question for study session 4

You are a purchasing manager. Explain what you would expect to report to your superiors on a monthly basis. Further, describe to what extent you would (or would not) report the same thing to your production and logistics manager.

Feedback on page 255

Revision question for study session 5

Alfred Chandler (1961) argued that: 'Structures should be designed to facilitate the strategic pursuits of a firm and, therefore, follows strategy'. Critically evaluate what he meant by this statement.

Feedback on page 255

Revision question for study session 6

Supply chain management assumes that the companies involved in the supply chain are willing to work closely together and are willing to develop partnership relationships. Discuss the validity of this assumption and explain why companies would want to develop partnership relationships.

Feedback on page 257

Revision question for study session 7

Bridges (cited in Robbins, 2003) predicts that in the future jobs will be designed on a temporary-contract basis to form project teams to complete a specific task. When the task is complete, the team will disperse. People are likely to work in more than one project team at once, keeping irregular hours. Networked computers will be relied upon heavily as a means of keeping in contact with other team members. Bridges concludes, 'Few of these employees will be working nine-to-five at specific work spots, and they'll have little of the security their grandfathers had'.

If Bridges' predictions of the future regarding job design are correct, describe how could this affect the purchasing and supply positions.

Feedback on page 257

Revision question for study session 8

Using Hofstede's model of national culture and a nationality of your choice, evaluate how that culture affects the way in which business is conducted today.

Feedback on page 258

Revision question for study session 9

The management of a medium-sized company is considering buying a new computer numerically controlled (CNC) machine. This is a completely new type of technology for the company. Describe the purchasing process stages involved and the disciplines that will probably be involved in each stage.

Feedback on page 259

Revision question for study session 10

(a) Explain how purchasing policies and processes can add value to a company.
(b) Describe what you consider to be the purchasing function's core and non-core activities.

Feedback on page 259

Revision question for study session 11

Explain, in the context of current management thinking, how employees can increase their level of power within their organisation.

Feedback on page 260

Revision question for study session 12

Discuss the assertion that the majority of conflicts arising in organisations are a result of poor communication.

Feedback on page 262

Revision question for study session 13

Critically evaluate the assertion that a certain level of conflict should be maintained within the organisation.

Feedback on page 263

Revision question for study session 14

Critically discuss the extent to which you believe that employee turnover is a cost to the business and should be avoided.

Feedback on page 264

Revision question for study session 15

Discuss how group cohesiveness affects an organisation's performance.

Feedback on page 265

Revision question for study session 16

'Technology and the internet are now regarded as major enablers and drivers of change.' Discuss.

Feedback on page 266

Revision question for study session 17

Critically appraise the following statement: 'Revolutionary change is brutal, expensive, and often fails'.

Feedback on page 268

Revision question for study session 18

'Resistance to change is an irrational response.' Critically evaluate what is meant by this statement in the context of managing change.

Feedback on page 269

Revision question for study session 19

Under UK/EU law, where a contract of employment exists – whether written or verbal – there are certain important 'implied duties' of both employer and employee. List and briefly explain *four* employer 'duties' relevant to your own employment situation, your organisation or the legislation governing contracts of employment in your own country. Use suitable examples to support your answer.

Feedback on page 271

Revision question for study session 20

According to Scarborough (2003), effective knowledge management within the organisation can provide organisations with the key source for competitive advantage by enabling them to differentiate themselves to customers and stakeholders. Explain and critically evaluate this point of view, using practical examples to illustrate your answer.

Feedback on page 272

Feedback on revision questions

Feedback on revision question for study session 1

There are many claims that effective leadership is said to differentiate successful organisations from their weaker competitors. The definition of leadership distinguishing it from management remains somewhat ambiguous.

> 'Many attempts to clarify modern leadership have caused conflicting viewpoints to emerge which create diverse styles and tend to justify a general opinion that very little is known about the subject' (Betts, 2004).

The literature surrounding leadership is not only conflicting and confusing, it is limited as well. This could be due to the difficulties associated with studying a topic which is so diverse and has so many variables that are difficult to quantify. The actual definition of leadership continues to be controversial.

Avery (2002) classify leadership research into four main paradigms: classical, transactional, visionary and organic, which are arranged along a continuum with the latter being the most recent.

Classical leadership dates back to before the 1970s and relates to the unitarist approach where Legge (1995) believes that all who belong to the organisation have the same interests. With Classical leadership, one or a few people are dominant and followers carry out tasks through fear or shear respect. Classical leadership is still used today, a recent example would be Saddam Hussein leading Iraq through fear. Classical leadership focuses on the individual being at the top of the formal hierarchy, with the leader possessing more power than its followers. This type of leadership encompasses theories such as the 'trait approach', the 'great man theory' and the behavioural theories.

Initially, during the 1950s, leadership researchers attempted to link the success of a leader to specific personality traits and attributes, which was termed 'the trait approach'. This relates to the 'great man theory' which was also proposed in the 1950s and claimed that true leaders were born with certain personality traits. The reason for examining personality traits could possibly be attributed to leaders having distinctive features at the time of the research. For example, Hitler was particularly authoritative, which could be considered a trait of successful leaders. Unfortunately the trait approach revealed little conclusive evidence – as Betts (2004) points out, 'characteristics are very difficult to classify because leaders are affected by their followers, conditions and situations'. This dated approach to leadership has one major flaw in that it ignores women and diversity issues. It attempts to simplify a complicated issue. This is supported by Knights and Willmott (1992) who argue 'it is all too often that complex and contradictory social practices are reduced to a set of mathematical variables'.

Caldwell (2003) attempts to distinguish between change managers and change leaders stating:

> 'change leaders are those executives or senior level managers at the very top of the organisation who envisage, initiate or sponsor strategic change of a far-reaching or transformational nature. In contrast, change managers are those middle-level managers and functional specialists who carry forward and build support for change within business units or key functions.'

Leadership research is limited, partly due to the romanticism of the trait approach. It is too restricted and narrow minded. Rather than looking at the bigger picture, researchers focused on specific traits, diverting their attention from the real issues surrounding leadership. This theory along with other traditional theories is lacking in many areas. Knight and Willmott (1992) stress 'what is not seen in orthodox studies is the presence of power and subjectivity'. This approach also lacks any practical application for managing change.

Amongst the classical approach are universal theories of leadership. Most renowned for their universal theory was the work of Blake and Mouton (cited in Burnes, 2004) with their 'managerial grid', later called the 'leadership grid'. Blake and Mouton examined how concern for people and business interacted and as a result produced a grid with five possible leadership styles. The first style is team management with a high concern for people and production. This style attempts to accomplish high performance through high job satisfaction. Country club management relates to a high concern for people but a low concern for business. The third style is middle-of-the-road management with a moderate concern for both, whereas task management (style four) represents a high concern for production but low concern for people. Style five is impoverished management which has a low concern for both, using minimal effort to achieve the desired results. Obviously team management is the preferred style which is a win-win situation for both parties involved.

Blake and Mouton are of the opinion that a leader's main style is attributed to the leader's value and belief system, the culture of the organisation, as well as chance and the fact that a leader can switch their style according to the situation. Burnes (2004) points out that there is little empirical evidence supporting this or any of the universal theories due to the difficulty in relating leadership effectiveness to traits. However, Kanter (cited in Burnes, 2004) believes in the one best fit – the universal theory – and uses the notion that all organisations operate in a turbulent environments. It is unrealistic, however, to present a general solution for all leaders in different situations in all organisations. This is supported by Hofstede (cited in Burnes, 2004) who believes that culture differs from one country to another and therefore the behaviour in a particular country and what is accepted is not necessarily appropriate for all cultures; Hofstede stated that universal rules do not in fact apply.

One limitation of the classical paradigm is that it is slow to react to change as classical leadership is most appropriate in organisations operating in stable environments. Another limitation is that one or a few dominant individuals having an authoritative, autocratic structure can hinder innovation as followers are not consulted, they just carry out the task.

Transactional leadership considers followers as individuals, acknowledging their skills and needs. Followers are consulted and negotiate with the leader but the leader has the final say. This paradigm was dominant during the 1970s through to the mid 1980s and operates on the basis that employees are rewarded for good performance, using incentives to motivate such as monetary rewards and promotions. This paradigm is most appropriate in organisations operating in a stable environment who introduce incremental changes.

Transformational/visionary leadership moves away from the norm bringing about radical change using the concept of business process re-engineering (BPR). Transformational leadership is characterised by the leader's personality to induce change, to create a vision. Rather than reaching objectives using extrinsic factors, transformational leaders attempt to motivate individuals by giving them the freedom of choice to satisfy their needs. This relates to Maslow's hierarchy of needs. This paradigm takes into account change, which much of the previous literature ignores.

> 'Types of outstanding leadership such as transformational, characteristic and visionary are becoming more and more important to organisations as workforces become more diverse, technology improves and international competition heightens.' (Smith, 2002)

The organic paradigm reflects the pluralist perspective, acknowledging diversity. It moves away from the notion that one leader is best, and believes that leaders in a group can emerge naturally at any time rather than being appointed. An organisation operating using this paradigm would have a particularly flat structure. 'Leadership will need to operate more through vision and values permeating the entire culture', Gayle and Avery (2004) state. However, this paradigm lacks the detail of how this culture will prevail. Also, with this approach, conflicts could occur unless one leader is designated and that person has the final say. Knights and Willmott (1992) are of the opinion that institutional theory has made a significant contribution to leadership literature. This perspective defines leadership as a process which shapes values and beliefs and that individuals are encouraged by the leader to reach the organisation's objectives. They state:

> 'common to the diversity of models and theories of leadership, including need achievement theory, path goal theory, normative decision-making theory, cognitive resource theory and transformational theory is a minimal regard for the historical, cultural/political and existential conditions of leadership processes.'

However, the institutional approach is not critical of the normative consensus.

Gayle and Avery (2004) advocate that leadership styles have shifted from classical and transactional forms to transformational and organic approaches. Leadership in practice, however, is not as advanced as the literature suggests. It could be argued that transactional leadership, where employees are considered as followers, is still very much the dominant paradigm. Unfortunately, this management style is not consistent with expectations of the workforce today.

Feedback on revision question for study session 2

According to Van Weele (2005), there are four different Directives:

- the Public Supplies Directive;
- the Public Works Directive;
- the Public Services Directive;
- the Utilities Directive.

The information to answer this question is available for free on the internet. You should use an appropriate search engine (for example Google) to find relevant websites and use the information thereon as the basis for formulating your answer.

Feedback on revision question for study session 3

This question relates to ethics in purchasing, for example what is acceptable and what is not. Most professional associations (for example CIPS, the Chartered Institute of Marketing (CIM) and so on) have ethical codes and guidelines for ethical behaviour. According to Van Weele (2005), the respect for the purchasing profession can be undermined by improper action on the part of its members with regard to gifts, gratuities or favours. What is clear is that people in purchasing should not (normally) accept any money, gift or favour that might influence, or be suspected of influencing, their buying decisions.

- Gifts from a supplier: acceptable for gifts (not being money) with low monetary value (less than €25–€30). If the gifts are of high value then buyers should not accept them.
- Invitation to dinner: acceptable if it is for the purpose of discussing business or if it is a dinner that is part of the annual supplier day. Invitations from suppliers for very exclusive and expensive dinners should not be accepted.
- Personal friendships with supplier sales representatives: difficult to avoid in some cases. Acceptable, but under the condition that both decide to leave negotiations or other business issues to other company representatives.
- Extending deadlines for competitive bids to one of your suppliers: acceptable only when you also extend the deadline for other suppliers.
- Offering the right of first refusal to your current supplier: the right of first refusal gives the holder the right to meet any other offer before the

proposed contract is accepted. Only acceptable when communicated very clearly beforehand to the bidders. The process has to be transparent and clear for everybody.

Feedback on revision question for study session 4

Here, your answer should include reference to some of the following (or similar, in relation to your own organisation and so on):

- Monthly reports to the general manager might include indicators for numbers of new contracts, internal compliance to these contracts, realised savings for the company, potential supply risks, delivery performance, internal customer satisfaction and quality of the purchased items.
- In general, it is very important to differentiate reporting. A general manager is interested in different indicators than the production or logistics manager. For example, the production manager is more interested to learn about supplier and product quality, preventing quality costs, process improvements, product innovations, and so on.
- The logistics manager is likely to be more interested in information about delivery performance (for example timely delivery, quantities delivered, materials shortages), inventories, waste in the supply chain, just-in-time deliveries, and so on.
- By differentiating communication, the purchasing manager can establish better relationships with these important stakeholders in the purchasing process. The production and logistics managers will better understand the impact of the purchasing process on their function/department, and might involve the purchasing department earlier in their purchasing decision making.

Feedback on revision question for study session 5

You are required to explain how organisations should configure their structure in relation to their overall (strategic) objectives. Alfred Chandler argues that strategy begets structure and not the other way around. Good answers will therefore pick up on the point that successful strategy implementation and achievement of objectives and so on is dependent upon appropriate supporting organisational and functional structures – and that inappropriate or outmoded structures/approaches will not see strategic objectives realised.

Answers should consider the following:

- An organisation's structure is a means to help management achieve its goals and objectives. As objectives are derived from the organisation's strategy, it is common sense that strategy and structure are directly related. However, structure should not dictate how a strategy is executed. It should, instead, always pursue strategy.
- According to Hannagan (2005), 'the object of [organisational] design is to create an organisational structure which fits with its objectives, its resources and its environment'. This infers [implies] that strategy should

be formulated first, in order to designate people and other resources. Having decided upon what strategy to employ, an organisation can therefore then make decisions regarding roles, responsibilities and resources and distribute them accordingly to achieve the desired strategy. In this sense, structure is used to facilitate strategy, which appears to be a rational and logical approach.

However, the most crucial reason for structure to proceed after strategy formulation is so that an organisation can evolve and stay competitive. This is because certain strategies may not be feasible with particular structures and therefore could impede and hinder the company from moving forward. For example, a hierarchical structure is unlikely to be suitable for stockbrokers who have to react quickly to the changing market. Robbins and Decenzo (2004) exemplify this point:

> 'if an organisation focuses on providing certain services – say, police protection in a community – its structure will be one that promotes standardisation and efficient services. Similarly, if an organisation is attempting to employ a growth strategy by entering into global markets, it will need a structure that is flexible, fluid and readily adaptable to the environment. Accordingly, organisation structure should follow strategy. And if management makes a significant change in its organisation's strategy, it will need to modify structure to accommodate and support that change.'

- According to Deresky (2006), 'considerable research has shown that a firm's structure must be conducive to the implementation of its strategy. In other words, the structure must "fit" the strategy, or it will not work'. Alfred Chandler, in particular, is renowned for his extensive research regarding the strategy–structure relationship. Interestingly, his findings revealed that changes in corporate strategy preceded and often lead to changes in an organisation's structure.

- Chandler's research discovered that changes in strategy cause new administrative problems and therefore require an alteration or new structure to accommodate the new strategy. He discovered that structure was likely to follow the firm's growth strategy, but often not until inefficiency and internal problems lead to structural adjustment being necessary. His findings were consistent, whereby companies adopted a new strategy and then they experienced new administrative problems and issues. This in turn caused a decline in productivity and consequently the company would then shift to a more appropriate organisational structure. Productivity and profitability would then show signs of improvement.

- However, Brooks (2003) critiques Chandler's findings and, contrary to his research, is of the opinion that 'structure will in some way contribute to the creation of a strategy'. 'In those times [the 1950s], the idea that an organisation could rationally determine its strategy and then put in place a structure to help achieve it was a reasonable one.' He argues that whilst this mode of thought may have been useful in the past (as planning and implementation of deliberate strategies was the accepted practice), it is now redundant. He concludes that change, however, occurs nowadays at an unprecedented rate and therefore the notion that managers can plan so far ahead is unrealistic. 'Strategy is no longer seen as a linear, detached process, and is increasingly seen as something that emerges from the organisation's efforts to stay competitive.' Despite Brooks' disapproval, strategy undoubtedly should precede structure. Whilst the environment may not be as predictable as it once was, long-term planning still has its place within an organisation.

Feedback on revision question for study session 6

This assumption is not so valid in many supply markets.

Mutual trust between buyer and supplier takes time and is often difficult to achieve.

Broken promises, abuse of trust and conflicts can sour relationships.

In many supply markets, suppliers form cartels (that is, silent agreements on pricing behaviour and division of markets), thus forming relationships with one another rather than with their buyers/customers.

Many suppliers avoid any discussion relating to improving their performance for their clients. Rather, they spend time and money on 'currying favour' with customers by offering fringe benefits such as invitations to sports events, exhibitions and trade fairs. This does not necessarily improve the relationship between supplier and buyer, nor does it always lead to improved supplier performance.

More often than not, suppliers pass on cost increases automatically to the next in line.

Conditions under which companies are willing to develop partnerships relate to:

- where mutual trust exists between buyer and supplier;
- shared balance of power between buyer and supplier;
- high interdependency between buyer and supplier;
- where both parties are committed for the long term;
- a fair sharing of risk and rewards;
- open sharing of strategies, knowledge, technology and so on.

Feedback on revision question for study session 7

According to Waller (2003):

'Purchasing is the buying of materials or services from an outside source and thus involves the transfer of goods from one distinct entity to another. The purchasing activity is the upstream part of the supply chain. A client's requirement is negotiated with marketing, this establishes the basis for operating plans and then production decides what needs to be purchased. In order to make an unbroken supply chain, purchasing, marketing and production must work in a team to ensure delivery dates are met.'

The key objectives of the purchasing function are as follows:

- to supply the organisation with a steady flow of materials and services to meet its needs;
- to ensure continuity of supply;
- to obtain, efficiently, the best value for every unit of expenditure;
- to manage inventory so as to give the best service at the lowest cost;
- to maintain sound cooperative relationships with other departments;
- to develop staff, policies, procedures and organisation to ensure the achievement of the foregoing;
- to link to the operations management and planning functions in order to obtain those items required by the operating system for the efficient and effective production of products or (where appropriate) provision of services.

The purchasing department is also responsible for maintaining a supplier database with records of products offered, quality, price and delivery times. This aspect of the job will be relatively easy to carry out, providing networked computers are used.

It appears that many aspects of the purchasing and supply position would remain unaffected by Bridge's preconceived notions of future job design. However, a major aspect of the purchasing function – to maintain sound, cooperative relationships – would be of high concern. Relationship building with marketing and production (internally) and suppliers (externally) would be very difficult purely by email. Whilst the latest video technology enables virtual meetings, interaction is not quite the same. Relationships with key suppliers will be in jeopardy. Using email it is difficult to really get to know a person and create, let alone build, a relationship. Conversation is likely to be in less depth with suppliers using technology, which implies that it will be more difficult to build a rapport with the supplier and find out about new products coming to market. Communicating by email and other technology applications brings with it a host of other problems too. For example, networks can fail and email can go unread.

Forming different teams every time a task is undertaken will bring with it inconsistent methods and confusion within the organisation. More time will be spent recruiting and relationships will be severed each time the team disbands. Team members could become complacent regarding the quality of their work as they know that they are only contracted short term and others will be left to pick up the pieces. Whilst new team formations will undoubtedly bring new blood and fresh insights into the organisation, so many other aspects of the purchasing and supply function will be compromised if Bridge's projections are to be realised. On the other hand, if technology freed up buyers' time so that they could maintain and build relationships with suppliers, then it would add real value to the company.

Feedback on revision question for study session 8

Your answer should relate to:

- Power, distance and authority – informal or strict ranking?

- Uncertainty avoidance.
- Individualism/collectivism – centralised decision making? Spontaneous, risk taking/careful and considerate?
- Masculinity/femininity – negotiation style: polite and friendly vs. competitive or frank? Straight down to business or socialising first? Gender equality?
- Long-term/short-term relationships – goal orientated, aggressive negotiator or long-term relationship builder?

Your answer should also include other accepted behaviours, for example is it acceptable to talk about politics, religion and so on?

Feedback on revision question for study session 9

The company will go through the following stages in the purchasing process:

- problem identification: the request for buying a new CNC machine is likely to be initiated by one of the technical departments of the company (for example engineering, maintenance, production);
- determining specification: the technical department will determine the technical specification. In some instances suppliers will be involved in this process. The finance department will have a role in requesting the budget for this machine;
- supply market research and supplier qualification: likely to be carried out by the technical department with support from the purchasing department;
- requesting quotations and bid evaluation: usually initiated by the purchasing department (or project team where relevant);
- negotiation with suppliers regarding features, delivery and general terms and conditions: carried out by the purchasing department (or project team);
- selection of the supplier: based on the quotations and the first negotiation round, the purchasing/project team usually selects the preferred supplier. (In a medium-sized organisation, it may be that a member of the management team will conduct any price negotiations. In larger firms, this is likely to be done by the project buyer);
- preparing contracts: normally drawn up by the purchasing department in close collaboration with the legal department;
- follow up and expediting the order: the purchasing department in collaboration with the production/engineering department;
- invoice control: where invoices and orders do not match, the purchasing department contacts the supplier for clarification.

Feedback on revision question for study session 10

(a) Purchasing policies and processes can add value and contribute to business success in three main ways:
   (i) policies can improve sales margins through realising substantial cost savings (for example introducing new suppliers, competitive

tendering, looking for substitute materials). Savings accrued in purchasing add value to the bottom line;

(ii) through sound financial, quality and logistics arrangements with suppliers, purchasing can contribute to a higher capital turnover ratio (for example longer payment terms, reduction of inventories, quality improvement and leasing instead of buying equipment);

(iii) if requested, suppliers can contribute to the company's innovation process. Even small improvements in the relationship with suppliers may have a significant impact on the company's return on net sales.

(b) According to Van Weele (2005), purchasing can be defined as: 'managing the company's external resources in such a way that the supply of all goods, services, capabilities and knowledge which are necessary for running, maintaining and managing the company's primary and support activities is secured at the most favourable conditions.'

From this definition it may be derived that the purchasing function covers the following core activities:

(i) determining the specification;
(ii) selecting the most suitable supplier;
(iii) preparing and conducting negotiations with suppliers in order to establish an agreement;
(iv) placing orders by selected suppliers;
(v) monitoring and controlling the orders (expediting);
(vi) following up and evaluation.

The purchasing function does not include responsibility for:

(i) materials requirement planning;
(ii) materials scheduling;
(iii) inventory management;
(iv) incoming inspection and quality control.

Feedback on revision question for study session 11

According to Betts (2000) power is usually defined as 'the ability to get things done; it implies capability ... [whereas authority] is conferred by management'. Power relates to leadership and concerns the ability to control or influence others. Traditionally, it was assumed that the rights inherent in one's formal position in an organisation were the sole source of influence. It was believed that managers were the only ones who possessed power, for example the only ones with the ability to influence decisions. Managers were only minimally dependent on those with expertise. Robbins and Decenzo (2004) state that historically 'the higher a manager's position in the organisation, the more influence he or she had. However, those conditions no longer hold'. This is also supported by Buchanan and Huczynski (2004) who stress 'prestige job titles no longer confer legitimacy on bosses' orders. Employees have their own sources of power, which they can use to undermine a leader's position'.

There are several types of power that exist. French and Raven (cited in Buchanan and Huczynski, 2004) are notorious for their research regarding power. They identified seven types. In particular, the most common types that were used over 30 years ago were coercive and legitimate power. Coercive power is where power was exerted over subordinates using fear, punishment and threatening behaviour. Legitimate power is based on the structural hierarchy of the organisation and the perception of subordinates to obey their senior mangers. On this basis, the more senior managers are, the more power they possess. Betts stresses that with these types of power, success is only short lived. For example, 'if a supervisor relies purely on authority power, or position power, he or she might be successful for a while, provided the situation is favourable'.

Alternatively, expert power is based on a person's expertise, knowledge and skill. This relates to the well-known phrase 'knowledge is power'. If this skill and expertise is acknowledged by others, then the person will have power. When help is offered to those in need, this type of power is viewed in a positive light. However, it can be perceived negatively when used in a condescending manner towards others.

Referent power refers to the personality or charisma someone has. These people will have power as people admire and respect them. Hannagan (2005) states:

> 'studies by Pierce and Robinson (1987), for example have shown that the most effective managers today rely more on expert, referent and connection power than on coercive, legitimate, reward or information power. Leaders now tend to use personal power rather than positional power as management structures have become flatter and management practice more open.'

His findings therefore illustrate that in order to develop power, employees must either be charismatic, have the ability to network and/or have expertise in a particular area, which is recognised by others (which implies it is who you know and what you know).

Betts (2000) recommends several methods of developing power. He believes in 'learning expertise in a new technology or discipline, which is recognised as a critical feature for company survival or development'. Also important is:

> 'achieving effective performance by working hard, developing new roles and proposing new ideas. Establishing strong relationships with influential people outside the company who are able to exert pressure in some way.'

Finally, Betts suggests that in order to develop more power, it is necessary to create, 'a better impression through a variety of means, such as improving speech, education, technical and social skills, dress, manner and social work'.

Benfari, Wilkinson and Orth (cited in Buchanan and Huczynski, 2004) argue that referent power is both important and an under-utilised source of power. They suggest that to improve your referent power, you should:

- get to know the motives, preferences, values and interests of your colleagues;
- build relationships using shared motives, goals and interests;
- respect differences in interests and do not attack another person's style;

- give 'positive strokes', use reward power, confirm others' competence;
- invite reciprocal influence, show that you respect the opinion of others;
- share information, give your expertise, particularly where you stand to benefit;
- minimise concerns with status, put signs of office aside, people relate to equals;
- develop communication skills, people value clear and consistent messages;
- get to know how people react to stress and crisis;
- get to know the informal political structure of your organisation.

Whilst there has been a shift in perception regarding who can gain power, the shift in practice is not as far advanced as the academics would suggest. Indeed, positional power is still prevalent. Common themes amongst the literature suggest that in order to be influential, it is necessary to possess sound interpersonal skills in order to network and build relationships as well as the expertise in an area that others lack and the willingness to share this with others. In addition to this, to develop power it is necessary to have some charisma.

Feedback on revision question for study session 12

According to Buchanan and Huczynski (2004), conflict is 'a state of mind. It has to be perceived by the parties involved. If two or more parties are not aware of a conflict, then no conflict exists'.

The causes of conflict within an organisation are many and varied, but poor communication is the source most commonly attributed to conflict. As Robbins (2003) finds:

> 'a popular myth in organisations is that poor communication is the primary source of conflicts. And certainly problems in the communication process do act to retard collaboration, stimulate misunderstandings, and create conflicts. But a review of the literature suggests that within organisations, structural factors and individual value differences are probably greater sources of conflict.'

Individual value differences are a result of the person's family background, education and experiences. Alternatively, structural factors relate to problems of integration, for example task interdependency. With structural differentiation, employees tend to disagree over organisational objectives and allocation of resources. These conflicts, however, are not a signal of poor communication. Rather, they are attributed to the organisational structure and bureaucratic procedures.

Robbins and Decenzo (2004) observe that many people make the mistake of equating:

> 'good communication with having others agree with their views. What might at first look like an interpersonal conflict based on poor communication is usually found, upon closer analysis, to be

a disagreement caused by different role requirements, unit goals, personalities, value systems, or similar factors.'

They conclude that 'as a source of conflict for managers, poor communication probably gets more attention than it deserves'.

Robbins and Decenzo (2004) point out 'people are often quick to assume that most conflicts are caused by a lack of communication, but, as one author noted, there is usually plenty of communication going on in most conflicts'. Robbins (2003) believes:

'many conflicts attributed to poor communication are on, closer examination, due to value differences … When managers incorrectly treat a value-based conflict as a communication problem, the conflict is rarely eliminated. On the contrary, increased communication efforts are only likely to crystallise and reinforce differences.'

Undeniably, a lack of communication can be a source of conflict within an organisation. However, it is unlikely to be the main source. Robbins (2003) recommends that 'managers should look first to structural or value-based explanations because they are more prevalent in organisations'.

Conflict is pervasive in organisations. Regardless of what sources of conflict manifest within the organisation, Nelson and Quick (1996) stress that 'conflict is pervasive [rife] in organisations. To manage it effectively, managers should understand the many sources of conflict'.

Robins and Decenzo (2004) state that 'because your approach to resolving a conflict is likely to be determined largely by its causes, you need to determine the source of the conflict'.

Feedback on revision question for study session 13

Conflict is usually associated with aggressive, dysfunctional behaviour. The shear idea of maintaining a level of conflict therefore appears ridiculous. As Robbins and Decenzo (2004) point out, 'for almost all of us, the term conflict has a negative connotation, and the idea of purposely creating conflict seems to be the antithesis of good management'. Stimulating conflict does not mean in the sense of creating upset and anxiety. Rather, it refers to keeping an organisation forward thinking and responsive to market demands. Indeed, in some cases conflict is unhelpful. Stimulating functional conflict, however, can be considered constructive. The goal of conflict management is essentially to keep conflicts productive. As Zornoza et al (2002) recognises: 'Conflict management operates on the basis that conflict can be positive and thus focuses on directing conflict toward constructive dialogue'.

Townsend (1970) actively encourages conflict. He argues that:

'compromise is usually bad. It should be a last resort. If two departments or divisions have a problem they can't solve and it comes up to you, listen to both sides and then, unlike Solomon, pick one or the other. This places solid accountability on the *winner* to make it work.'

Deutsch (cited in Chen and Tjosvold, 2005) proposes two approaches to managing conflict: cooperative and competitive conflict management. Cooperative conflict is viewed as a mutual problem that requires a mutual solution. As one party moves towards achievement their goals, so does the other party. The emphasis on cooperative goals leads to mutual exchange and an open-minded discussion that in turn help develop useful, mutually beneficial resolutions that reaffirm the relationship. Therefore, in this instance, conflict is productive.

Whereas a cooperative style tends to result in a win-win situation, the competitive approach believes that, as one party moves towards the achievement of their goals, the other party fails (win-lose). Because each party is so compelled to win, discussion is avoided. The consequences tend to lead to weakened relationships and deadlock or imposed solutions. It is likely that the party who is perceived to be the loser will be frustrated. This kind of conflict management is not very productive.

The notion of maintaining a certain level of conflict reflects the interactionist perspective. This approach actively encourages conflict believing that harmonious and overly cooperative organisations are likely to become complacent, static and reluctant to change. Conflict instigates discussion and idea generation regarding the organisation's goals and use of resources. As Chen and Tjosvold (2005) point out, 'Diversity, when properly harnessed, promotes the "creative abrasion" of dialogue and debate that in turn stimulates innovation'. Consequently, managing conflict in this light keeps firms self-critical, creative and therefore competitive.

There is much evidence to suggest that conflict, when managed effectively, can enhance decision processes in organisations, leading to improved decision outcomes and the development of a more cohesive approach towards the achievement of functional or organisational objectives. When managed ineffectively, however, conflict results in dysfunctional behaviours and low group productivity. Unfortunately, whilst there is plenty of documentation regarding resolving conflict, there is little on the subject of stimulating it. It is strongly recommended, therefore, that those who demonstrate original thinking and contribute innovative ideas should be rewarded in the presence of their colleagues.

Feedback on revision question for study session 14

Abbassi and Hollman (cited in Stovel and Bontis, 2002) define employee turnover to be 'the rotation of workers around the labour market; between firms, jobs and occupations; and between the states of unemployment and employment'.

A low level of employee turnover incurs the obvious costs of recruitment, selection, training and development as well as hindering productivity and the quality of service provided for a short period. Taylor (2002) concluded from his research that 'for most organisations, turnover in excess of 5–10% has more negative than positive consequences'. In addition to this, Johnson et al (cited in Stovel and Bontis, 2002) state that 'research estimates indicate that hiring and training a replacement worker for a lost employee cost approximately 50% of the workers annual salary'. Although Curtis and Wright (2001) estimate the costs to be nearer 150%!

However, the financial implications are only half the story. The problem of employee turnover is exacerbated when employees leaving the organisation not only take their skills but also inside information specific to the organisation and place them in the hands of the competitor. Stovel and Bontis (2002) warn that 'voluntary turnover often results in departing employees migrating to competing firms, creating an even more critical situation, since this knowledge can now be used against the organisation'. Worse still, many employees who leave a firm, sales personnel in particular, often take their business contacts with them. Johnson et al (2000) believe the loss of sales people can have a serious impact upon the organisation. They argue, 'it is not just the cost in time and money that comes with recruiting and training a new sales person, it is the loss of crucial market intelligence, customer relationships and sales knowledge'.

Voluntary turnover is likely to put pressure on existing staff leading to lower staff morale. Hendrie (2004) stresses that 'the workers left in the business can feel naturally aggrieved as they are left to pick up the pieces'.

Whilst a high level of employee turnover can be considered to be detrimental to a company, it can also be acknowledged as beneficial. Taylor (2004) found that some organisations with a low turnover and a stagnating atmosphere made it difficult for employees to embrace change. Turnover can be healthy for organisations as it fosters new ideas and skills, bringing fresh blood into the organisation. According to Johnson et al (2000), there are many positive outcomes associated with turnover: 'The prevention of stagnation and complacency, the facilitation of change and innovation and generation of new ideas that new employees bring into the corporation should be recognised'. Mobley (cited in Johnson et al, 2000) points out that 'turnover can provide the opportunity to supplant poor performers with more capable replacements' which could effectively improve the business's productivity.

Feedback on revision question for study session 15

Nelson and Quick (1996) define group cohesion as the 'interpersonal glue that makes members of a group stick together'. Brooks (2003) describes group cohesiveness as 'the pulling power of the group, its magnetism, its ability to retain its members'. He maintains that 'in a cohesive group, group identity is clear, interpersonal relationships are good and people place value upon being a member of the group'.

Cohesive groups gel together and therefore there is less likely to be tension within the group. They tend to develop greater levels of cooperation amongst themselves, which results in group effectiveness. A cohesive group is also claimed to have higher rates of job satisfaction and lower levels of absenteeism and employee turnover. Groups with little cohesion are more likely to experience difficulty exercising control over their members and enforcing their standards of behaviour and performance. Therefore, in many respects, group cohesion positively benefits the organisation in the sense that it can improve organisational productivity.

The size of the group has an impact on group cohesiveness. Larger groups tend to be less effective as they will find it harder to communicate and they are more likely to suffer form absenteeism. With large groups members tend to feel less involved.

Whilst cohesive groups clearly contribute to an organisation's performance, strongly cohesive groups can in fact be a hindrance to the organisation. Brooks (2003) asserts that 'they start to look in on themselves too much and can become very defensive and protective of their territory and jealous of, or even aggressive towards other groups'. A very cohesive group can be unwelcoming to new members, can be manipulative and reject and refuse any new ideas. Most importantly, a strongly cohesive group can become resistant to change and towards management as they feel safety in numbers.

For this reason, Brooks (2003) stresses, 'it must come as no surprise, either that these over-cohesive groups are viewed as awkward, overbearing and bombastic by others'.

Despite the intention that groups are formed in order to be more creative and innovative than an individual working alone, the irony of it is that people belonging to over-cohesive groups often prefer to go along with the group's decision, rather than what they genuinely believe. Members do this in order to feel included and involved. Janis (cited in Brooks, 2003) refers to this dysfunctional trait as 'groupthink' – 'a mode of thinking in which people engage when they are deeply involved in a cohesive group, in which strivings for unanimity override motivations to realistically appraise alternative courses of action'. Nelson and Quick (1996) view groupthink in a particularly negative light stating that 'cohesive groups tend to avoid conflicts and to demand conformity. Other antecedents include directive leadership, high stress, insulation of the group and lack of methodical procedures for developing and evaluating alternatives'.

Whilst a certain level of cohesiveness clearly benefits organisations, strongly cohesive groups can actually be counter-productive. Managers should be wary of strongly cohesive groups forming.

Feedback on revision question for study session 16

The sophistication of information technology (IT) has had a major impact on society as a whole. Deresky (2006) points out:

> 'of all the developments propelling global business today, the one that is transforming the international manager's agenda more than any other, is the rapid advance in information technology. The speed and accuracy of information transmission are changing the nature of the global manager's job by making geographic barriers less relevant. Indeed, the

necessity of being able to access IT is being increasingly recognised by managers and families around the world, who are giving priority to being "plugged in" over other lifestyle accoutrements.'

The internet in particular has revolutionised the way businesses operate today. Thompson and Strickland (2003) believe:

'The internet is opening up new market opportunities, affecting competition, creating a fundamentally different business environment, and prompting companies to incorporate the capabilities of online technology to transform the way they do business.'

The use of the internet is widely acclaimed for boosting the productivity of firms. Furthermore, the internet is impelling electronic commerce across the globe allowing companies to communicate electronically with their customers, employees and partners as well as their distributors and suppliers.

With the advent of the internet, firms can compete on a global basis, which would otherwise be difficult to do. For example, organisations can trade online rather than bear the cost of setting up operations. As Griffen and Pustay (2003) explain: 'Today a well-developed website can draw consumers without the need to establish a physical presence in each country'. Using the internet allows companies to captivate a wider audience. For example, customers from the other side of the world are able to purchase a product that otherwise they would not have had access to unless they travelled to the point of sale. Firms can also reduce their advertising costs. This can be beneficial to smaller organisations in particular, allowing them to compete with larger organisations for market share. E-commerce has made market research more efficient by increasing the opportunities to identify and address customer trends and target these accordingly (Aldin et al, 2004). With the increased use of email and knowledge of individual customers' buying habits, target marketing of goods and services is now more easily achievable.

Thomas and Strickland (2003) emphasise that:

'the internet is unquestionably spawning a sweeping business revolution that alters industry boundaries, opens up all kinds of new business-to-business and business-to-consumer market opportunities and threats, sparks competition from new and entirely different breeds of enterprises, and mandates fundamental changes in business practices.'

However, whilst the internet is one of the most prevalent forces of change, there are many other factors that are responsible for driving change. These include:

- globalisation;
- changes in consumer tastes and lifestyles; and
- changes in legislation and government policies.

Changes in labour demographics, the composition of the workforce, Japanisation in addition to changing domestic and global economic trading conditions and dynamic competition also instigate change. Although Cronin (1995) stresses that 'those organisations who do not embrace the internet will be increasingly isolated as managers become increasingly dependent on information to operate and control their business'.

Feedback on revision question for study session 17

The revolutionary (or *punctuated equilibrium*) approach to planning change, according to Romanelli and Tushman (cited in Burnes, 2004) depicts organisations as 'evolving through relatively long periods of stability (equilibrium periods) in their basic patterns of activity that are punctuated by relatively short bursts of fundamental change (revolutionary periods)'. Revolutionary/transformational change takes a 'clean sheet approach' to the organisation, making abrupt changes, which occur over a relatively short period of time.

Revolutionary change has a reputation for being brutal, expensive and associated with high failure rates, but the current negativity surrounding revolutionary change is not a true reflection of its value within organisations. In many instances, this type of change is the only resort. Indeed, frame-breaking change can be construed as a brutal and a traumatic experience for employees as it involves a considerable amount of change to cope with over a short space of time. However, slow and continuous change can get bogged down with politics, and pockets of resistance may have time to form, thus hindering progression and adaptation.

The brutality of revolutionary change is also illustrated by managers' actions. For example, management start from scratch, redesigning processes in order to make efficiencies within the firm, only to later make many redundancies. Buchanan and Huczynski (2004) state 'in America, re-engineering quickly earned a "slash and burn" reputation for the job losses or "downsizing" that applications typically caused'.

Many academics claim that this type of change is expensive to conduct. However, this could be due to the fact that management have to take a clean sheet approach and as a result have to redesign entire processes. It can result in real savings being made as processes are made more efficient and effective. Whilst this approach is often termed as 'expensive', the savings accumulated are often overlooked.

The alternative to revolutionary change is evolutionary or 'continuous' change.

The evolutionary (or *incremental*) approach to planning change is where strategy evolves through an accumulation of relatively small changes over time. It proposes that one problem should be dealt with at a time in order to fine-tune the organisation. However, this approach also has its flaws and does not offer a coherent approach to revolutionary change. It does not alter mindsets or shake up the organisation, it allows it to just drift along. It involves the organisation and its employees in continual change which can cause reform fatigue for employees as they are constantly subject to change.

Whilst it is thought of as less risky, it does take a long time for the small changes to accumulate and be visible.

If an organisation operates in a stable environment and is successful, frame-breaking change is unnecessary. If, however, the organisation is performing poorly or the environment changes substantially, frame-breaking change may be the only way to realign the organisation with its competitive environment. Brutal, drastic action may be the only way forward. Faced with environmental threat, organisations with strong convergent momentum (proponents of continuous change) may not register the threat, or may respond by increased conformity to the status quo. A paradoxical result of long periods of success may be heightened organisational complacency, decreased organisational flexibility and a stunted ability to learn.

Feedback on revision question for study session 18

Resistance to change is a common and natural response. Change involves moving away from what is familiar and common practice to employees, and therefore causes them to be wary and fearful. Mullins (2005) makes the point that:

> 'Fears may be expressed over such matters as employment levels and job security, deskilling of work, loss of job satisfaction, wage rate differentials, changes to social structures and working conditions, loss of individual control over work, and greater management control.'

Burnes (2004) stresses that 'one of the major mistakes companies can make when introducing change is to fail to recognise, and deal with, the real and legitimate fears of the managers and staff'. Resistance to change is therefore by no means an illogical or a rare reaction. However, it does pose as a real problem to management as it can hinder adaptation and progress and therefore must be addressed.

Robbins (2003) believes that despite resistance having some definite downfalls, resistance can be a positive response: 'It provides a degree of stability and predictability to behaviour. If there weren't some resistance, organisational behaviour would take on the characteristics of chaotic randomness.' He continues, pointing out that 'resistance to change can also be a source of functional conflict. For example, resistance to a reorganisation plan or a change in a product line can stimulate a healthy debate over the merits of the idea and result in a better decision'. Robbins and Decenzo (2004) are of the opinion that 'if the employee expresses his or her resistance positively (clearly expressing it to the change agent, along with substantiation), this form of resistance can [actually] be beneficial to the organisation'.

Kubler-Ross (cited in Buchanan and Huczynski, 2004) found that it was natural for people reacting negatively towards change to often experience several stages of resistance before final acceptance. Kubler-Ross extensively researched the emotional states of the terminally ill. She observed that 'we deal with loss by moving through a series of stages, each characterised by a particular emotional response' which she refers to as the 'coping cycle' (see figure 21.1). More recently, it was noticed that these responses are not exclusive to the terminally ill but are typical to those reacting negatively to a change in circumstances.

Figure 21.1: The coping cycle

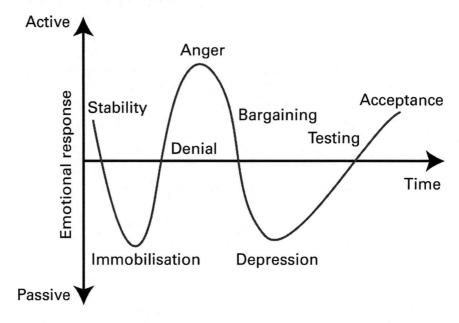

The various emotional responses relating to each of the stages in this model are:

- The denial stage: http://changingminds.org/disciplines/change_management/kubler_ross/denial_stage.htm: reluctance to confront reality, that is, there is still a chance things will return to normal.
- The anger stage: http://changingminds.org/disciplines/change_management/kubler_ross/anger_stage.htm: frustrated feelings especially towards scapegoats. 'Why me' reaction.
- The bargaining stage: http://changingminds.org/disciplines/change_management/kubler_ross/bargaining_stage.htm: exerts effort to negotiate and to mitigate loss.
- The depression stage: http://changingminds.org/disciplines/change_management/kubler_ross/depression_stage.htm: final realisation of what is happening. 'There's nothing that can be done, I'm stuck like this.'
- The testing stage: http://changingminds.org/disciplines/change_management/kubler_ross/testing_stage.htm: seeks solutions.
- The acceptance stage: http://changingminds.org/disciplines/change_management/kubler_ross/acceptance_stage.htm: comes to terms with situation and moves forward.

In order to manage change effectively, the importance of education and communication, participation and involvement as well as facilitation and support must be realised. Despite management's efforts and best intentions, it must be acknowledged that not all employees will accept change.

Feedback on revision question for study session 19

Duties of employer

Any *four* from the following list.

1 'Duty to provide work: Where there is a right to work, jurisprudentially there must be a corresponding duty on an employer to allow an employee to exercise that right, as for every right there must be a corresponding duty. In the area of employment, it has been stated by the majority of judges that there is no right to work and therefore no duty of the employer to provide work, except in certain cases, for example:
    (a) where the work is needed to maintain the employee's publicity and reputation;
    (b) where the work is needed to enable the employee to earn the wage;
    (c) where the nature of the work is such that the employee needs to work to maintain or develop their skills etc.' (Lockton, 2003)

2 'Duty to pay wages: Although there is no general duty on employers to provide work, their duty to pay wages is fundamental to the bargain, and if persistently broken will entitle an employee to sue for a repudiatory breach of contract. Normally, the contract itself will state the amount of pay the employee is entitled to receive – and this will come from individual negotiation between the employer and the employee or from a collective agreement. Where the contract is silent as to the amount of pay the law will imply that reasonable remuneration should be paid.' (Lockton, 2003)

3 'Duty to indemnify: There is some legal argument as to whether the common law implies a duty that an employer should indemnify their employees against expenses incurred during the performance of their contract. While the majority of contracts will expressly cover the situation of travelling and accommodation expenses, a problem arises when the expense has not been envisaged by the contract, for example if a lorry driver is fined for overloading or for a defective tyre. There is an implied duty for an employer to indemnify *unless* the employee has chosen to perform their job in an unlawful way, and by doing this has incurred an expense such as a fine.' (Lockton, 2003)

4 'Duty in relation to references: Although employers are under no obligation to provide references for their employees, in practice most employers do. (In the UK, the majority of the House of Lords held that the writer of a reference owed a duty to the subject of that reference to exercise reasonable care.)' (Lockton, 2003)

5 'Duty of mutual respect: For many years (post industrial revolution) the employment relationship was thought of as being between a master and their servant rather than between an employer and employee. However, the law now imposes a duty on the employer to treat an employee with respect. This is often referred to as the duty of mutual respect, where the word 'mutual' demonstrates that the duty now applies to both parties and not merely to the employee. (The duty has really arisen –

in recent years – in the context of unfair dismissal, where the employee will argue that the employer's treatment has destroyed the trust and confidence that parties need to maintain the relationship, and as such the employee argues that there has been a constructive dismissal).' (Lockton, 2003)

Duty to ensure the employees' safety – extent of the duty

The ordinary employees' safety is protected in two ways:

- 'First, by the common law of negligence, which requires that an employer takes reasonable care to protect their employees, who are reasonably foreseeable victims should the duty of care be broken. (This duty is translated into an implied term in the contract of employment and if broken can be seen as a repudiatory breach of contract.)' (Lockton, 2003)
- 'In addition to the common law implied term, statute protects employees in the form of The Health and Safety at Work Act 1974. Whereas common law exists to compensate the employee if injured, The Act exists to *prevent the injury happening in the first place*, and creates criminal, not civil, liability.' (Lockton, 2003)

The two systems compliment one another and interrelate so that often an employee will allege both a breach of contract and a breach of statute.

Feedback on revision question for study session 20

The majority of academics advocate that knowledge management is the key for organisations to have sustainable competitive advantage. This notion of achieving competitive advantage through personnel is by no means a new concept. Recent interest has probably been aroused due to the fast-growing service sector. Little, Quintas and Ray (2002) state:

> 'in a world where markets, products, technologies, competitors, regulations and even societies change rapidly, continuous innovation and the knowledge that enables innovation has become an important source of sustainable competitive advantage.'

Currently, existing definitions of KM are ambiguous and exhibit discrepancies. Gates (1999) states: 'KM has been infused with almost any meaning someone wants to associate with it'. Drucker (2002) defines KM as 'the coordination and exploitation of knowledge resources to create benefit and competitive advantage'.

KM consultant Nir (cited in Kaplan, 2002) found that a common misconception with KM is that it refers solely to IT applications: 'Usually people begin a KM project by focusing on technology needs, but the key is people and processes'. Call (2005) states that 'it is important to realise that KM is less of a technical problem and more of a cultural issue'.

Too much emphasis on technology can be to the detriment of KM programmes. Kaplan (2002) found that a KM system that integrated a collaborative software package, a naval war game software tool and

Microsoft's exchange server with internet, video and chat capabilities was unsuccessful. Users were overwhelmed and as a result became frustrated: 'The technology bogged them down. We had gadgets and tools, but it became clear we had given them too much IT'. KM programmes approached in this manner will result in underutilised systems and will actually encourage employee turnover. For this reason, Chourides (2004) recommends that 'the human element and the technological aspect of KM needs to work in association and in balance to achieve and sustain competitive advantage'. Therefore, IT should facilitate KM initiatives but not rely upon them.

Unfortunately, relatively few firms realise the potential of KM. Rossett's (2002) research revealed that 50% of all KM incentives fail. This is hardly surprising as Call (2005) concluded that many companies involved in undertaking a KM initiative do so without a clear understanding of what KM is or what a successful implementation entails. Conversely, De Wit and Meyer (2004) postulate that the reason why KM initiatives fail is that little is done to take advantage of the knowledge. They describe organisations' efforts as treating knowledge as 'steel' – 'a resource to be gathered, shared and distributed' – implying little action is taken. They continue, 'what firms have not done very much is build knowledge and services or develop new products or services based on knowledge'.

It is unfortunate that many companies have attempted to install KM systems and have invested heavily in IT systems such as expert databases and intranet sites, only then to foist them on a workforce. Employees often resist such introductions leading to inevitable failures.

KM concerns the transfer of both tacit and explicit knowledge. Nonaka (cited in Jones et al, 2003) defines tacit knowledge to be 'subjective and experience based', whereas explicit knowledge refers to 'objective and rational knowledge that can be expressed in words or numbers'. Jones et al (2003) posits, 'it appears to be the ability of a firm to codify and share its tacit knowledge that creates sustainable competitive advantage'.

Organisations should realise that using IT is not necessarily the best way to transfer knowledge. People do not enjoy reading copious amounts of information to enable them to do something. Information is often better understood when people are involved in a particular activity. As the proverb suggests: 'Show me, tell me, involve me and I'll understand'. Experience (tacit knowledge) is often transferred by observation, stories and interaction. De Wit and Meyer (2004) state, 'a recent study of 1,000 employees reported that most workplace learning goes on unbudgeted, unplanned and uncaptured by the organisation. Up to 70% of workplace learning is informal'.

KM programmes, if implemented carefully and correctly, can indeed help an organisation sustain competitive advantage. Each company is unique and what constitutes an effective KM programme at one company may be ineffectual at another. However, the principle of KM – concerning 'continuous improvement' in order to sustain competitive advantage – is applicable to all organisations, especially the growing service sector where personnel is the only real differentiating factor.

273

References and bibliography

This section contains a complete A-Z listing of all publications, materials or websites referred to in this course book. Books, articles and research are listed under the first author's (or in some cases the editor's) surname. Where no author name has been given, the publication is listed under the name of the organisation that published it. Websites are listed under the name of the organisation providing the website.

Academy of Management Executive (2004) 'Changing Organizational Structures: An interview with Rosabeth Moss Kanter'. Vol 18, 2 May, pp 92-111.

Adair, G (1984) 'The Hawthorne effect: A reconsideration of the methodological artefact', *Journal of Applied Psychology*, 69, pp334–345.

Adair, J (1999) *Decision Making and Problem Solving*. London: CIPD.

Ahmed, PK and M Rafiq (2002) *Internal Marketing – tools and concepts for customer-focused management*, 1st edn. Oxford: Butterworth-Heinemann.

Aldin, N, P Brehmer and A Johansson (2004) 'Business development with electronic commerce: refinement and repositioning', *Business Process Management Journal*, 10, 1, pp 44–62.

Anonymous (2003) 'Making teamwork work', *Human Resource Management International Digest* (online), 11, 3, pp5–7 (Emerald: http://www.emeraldinsight.com).

Argenti, J (1990) *Practical Corporate Planning*. London: Allen and Unwin.

Argyris, C (1960) *Understanding organizational behavior*. Homewood, IL: Dorsey Press.

Arnold, J, J Silvester, F Patterson, IT Robertson and C L Cooper (1998) *Work Psychology*. London: Pitman.

Avery, GA (2004) *Understanding Leadership*, 1st edn. London: Sage.

Balogun, J and V Hope Hailey (2004) *Exploring Strategic Change*, 2nd edn. Essex: FT Prentice Hall.

Bamford, D and P Forrester (2003) 'Managing planned and emergent change within an operations management environment', *International Journal of Operations and Product Management* (online), 23, 5 (Emerald: http://www.emeraldinsight.com).

Bateman, B, FC Wilson and D Bingham, 'Team effectiveness – development of an audit questionnaire', *Journal of Management Development* (online), 21, 3 (Emerald: http://www.emeraldinsight.com).

Beardwell, L and L Holden (2001) *Human Resource Management – a contemporary approach*, 3rd edn. Essex: FT Prentice Hall.

Belbin, RM (1981) *Management Teams*. Oxford: Butterworth-Heinemann.

Belbin, RM (1993) *Team Roles at Work*. Oxford: Butterworth-Heinemann.

Belbin, RM in GA Cole (2000) *Management – Theory and Practice*, 5th edn. London: Continuum.

Bell, RR and FS Mclaughlin (1977) 'Span of control in organisations', *Industrial Management*, 19, 5, p23.

Bennet, R (1997) *Management*, 3rd edn. London: Financial Times Pitman.

Betts, PW (2000) *Supervisory Management*, 7th edn. Essex: Pearson Education Ltd.

Bickerton, P, M Bickerton and K Simpson-Holley (2001) *Cyberstrategy*. Woburn: Butterworth-Heinemann.

Bijlsma-Frankema, K (2001) 'On managing cultural integration and cultural change processes in mergers and acquisitions', *Journal of European Industrial Training* (online), 25, 2 (Emerald: http://www.emeraldinsight.com).

Blanchard, K (2004) *Leadership and the One Minute Manager*. London: HarperCollins.

Bocij, P, D Chaffy, A Greasley and S Hickie (2003) *Business Information Systems*, 1st edn. Essex: Pearson Education Limited.

Bohte, J and K Meier (2001) 'Structure and performance of public organisations: task difficulty and span of control', *Public Organisation Review*, cited in *Administration & Society*, 2005, 36, pp648–660.

Bradley, A (2005) 'E-procurement: a long way to go', *Supply chain management*, p15.

Brech EFL (1975) *Principles and Practice of Management*, 3rd edn. London: Longman.

Brooks, I (2003) *Organisational Behaviour – Individuals, Groups and Organisation*, 2nd edn. Essex: FT Prentice Hall.

Brown, A (1995) *Transforming Company Culture: getting your company from where you are now to where you want it to be*, 1st edn. London: McGraw-Hill.

Brown, S, R Lamming, J Bessent and P Jones (2000) *Strategic Operations Management*. Oxford: Butterworth-Heinemann.

Buchanan, D and A Huczynski (2004) *Organisational Behaviour – an introductory text*, 5th edn. Essex: Pearson Education Ltd.

Burnes, B (2004) *Managing Change*, 4th edn. Essex: Pearson Education Ltd.

Burnes, T and GM Stalker (1961) *The Management of Innovation*. London: The Tavistock Institute.

Caldwell, R (2003) 'Change leaders and change managers: different or complementary?', *Leadership and Organization Development Journal* (online), 24, 5 (Emerald: http://www.emeraldinsight.com).

Call, D (2005) 'Knowledge management – not rocket science', *Journal of Knowledge Management* (online), 9, 2 (Emerald: http://www.emeraldinsight.com).

Carnall, CA (2003) *Managing Change in Organisations*, 4th edn. Essex: Pearson Education Ltd.

Cawsey A and R Dewar (2004) *Internet Technology and E-commerce*. Hants/New York: Palgrave Macmillan.

Cawthray, B (1984) 'Teambuilding for senior managers 2', *Outlines for Developing Managers*, 2.07.

Chandler, AD (1962) *Strategy and Structure: chapters in the history of the American industrial enterprise*. Cambridge, Mass.: MIT Press.

Chase, RB, NJ Aquilano and FR Jacobs (2001) *Operations Management for Competitive Advantage*, 9th edn. New York: McGraw-Hill.

Chen, G, C Liu and D Tjosvold (2005) 'Conflict management for effective top management teams and innovation in China', *Journal of Management Studies*, 42, 2, pp277–300.

Chen, G and D Tjosvold (2002) 'Conflict management and team effectiveness in China: the mediating role of justice', *Journal of Management Studies*, 19, 4, pp557–572.

Cheng, Y (2000) 'First line management in small and medium sized enterprises in the UK and China', PhD Thesis. Derby, UK: Derbyshire Business School, The University of Derby.

Chorides, P (2004) 'Best practice in knowledge management: an empirical study of the critical success factors in the creation of a knowledge management', PhD Thesis, Derbyshire Business School: The University of Derby.

Cole, GA (1996) *Management Theory and Practice*, 5th edn. London: Continuum.

Confederation of British Industry (undated publication) *Focus on the first line: the role of the supervisor*, 1st edn. Sussex: Ditchling Press Ltd.

Cook, RA and JL Goff (2002) 'Coming of age with self-managed teams: dealing with a problem employee', *Journal of Business and Psychology*, 16, 3, pp485–495.

Cronin, M (1995) *Doing Business on the Internet*, 1st edn. London: International Thompson Publishing.

Cully, M et al (1999) *Britain at Work*. London: Routledge.

Curtis, S and D Wright (2001) 'Retaining employees – the fast track to commitment', *Management Research News* (online), 24, 8 (Emerald: http://www.emeraldinsight.com).

Dastmalchian, A, S Lee and I Ng (2000) 'The interplay between organizational and national cultures: a comparison of organizational practices in Canada and South Korea using the competing values framework', *International Journal of Human Resource Management* (online), 11, 2.

Davison, B (2003) 'Management span of control: how wide is too wide?', *Journal of Business Strategy*, 24, 4, pp22–29.

De Wit, R and R Meyer (2004) *Strategy: Process, Content and Context*, 3rd edn. London: Thomson Learning.

Deal, TE and AA Kennedy (1982) *Corporate Cultures: The Rites and Rituals of Corporate Life*. Harmondsworth: Penguin Books.

Deise, M, C Nowikow, P King and A Wright (2000) *E-Business from Tactics to Strategy*. Canada: John Wiley and Sons Inc.

Deresky H (2006) *International Management: Managing Across Borders and Cultures*, 5th edn. Jersey: Pearson Education Ltd.

Dexter, B (2003) '21st century schizoid manager? Contradictory elements in the role of the first line manager', 18th Annual Employment Research Unit Conference, Cardiff Business School, 10–11 September (2003). University of Derby: Derbyshire Business School.

Drennan, D (1992) *Organisational Culture*, 1st edn. London: Pitman Publishing.

Drucker, P (1954), *The Practice of Management*. Oxford: Heinemann.

Drucker, P (1989) *The Practice of Management*, 3rd edn. Oxford: Heinemann Professional.

Drucker, P (1955) 'The promise of automation: America's next twenty years, part II,' *Harpers*, 210, March: 41-47.

Drucker, P (2002) *Managing in the Next Society*. Oxford: Butterworth Heinemann.

Elsayed-Elkhouly, SM, H Lazarus and V Forsythe (1997) 'Why is a third of your time wasted in meetings?', *Journal of Management Development*, 16, 9, pp672–676.

Etzione, A (1964) *Modern Organizations*. Englewood Cliffs, NJ: Prentice-Hall.

Fayol, H (1949) *General and Industrial Management*. London: Pitman.

Fletcher, C (2004) *Appraisal and Feedback; making performance review work*. CIPD.

Follett, MP (1918) *The New State*. New York: Longman Green and Co.

Garen, J (1999) 'Unions incentive systems and job design', *Journal of Labour Research*, 20, 4, pp589–603.

Gates, W (1999) *Business at the Speed of Thought: Succeeding in the Digital Economy*. New York: Warner Books.

Gilbert, TF (1966) *Human competence: Engineering worth performance*. Silver Spring, MD: International Society for Performance Improvement.

Gosling, J and H Mintzberg (2003) 'The five minds of a manager', *Harvard Business Review*, 11, pp54–63.

Greasley, A (1999) *Operations Management in Business*, 1st edn. Cheltenham: Stanley Thornes (Publishers) Ltd.

Greenberg, J and RA Baron (2003) *Behaviour in Organisations*, 8th edn. New Jersey: Pearson Education Ltd.

Greiner, LE (1972) 'Evolution and revolution as organisations grow', *Harvard Business Review*, 76, 3, pp55–68.

Griffin, R and M Pustay (2003) *International Business*. New Jersey: Pearson Education.

Guest, D (1977) ' Human Resource Management and Performance: a review and research agenda', *The International Journal of HRM*, Vol 8, No 3, pp 263-76.

Hales, CP and D Knowles (2003) 'Anchored in supervision but drifting into management: continuity and change in the role of first line managers', 18th Annual Employment Research Unit Conference, Cardiff Business School, 10–11 September (2003). University of Westminster: Westminster Business School.

Handy, C (1976) *Understanding Organisations*, 1st edn. Harmondsworth: Penguin Books.

Handy, C (1993) *Understanding Organisations*, 4th edn. London: Penguin.

Hannagan, T (2005) *Management – Concepts and Practices*, 4th edn. Essex: FT Prentice Hall.

Harrison, FE (1999) *The Managerial Decision-Making Process*, 5th edn. New York: Houghton Mifflin.

Hayes, J (2002) *The Theory and Practice of Change Management*, 1st edn. Basingstoke: Palgrave.

Hendricks, M (2001) 'Span control', *Entrepreneur*, January.

Hendrie, J (2004) 'A review of a multiple retailer's labour turnover', *International Journal of Retail and Distribution Management* (online), 32, 9 (Emerald: http://www.emeraldinsight.com).

Herguner, G and NBR Reeves (2000) 'Going against the national cultural grain: a longitudinal case study of organizational culture change in Turkish higher education', *Total Quality Management*, 1, 1, pp45–56.

Hodge, DD (2003) 'The only constant is change: transforming the UW undergraduate experience'. Discussion paper used as basis for talk at Downtown Seattle Rotary Club, 12 March. University of Washington College of Arts and Sciences.

Hofstede, G (1980) *Culture's consequences: International differences in work-related values*. Newbury Park, CA: Sage.

HRH The Duke of Edinburgh 'Introduction', in CN Parkinson (2002) *Parkinson's Law*. London: Penguin Modern Classics.

Izar, R (1991) *Accounting, Costing and Management*. Oxford: Oxford University Press.

Jay, A (2004) 'Safeway hits Morrison's profits', *The Guardian*. London: Guardian Newspapers Ltd.

Jennings, D and S Wattam (1994) *Decision Making: An Integrated Approach*, 1st edn. London: Pitman Publishing.

Jobber, D (2001) *Principles and Practice of Marketing*, 3rd edn. England: McGraw-Hill.

Johnson, G and Scholes K (1999) *Exploring Corporate Strategy*, 5th edn. London: Prentice Hall.

Johnson, J, R Griffeth and M Griffin (2000) 'Factors discriminating functional and dysfunctional salesforce turnover', *Journal of Business and Industrial Marketing* (online), 15, 6 (Emerald: http://www.emeraldinsight.com).

Jones, NB, RT Herschel and DD Moesel (2003) 'Knowledge champions to facilitate knowledge management', *Journal of Knowledge Management* (online), 7, 1 (Emerald: http://www.emeraldinsight.com).

Kaplan, R and D Norton (1996) *The Balanced Scorecard*. Harvard: Harvard Business School Press.

Kaplan, R and D Norton (2005) 'The Balanced Scorecard: Measures that Drive Performance', *Harvard Business Review*. Jul 1.

Kaplan, S (2002): 'KM - The Right Way' *CIO Magazine*, July 15, 2002 edition. Framingham, MA

Kessapidou, S and NC Varsekelis (2003) 'National culture and its impact on the choice of managing director in international production: the case of foreign firms in Greece', *International Journal of Human Resource Management*, 14, 2, pp285–295.

King, N and N Anderson (1995) *Innovation and Change in Organizations*, 1st edn. London: Routledge.

Knights, D and H Willmott (1992) 'Conceptualising leadership processes: a study of senior managers in a financial services company', *Journal of Management Studies*, 29, 6, p761.

Koontz, H and H Weihrich 1990. *Essentials of Management*, 5th edn. Singapore: McGraw-Hill.

Kotter, J and J Heskett (1992) *Culture and Performance*. New York: Free Press.

Kotter, JP (1990) *A Force for Change: How Leadership Differs from Management*. New York: Free Press.

Lao Tzu (Old Master) (ca. 600 BCE) *The Art of War*.

Laudon J and K Laudon (2003) *Essentials of Management Information Systems*. Jersey: Prentice Hall.

Lax, DA and JK Sebenius (1986) *The Manager as Negotiator: Bargaining for Cooperation and Competitive Gain*. NY: Free Press.

Leat, M (2003) *Exploring Employee Relations*, 1st edn. Oxford: Butterworth-Heinemann.

Legge, K (1995) *Human Resource Management: rhetoric and realities*. Basingstoke: Palgrave.

Lewin, K (1947/1976) 'Frontiers in group dynamics', in Cartwright, D (ed) *Field theory in social science: Selected theoretical papers by Kurt Lewin*. Chicago: University of Chicago Press.

Little, SE, P Quintas and T Ray (eds) (2001) *Managing Knowledge: an essential reader*. London: Sage Publications Ltd.

Locke, EA (1968) 'Towards a theory of task motivation and incentives,' *Organizational behavior and performance*. 3, 157-189.

Lockton, DJ (2003) *Employment Law*, 4th edn. Basingstoke: Palgrave Law Masters, Palgrave Macmillan.

Loo, R and K Thorpe (2003) 'A delphi study forecasting management training and developing for first line nurse managers', *Journal of Management Development* (online), 22, 9 (Emerald: http://www.emeraldinsight.com).

Luffman, G, E Lea, S Sanderson and B Kenny (1996) *Strategic Management – an analytical introduction*. Oxford: Blackwell.

Macneil, C (2001) 'The supervisor as a facilitator of informal learning in work teams', *Journal of Workplace Learning* (online), 13, 6 (Emerald: http://www.emeraldinsight.com).

Mason-Jones, R and DR Towill (1997) 'Information enrichment: designing the supply chain for competitive advantage', *Supply Chain Management*, 2, 4.

Maybe, C and B Mayon-White (1993) *Managing Change*, 2nd edn. London: The Open University/Paul Chapman Publishing.

Mayo, A (1995) 'Economic indicators of HRM', in Tyson, S (ed) *Strategic Prospects for HRM*. London: IPM.

McGregor, D (1960) *The Human Side of Enterprise*. New York: McGraw-Hill.

McLaney, E and P Atrill (2002) *Accounting, An Introduction*. Harlow: Pearson Education Ltd.

Mendibil, K and J Macbyrde (2005) 'The dimensions of management team performance', *Production Planning and Control*, 16, 2, pp208–225.

Miles, S and G Mangold (2002) 'The impact of team leader performance on team member satisfaction: the subordinates perspective', *Team Performance Management: An International Journal* (online), 8, 5 (Emerald: http://www.emeraldinsight.com).

Milligan, J, D Longbottom and N Ellis, 'Suppliers – partnership or independence? Extending the boundaries of best practice to strategy and inter-organisational relationships'. Paper presented at the 6th Annual Asia Pacific Conference on Quality Management, RMIT, Melbourne, Australia (February 1999).

Mintzberg, H (1973) *The Manager's Working Roles, the Nature of Managerial Work*. Longman.

Moody Jennings, M (1996) *Case Studies in Business Ethic*, 2nd edn. US: West Publishing Company.

Mintzberg, H (1979) *The Structuring of Organizations*. Englewood Cliffs, NJ: Prentice-Hall.

Moore, M (1995) *Creating Public Value: Strategic Management in Government*. Cambridge MA: Harvard University Press.

Muhlemann, A, J Oakland and K Lockyer (1992) *Production and Operations Management*, 6th edn. London: Pitman Publishing.

Mullins, JL (2005) *Management and Organisational Behaviour*, 7th edn. England: FT Prentice Hall.

Nozick, R (1974) *Anarchy, State and Utopia*. Blackwell.

Nelson, DL and JC Quick (1996) *Organizational Behaviour: The Essentials*, 1st edn. US: West Publishing Company.

Nonaka, I and H Takeuchi (1995) *The Knowledge Creating Company*. Oxford: Oxford University Press.

Orpen, C (1994) 'Empowering the supervisory role', *Work Study* (online), 43, 2 (Emerald: http://www.emeraldinsight.com).

Osborne SP and K Brown (2005) *Managing Change and Innovation in Public Service Organisations*. USA: Routledge.

Parker, R (2005) 'Going through changes', *Supply Chain Management*, November, pp28–29.

Peppard, J and P Rowland (1995) *The Essence of Business Process Re-engineering*. London: Prentice Hall.

Peters, TJ and RH Waterman (1982) *In Search of Excellence: Lessons from America's Best-Run Companies*. New York: Harper and Row.

Porter, ME (1985) *Competitive Advantage: creating and sustaining superior performance*. New York: The Free Press.

Porter, ME (2001) 'Strategy and the internet', *Harvard Business Review*, 79, 3, pp62–78.

Pugh, DS, DJ Hickson and CR Hinings (1971) *Writers on Organizations*, 2nd edition. Harmondsworth: Penguin.

Randall, L and M Senior (1992) *Managing and Improving Service Quality and Delivery*. Cheltenham: Stanley Thornes.

Robbins, SP (2003) *Organisational Behaviour*, 10th edn. New Jersey: Pearson Education Ltd.

Robbins, SP and DA Decenzo (2004) *Fundamentals of Management – essential concepts and applications*, 4th edn. New Jersey: Pearson Education Ltd.

Rodrigues, CA, N Bu and B Min (2000) 'Learners' training approach preference: National culture as a determinant', *Cross Cultural Management*, 17, 1, pp23–30.

Scarborough, H and J Swan (2003) 'Discourses of Knowledge Management and Organisational Learning, Their Production and Consumption', in Easterby-Smith, M and M Lyles (eds) *The Blackwell Handbook of Organizational Learning and Knowledge Management*. Oxford: Blackwell Publishing

Schneider, SC and JL Barsoux (1997) *Managing across Cultures*, 1st edn. Hertfordshire: Prentice Hall Europe.

Schraeder, M and D Self (2003) 'Management decision. Enhancing the success of mergers and acquisitions: an organizational culture perspective' (online), 41, 5 (Emerald: http://www.emeraldinsight.com).

Senior, B (1997) *Organisational Change*. London: Pitman.

Senior, B (2002) *Organisational Change*, 2nd edn. Harlow: FT Prentice Hall.

Senior, B and S Swailes (2004) 'The dimensions of management team performance: a repertory grid study', *International Journal of Productivity and Performance Management*, 53, 4, pp317–333.

Shah A (1998) *Management*, 3rd edn. New York: McGraw-Hill.

Shelton, D, R Hall and J Darling (2003) 'When cultures collide: the challenge of global integration', *European Business Review* (online), 15, 5 (Emerald: http://www.emeraldinsight.com).

Sisaye, S (2004) 'Teams and management control systems: a synthesis of three organisational development approaches', *Leadership and Organization Development Journal*, 25, 3, pp172–185.

Slack, N, S Chambers, C Harland, A Harrison and R Johnson (1995) *Operations Management*. London: Pitman.

Slatter, S (1990) 'Common Pitfalls in Using the BCG Product Portfolio Matrix', *London Business School Journal*, winter, pp18–22.

Smith, M (2003) 'Changing an organization's culture: correlates of success and failure', *Leadership and Organization Development Journal* (online), 24, 5 (Emerald: http://www.emeraldinsight.com).

Smith, P and CI Barnard (1938) *The Functions of the Executive*. Cambridge, MA.: Harvard University Press.

Standing, C (2000) *Internet Commerce Development*. London: Artech House.

Stewart, J and S Ranson (1988) 'Management in the Public Domain,' *Public Money and Management*, Spring/Summer.

Stock, JR and DM Lambert (2001) *Strategic Logistics Management*, 4th edn. Singapore: McGraw-Hill.

Stokey, E and R Zeckhauser (1978) *A Primer for Policy Analysis*. New York: WW Norton and Co.

Stone, D (1988) *Policy Paradox and Political Reason*. Glenview, IL: Scott Foresman.

Stoner, JA and RE Freeman (1992) *Management*, 6th edn. New Jersey: Prentice Hall International Inc.

Stovel, M and N Bontis (2002) 'Voluntary turnover: knowledge management – friend or foe?', *Journal of Intellectual Capital* (online), 3, 3 (Emerald: http://www.emeraldinsight.com).

Strachan, PA (1996) 'Managing transformational change: the learning organization and teamworking', *Team Performance Management*, 2, 2, pp32–40(9).

Swailes, B, and S Swailes (2004) 'The dimensions of management team performance: a repertory grid study', *International Journal of Productivity and Performance Management*, 53, 4, pp317–333.

Tassabehji, R (2003) *Applying E-commerce in Business*, 1st edn. London: Sage.

Taylor, S (2002) *The Employee Retention Handbook*, 1st edn. London: Chartered Institute of Personnel and Development.

Taylor, S (2004) 'Recruitment, retention and turnover (2004): a survey of the UK and Ireland' (online). London: Chartered Institute of Personnel and Development (CIPD: http://www.cipd.co.uk).

Teale M, V Dispenza, J Flynn and D Currie (2003) *Management Decision-making: towards an integrative approach*, 1st edn. Essex: FT Prentice Hall.

Teets, JW in FR David (2005) *Strategic Management – concepts and cases*, 10th edn. New Jersey: Pearson Education.

Thacker, R (1997) 'Team leader style: enhancing the creativity of employees in teams', *Training for quality*, 5, 4, pp146–149.

Theaker, A (2002) *The Public Relations Handbook*. New York: Routledge.

Thompson, AA and AJ Strickland (2003) *Strategic Management Concepts and Cases*, 13th edn. New York: McGraw-Hill.

Thornhill, A, P Lewis, M Saunders and M Millmore (2000) *Managing Change: a human resource strategy approach*. Harlow: FT Prentice Hall.

Townsend, R (1971) *Up the Organisation*, 1st edn. Great Britain: Michael Joseph Ltd.

Tuckman, BW and MAC Jensen (1977) 'Stages of small group development revisited', *Group and Organizational Studies*, 2, 419–27

Urwick, LF (1956) 'The Manager's Span of Control.' *Harvard Business Review*, pp 39-47.

Van Weele, AJ (2005) *Purchasing and Supply Chain Management: analysis, strategy, planning and practice*, 4th edn. London: Thomson Learning.

Van Wendel De Joode, R (2004) 'Managing conflicts in open source communities', *Electronic Markets*, 14, 2, pp104–111.

Vollman, TE and C Cordon (1998) 'Building successful customer–supplier alliances', *Long Range Planning*, 31, 5, pp684–694.

Waller, DL (2003) *Operations Management: a supply chain approach*, 2nd edn. London: Thompson Learning.

Webber, S (2002) 'Leadership and trust facilitating cross-functional team success', *Journal of Management Development* (online), 21, 3 (Emerald: http://www.emeraldinsight.com).

Wild, R (2002) *Operations Management*, 6th edn. London: Continuum.

Williams, A, P Dobson and M Walters (1989) *Changing Culture: new organizational Approaches*, 1st edn. Wiltshire: Dotesios Printers Ltd.

Young, A (1986) 'The manager's handbook: the practical guide to successful management'. London: Guild Publishing, 1, 3, pp341–354.

Zaleznik, A (1977) 'Managers and leaders: Are they different?' *Harvard Business Review*, May-June.

Zornoza, A, P Ripoll and JM Peiro (2002) 'Conflict management in groups that work in two different communication contexts', *Small Group Research*, 33, 5, pp481–508.

Index